D1523717

THE CHOICE THEORY OF CONTRACTS

This concise landmark in law and jurisprudence offers the first coherent, liberal account of contract law. *The Choice Theory of Contracts* answers the field's most pressing questions: What is the "freedom" in "freedom of contract"? What core values animate contract law and how do those values interrelate? How must the state act when it shapes contract law? Hanoch Dagan and Michael Heller – two of the world's leading private law theorists – show exactly why and how freedom matters to contract law. They start with the most appealing tenets of modern liberalism and end with their implications for contract law. This readable, engaging book gives contract scholars, teachers, and students a powerful normative vocabulary for understanding canonical cases, refining key doctrines, and solving long-standing puzzles in the law.

HANOCH DAGAN is one of the world's leading private law theorists. He is the Stewart and Judy Colton Professor of Legal Theory and Innovation and former dean of the Tel Aviv University Faculty of Law. Dagan has written five books across the landscape of private law topics and has published more than seventy articles in major law reviews and journals. His most recent book is *Reconstructing American Legal Realism & Rethinking Private Law Theory* (2013).

MICHAEL HELLER is one of America's leading authorities on property. He is the Lawrence A. Wien Professor of Real Estate Law and former Vice Dean for Intellectual Life at Columbia Law School. In *The Gridlock Economy: How Too Much Ownership Wrecks Markets, Stops Innovation, and Costs Lives* (2008), Heller sets out a market paradox that he discovered: private ownership usually creates wealth, but too much ownership has the opposite effect – it creates gridlock.

The Choice Theory of Contracts

HANOCH DAGAN

Tel Aviv University

MICHAEL HELLER

Columbia Law School

CAMBRIDGE
UNIVERSITY PRESS

University Printing House, Cambridge CB2 8BS, United Kingdom

One Liberty Plaza, 20th Floor, New York, NY 10006, USA

477 Williamstown Road, Port Melbourne, VIC 3207, Australia

4843/24, 2nd Floor, Ansari Road, Daryaganj, Delhi – 110002, India

79 Anson Road, #06–04/06, Singapore 079906

Cambridge University Press is part of the University of Cambridge.

It furthers the University's mission by disseminating knowledge in the pursuit of
education, learning, and research at the highest international levels of excellence.

www.cambridge.org
Information on this title: www.cambridge.org/9781107135987
10.1017/9781316477045

© Hanoch Dagan and Michael Heller 2017

First published 2017

Printed in the United States of America by Sheridan Books, Inc.

A catalogue record for this publication is available from the British Library.

ISBN 978-1-107-13598-7 Hardback
ISBN 978-1-316-50170-2 Paperback

For Ifat
H.D.

For Debora, Ellie, and Jonah
M.H.

Contents

Preface

We aim to persuade you to adopt a liberal view of contract law. To achieve this goal, this book offers *choice theory*, an approach that departs from contemporary accounts in two ways: it analyzes the field as a whole and puts freedom back into "freedom of contract."

* * *

Our first departure is to explore contract as a whole, not just the narrow commercial issues that are of primary scholarly concern today. For millennia, contract law has been organized around a diverse array of off-the-shelf solutions for many of life's pressing contractual challenges – that is, around contract types for family, work, and home, along with commerce.

But then, in the late 1800s, classical legal thought in America began shifting contract's terrain. The transition culminated in the 1920s with Samuel Williston's multivolume treatise, *The Law of Contracts* – a work that still shapes the everyday law. Williston's goal was to unify a body of law whose fragmentation, in his view, obscured the field's basic principles. The result of his project was to give pride of place to commercial contracts, and as a by-product, render peripheral the diversity of other contract types.

Williston replaced the *unprincipled multiplicity* of the common law (and European civil law) with the *unprincipled uniformity* that dominates American contract law today. This shift had an unexpected implication: if contracts are for commerce, then the law should maximize utility, a goal understood primarily in terms of material benefits. Competing values like autonomy and community could be ignored because they came to be seen as outside the field.

But what if the values contracting parties actually care about are in conflict? It's here that the now-conventional scope of the field (the Willistonian project) and the now-dominant method of inquiry (efficiency analysis) fall short. Utility matters, but it is not the sole, or even the dominant, value people seek when contracting.

Despite Williston's success in reshaping the field, existing contract law still offers types that vary widely in their normative structures: some are indeed organized to promote utility, others to enhance community, but most aim to achieve a mix of these values. In large measure, what ensures contractual autonomy is people's continuing ability to choose from among diverse types within each important sphere of human interaction. Based on this descriptive reality, and the normative imperatives it suggests, we renew the focus on contract types and, in so doing, reject Williston's answer to the question, "What is contract?"

* * *

Our second departure is to offer a rigorous normative account of contract types. Freedom comes first. Ours is a liberal account that takes seriously contract's role in enhancing autonomy.

We are not the first on this path. Charles Fried, in his 1981 volume *Contract as Promise*, recovered autonomy as the moral core of contract. Departing from Williston's *unprincipled uniformity*, Fried aimed at *principled uniformity*. Fried argued correctly that autonomy matters centrally to contract – in this, he made an enduring contribution. But his specific arguments faltered because he missed the role of diverse contract types and because he grounded contractual freedom in a flawed, rights-based view. Despite decades of effort by Fried and by later liberal theorists, we can now say all rights-based arguments for contractual autonomy have failed.

This failure has high costs: if freedom drops away as a justification for contract, then what's left, mostly, is the efficiency approach. But a thorough-going efficiency theory of contract has never been persuasive. Other values cannot be banished altogether if, for example, you oppose slavery and endorse marriage. The challenge is to offer a normatively appealing way to situate efficiency analysis within a liberal framework. The first step in that project is to reject Fried's answer to the question, "What is freedom?"

* * *

We offer this book as a counterpoint to Williston and Fried. Choice theory shows how contract law can enhance individual autonomy while, at the same time, providing the economic and social benefits people seek in working together. Our approach returns analysis to the mainstream of twentieth-century liberalism – a tradition concerned with enhancing self-determination that is mostly absent in contract theory today. By showing how this tradition applies to contract law as a whole, choice theory moves from the *principled uniformity* that Fried attempted to the *principled multiplicity* that liberalism requires.

While not (yet) a restatement of contract law, choice theory offers numerous appealing doctrinal refinements and solves many long-standing puzzles in contract law and theory. It provides efficiency analysts of contract a more secure normative grounding for their work. And it offers teachers and students of contract law, for the first time, a coherent normative vocabulary that makes sense of the casebook canon. Choice theory shows why and how freedom matters to contract.

Introduction

As free people, we do not live each on our own island, isolated in perfect independence. We want and need each other to achieve life's worthy goals. Contract law provides a powerful means to achieve these goals. Through contract, we can recruit others to help write the stories of our lives.

There's a catch, however. Contracts require enforcement; enforcement entails coercion; and coercion seems at odds with freedom. So, is "freedom of contract" possible? Yes, the state can respect, indeed enhance, our autonomy even when it enforces our contracts. However, the truth of this proposition is not self-evident. The aim of this book is to show how a robust commitment to freedom justifies and shapes contract law in a liberal polity.

We start from the mainstream liberal tradition of the past century, that is, with concern for individual autonomy – with self-determination, with self-authorship, with ensuring to us, as individuals, the ability to write and re-write the story of our own lives. This deep and widely-shared sense of what it means to be free – the liberalism of Isaiah Berlin, H.L.A. Hart, and John Rawls – rightly dominates the most important political, legal, and philosophical debates.

Surprisingly, however, this approach has gone missing in recent generations of work on private law in general and contract law specifically. Other notions of contractual autonomy – say Kantian and libertarian ideas of personal independence – now have a powerful hold on the field. But they all necessarily fail for reasons we detail in Chapters 1 through 3. Similarly, foundational alternatives for liberalism itself, such as political liberalism, are not adequate to justify contract law, as we explain in Chapter 8, where we answer many objections to our theory.

We call our approach the *choice theory* of contract. In this view, the state enforces contracts not just to make society as a whole better off – that's the

1

efficiency rationale – but even more fundamentally to enhance people's autonomy so that they can make their lives meaningfully their own. Much of our task is to persuade you that any contract theory worthy of being called liberal must concern itself with autonomy defined in this sense, as self-determination.

Choice theory answers the most important questions of contract theory: What is the "freedom" celebrated in "freedom of contract"? How are individuals freer when the state coerces contract performance? What core values should contract law advance and how do those values inter-relate? Must the state take an active role in shaping contract law? If so, what is that role?

Existing approaches have failed to answer these fundamental questions. One observer goes so far as to say that "today there is no generally recognized theory of contract. The effort to develop a coherent explanation of contract seems to have reached an impasse."[1] There is no impasse. A doctrinally well-fit, conceptually coherent, and normatively attractive account of contract is in view. Choice theory starts with the most appealing, least controversial tenets of modern liberalism and ends with their implications for contract law.

FREEDOM OF CONTRACTS

The main tool that choice theory uses to point the way forward is an organizing framework we call "freedom of contracts." We would like to claim the ubiquitous phrase "freedom of contract" – without the "s" – but we leave the term aside because of its confounding negative liberty and *laissez faire* associations.

"Freedom of contracts" sums up the three irreducible elements necessary to contractual autonomy: (1) an overarching voluntariness principle, sometimes called freedom *from* contract; (2) the familiar freedom to bargain for terms *within* a contract; and (3) the long-neglected freedom to choose from *among* contract types. As we will show, attention to the third element – choice among types – is the key that can set contract theory on a sustainably liberal path.

We agree that the first element, voluntariness, is an essential aspect of free contracting, with a twist we'll get to in Chapter 8. Also, we acknowledge that the second component, bargaining for terms within a contract, is a nontrivial aspect of contracting. It's the overwhelming focus of current theory. At times, people really do want their own idiosyncratic deal and they need the law to do no more than enforce their joint agreement.

But bargaining for terms is not the dominant mode of contracting, and it should not determine, as it long has, the central meaning of contractual autonomy. Usually, when people voluntarily enter contracts, they are not designing their deal from scratch. For most of us, most of the time – if we get married, start a new job, or click "I accept" – contractual freedom means the ability to choose from among a sufficient range of off-the-shelf, normatively attractive contract types and then, perhaps, make a few contextual adjustments within the deal. In large measure, freedom means pursuing the valuable ends of our lives, not spending our resources dickering over contract terms and worrying whether others are taking advantage of us.

In other words, the mainstay of present-day contracting is the choice among types. By "types," we do not mean standard-form contracts or boilerplate terms as such. Forms or terms may reflect the parties' choice of a particular type (say, a franchise agreement); they may push a type in a certain direction (say, a landlord-provided lease), or they may point toward emergence of a new type (such as a cohabitation agreement). But standard forms and terms are not themselves types. They are particular instances of the types of relationships people contractually create, whether franchise or agency, commercial or residential lease, cohabitation or marriage.

Each type uses distinctive doctrinal features embedded in the law – not just in form contracts or boilerplate terms – to embody that type's particular normative concerns and stabilize its shared cultural meaning. To give just a few examples, consider doctrines such as waiting periods to dissolve marriage contracts, limitations on enforcement of employee noncompete agreements, and generous return rules in consumer transactions. From the perspective of most contract theory today – focused on freedom to bargain for terms inside a contract – such doctrinal rules may seem to be exceptions from a general norm, oddities needing rationalization, or even worse, they may be framed simply as limits on contractual freedom to be discarded.

By contrast, choice theory suggests that each of these doctrines, and many others, may be better understood as clues to and reflections of the divergent normative concerns of a particular contract type. By stabilizing their respective types, by making them more available and attractive to contracting parties, and by making available distinct choices about the structure of important relationships, such doctrinal rules can enhance contractual freedom.

Attention to the actually existing choice among types opens the door to a *liberal* and *general* theory of contract *law*. Let's introduce those three components in turn.

A LIBERAL THEORY

To qualify as liberal, contract theory must be grounded in an appealing conception of contractual "autonomy" – or "freedom" or "liberty" (we use these terms interchangeably for reasons that will become apparent by the end of Chapter 4). The problem is that contractual autonomy is not self-defining.

Just the opposite. Pinning it down is tough, much tougher than the concept's easy intuitive appeal suggests.[2]

1. *Autonomy through Choice.* The first theoretical aspiration of choice theory is to offer a liberal conception of contractual autonomy grounded in, and well-adapted to, the actual diversity of contract types. One element of this autonomy – reflecting the usual meaning of freedom of contract – involves supporting individuals as they pursue their own idiosyncratic deals. But contract law must do more if it is to expand meaningful choices in service of autonomy. It must also support freedom to choose from among diverse, normatively attractive contract types in each important area of human interaction. Free people are defined in part by the attractive choices they reject, not just those they select.

The implications of this claim are stark. It is here that choice theory offers its single most important and distinctive normative payoff: a state committed to human freedom must be proactive in shaping contract law, including ensuring availability of a diverse body of normatively attractive types. This commitment means that the state is sometimes obligated to support establishment of emerging types that serve minoritarian or utopian values – even when market demand for the new types is low. This support can take the form of enforcing novel contract types (say, judicially created cohabitation doctrines or privately drafted commercial surrogacy contracts) or removing legislative and regulatory hurdles to emerging contract types (such as Canada's "dependent contractors"). We illustrate this process in Chapter 11, and then, in Chapter 12, we explore some countervailing limits to expanding choice – based on cognitive, behavioral, structural, and political economy grounds and in response to concerns about comparative institutional competence.

2. *Mandatory Rules and Autonomy.* As a corollary to supporting new types, sometimes the state must also *restrict* choice within types. By stabilizing and channeling cultural expectations regarding types, such restrictions may be necessary to make them effective. This last point suggests a surprising payoff of choice theory: sticky defaults and even mandatory terms within a contract type can actually increase freedom, so long as – and this is crucial – law offers sufficient choice among types, a claim we justify and refine in Chapter 10.

A GENERAL THEORY

The second conceptual component of choice theory is to show how a liberal contract theory can also be a *general* one. To qualify as general, a theory must address the varied goods and diverse spheres of contracting.

1. *Intra-Sphere Multiplicity*. Accordingly, we reject the notion that any single value – utility, community, or even autonomy – suffices for a coherent general theory. Instead, we relocate most of the normative (and doctrinal) discussion to a more correct and productive level – relating to the diverse values that animate each type and the recurring dilemmas common to each sphere. For now, it suffices to note that by "sphere," we mean a core realm of human interaction in which contract law can enrich how individuals legitimately enlist others to their projects. The particular taxonomy of spheres we develop in Chapter 9 is wholly instrumental to this end of ensuring adequate choice among types. (Chapter 10 pins down "types," including how we know when a new "type" has emerged and when the range of types is "adequate.")

It should be no surprise that the values plausibly animating marriage, employment, and consumer transactions differ from each other and from those driving commercial transactions, and further that, the contract types within a single sphere offer individuals choices among divergent values. Indeed, the core requirement of choice theory is the availability of normatively attractive types with distinct value mixes that can serve as effective substitutes within each sphere – what we call *intra-sphere multiplicity*.

2. *Freedom for Economists*. One collateral benefit of this approach – and a major impetus for this book – is to offer efficiency-oriented contract scholars a more secure and defensible normative grounding for their work. Much of contract law is, and should be, driven by efficiency concerns. But a thoroughgoing efficiency theory of contract has never been persuasive. Autonomy and community concerns cannot be banished altogether if, for example, you oppose slavery and endorse marriage. So, how do these normative commitments interrelate?

Choice theory solves this puzzle. It shows how contract law can enhance individual autonomy while at the same time providing people with the economic and social benefits they seek. Thus, we recognize autonomy as contract law's ultimate value, as set out in Chapters 4 and 7. At the same time, we note that people usually do not enter into specific contracts to become freer. Sometimes, people contract to achieve "utility," as framed in Chapter 5. Other times, they seek "community" – the somewhat clunky term we define in Chapter 6 to encompass the social benefits of contracting, as distinct from utilitarian ones. Contractual autonomy operates primarily, but not entirely, to ensure that people can make effective choices among these values when they so choose.

For efficiency theorists, we offer a path back from the uncomfortable collectivist position implied by an exclusive focus on maximizing social welfare, and we give them a normatively appealing way to situate efficiency analysis within a liberal framework. Most efficiency theorists care about freedom, but they haven't had a compelling way to incorporate that concern into their models besides some hand-waving in its general direction.

We show the way: efficiency theorists must, at the least, adopt as friendly amendments five theoretical points in Chapter 8 and consider a somewhat larger number of novel doctrinal reforms sprinkled throughout the book and collected in the Conclusion. In short, freedom has a price.

A THEORY OF LAW

Finally, to qualify as a liberal and general theory of *law*, we consider seriously the distinctive reform program of choice theory. It boils down to two components: first, a liberal state is obligated to ensure intra-sphere multiplicity; second, the meaning of trans-substantive or "general" contract law concepts should vary according to the "local" animating principles of particular contract types. We consider these in turn:

1. *The State's Affirmative Role*. Prior autonomy-based theories have conflated ideal contract law with legal passivity, that is, with the commitment that law aim just to enforce the parties' wills and maybe cure discrete market failures.

By contrast, choice theory shows why a state committed to human freedom must actively enable people's relationships by shaping distinct contract types. Contract law has a crucial role to play in delivering on the liberal promise of freedom. The state may betray this autonomy-enhancing mission not only by having bad law or too much law; law's absence may undermine it just as well.[3] Put more sharply, choice theory shows that liberal states are affirmatively obligated to ensure an adequate range of contract types in each important sphere of human interaction – subject to concerns about comparative institutional competence discussed in Chapter 12.

Choice theory is at its strongest in analyzing new and emerging contract types – in areas as diverse as gestational surrogacy, employment in the sharing economy, and the partnership structure of law firms. While the market for contractual innovation is vibrant, particularly in the commercial sphere, there is no reason to believe that existing types either exhaust the variety of goods that people seek by contracting or are best configured to support their divergent goals.

2. *"Local" Contract Law.* A second implication of choice theory is to challenge the idea that "general" contract law principles should have a universal meaning across contract law.[4] The seeming incoherence of this view, which advocates multiplicity in the name of one underlying commitment to autonomy, dissolves once we appreciate its reliance on a familiar, autonomy-based commitment to pluralism. Our method has the virtue of providing a textured way to evaluate the fine doctrinal details of contract law, as we discuss in the back half of the book.

We show that the application of familiar contract concepts – including, for example, liquidated damages, efficient breach, and the duty of good faith and fair dealing – should vary depending on the normative concerns driving different contract types. Even voluntariness, the most trans-substantive contract concern, should be understood differently in different types, and the doctrinal tools used to protect this concern should vary accordingly. Further, we show how universal application of "general" contract law doctrines has led to doctrinal confusion in long-standing contract types. We give examples of how choice theory can improve our understanding of, for example, the law of agency, bailments, consumer transactions, fiduciaries, and suretyship – the ABCs of traditional, pre-Willistonian contract law.

A consistent commitment to autonomy as the normative foundation of contract implies that doctrinal interpretation and evaluation should, by and large, look to the "local" animating principles of existing contract types rather than to any "core" principle of contract law. While this stance may seem novel to some American contract theorists, it can be understood as a principled analogue to the ordinary, taxonomic civil law approach in which "the classification of the contract as a particular type[,] generates a set of abstract expectations as to what is central to that contract."[5]

CONTRACTS AS A WHOLE

It should be apparent already that choice theory makes two substantial departures from contemporary approaches to contract. As noted in the Preface, we are interested in the field as a whole and we take seriously the centrality of freedom to contract. A few more words on these departures may be helpful.

1. *The Willistonian Constraint.* In our view, contract theory seems to have reached "an impasse" primarily because the field of study has been so artificially constrained. If you ask theorists about marriage or surrogacy contract types, many answer: that's family law, not contracts. How about new forms of worker contracts? That's employment or labor law. Consumer

transactions? They're part of the regulatory state. Rather than embracing diverse types, contract theory has shrunk its focus to certain commercial transactions.

This conceptual shrinkage represents an ahistorical and misleading view of contract.[6] From Roman times nearly to the present, contract law was built on an appreciation of the role of existing and emerging contract types. Ancient Roman law itself was marked by a divide between "nominate" contracts (contract types) and "innominate" contracts (freestanding bargains), a distinction that persists in European civil law systems.[7] For example, German law today offers a taxonomy of "typical" contract types, each with its own tailored doctrines; it has methods for shunting analysis of "hybrid" or "mixed" contracts through the existing types; and it deploys recognition mechanisms for "atypical," "customary," and "new" types.[8] By contrast, contract theory in America has lost sight of this deep structure.

The story of how contract was transformed in America is beyond our scope here. It is enough to mention that this process shifted contract theory from concern with distinctive types to a trans-substantive, stylized, and seemingly universal approach. The transition began with the work of Christopher Columbus Langdell in the late 1800s, was crystalized in Samuel Williston's 1920 treatise *The Law of Contracts*, and was fully cemented in the 1932 *First Restatement of Contracts* (with Williston as Reporter).[9] Perhaps because of his abiding concern with creating a national, uniform legal architecture for commerce, Williston made many actual contracting practices seem peripheral – or outside of contract law altogether. This distinctive, early twentieth-century American trajectory elevated commercial transactions to the core of contract, and, as a byproduct, substantially obscured the generative role of diverse contract types.

Williston's aspiration to transcend contract types with "general" law is understandable and indeed laudable (especially if reframed as the "residual category of freestanding contracting" that we suggest in Chapter 8). But lawyers cannot rely on "general" contract law to engage with the key elements of employment, family, or other ordinary types of contract – even if the law were redesigned as we recommend. To rely on any general view would often constitute malpractice.[10] And yet, contract theory today is dominated by the notion of general contract law and is structured around the specific, not very representative, sphere of commercial contracting.

So, in brief, the first substantial departure for choice theory is to push back against the Willistonian notion that the core of contracting is dickering over terms within a commercial deal. Such transactions are surely important, but they are not the platonic type of any contracting sphere, not even – as it turns out – in a world of commerce, a world that has been increasingly affected by collaborative contracting, strategic alliances, and business networks, among many other innovative practices. While we are not the first to note the overlooked role of contract types – relational theorists following Karl Llewellyn's lead have also resisted the Willistonian move[11] – we are the first to offer a normative account that connects the multiplicity of types with its role in enhancing freedom.

2. *Teaching Contract Law.* Unfortunately, contract law teaching has followed Williston's commercial law push. The leading casebooks through which American law students learn contracts are all organized along trans-substantive lines and marginalize many noncommercial contracting practices from their explanatory field.[12] Each presents *Wood v. Lucy, Lady Duff-Gordon, Williams v. Walker-Thomas Furniture, Jacob & Youngs v. Kent, Hadley v. Baxendale, Taylor v. Caldwell*, and the same few dozen primary teaching cases (with minor variations) to drive home a Willistonian agenda supported by a thin utilitarian scaffolding. By our count, the strong majority of the roughly 1200 excerpted cases in the top six casebooks have a commercial focus.[13] No book contains even a single chapter devoted to noncommercial contract types and none offers a coherent framework for analyzing what is distinctive about contracting in the spheres of work, home, or intimacy.[14]

Wisps of conceptual and normative concern appear sporadically when the books note "deviations" from a trans-substantive application of concepts such as promissory estoppel, unconscionability, consideration, specific performance, or misrepresentation.[15] These deviations appear mostly as instances of judicial application of "public policy" or equitable powers in noncommercial contexts – in contrast to the vast majority of excerpted cases decided "at law" and used to illustrate rule-based, commercially oriented, trans-substantive principles.

It's a mistake, though, to say that cases decided on public policy or equity grounds are outliers from a coherent core. Public policy and equity tap into threads of contract law as deep as those decided at law. The challenge for students is that the casebooks do not offer them (or their professors) any coherent vocabulary for talking through what principles might animate public policy or equity. Are these concepts threaded coherently through contract law or are they just an ad hoc grab bag? When should we apply which principle?

In addition, the "general" law taught to 1Ls gives them no purchase on the diverse family, work, home, and consumer contract types they encounter in upper-level "contracts" classes and later in legal practice. Students begin their careers without a language for thinking through why contract law appears as it does and without tools for arguing how it should be shaped going forward – other than some undeveloped utilitarian commitments.

It may be worth noting that contract is a private law outlier. Other private law fields have not gone through quite the same flattening process. For example, property still focuses on recurring dilemmas of distinctive property types – that is, conveyancing, leasing, servitudes, co-ownership, and intellectual property – and the particular normative concerns underlying each of these property institutions. Torts, too, still retains some of the lumpy quality of pre-Williston contracts (notwithstanding the exaggerated teaching focus today on negligence).

The first-year contract law curriculum represents Williston's greatest victory. To the extent this book has a pedagogical purpose, it is to shift the conceptual framework and normative language that students – and later lawyers, judges, and scholars – bring to analyzing contract in America. To start, we reject Williston's answer to the question, "what is contract?"

THE NATURE OF CONTRACTUAL FREEDOM

Our second departure concerns the nature of contractual freedom. This is not a new problem. Some liberal contract theorists – notably Charles Fried in *Contract as Promise* – take Kant as their starting point. Others start with a libertarian philosopher like Robert Nozick. Depending on which aspect of freedom they celebrate, liberal theorists have given the resulting approaches names such as "promise theory," "transfer theory," and "consent theory." All these modern theories share a crucial element: they answer the question "what is freedom?" with a rights-based (or deontological) view of contract that excludes consequentialist (or teleological) elements.

While these theories make many useful contributions, as a group, they have reached a dead end. This is not to condemn deontological theories of private law in general. It may be possible, for example, to construct a persuasive deontological approach to tort law. Our claim is more targeted: despite several decades of sustained effort, rights-based theories of contractual autonomy, and the ambitious reform programs they advance, have failed. It is time to move on.

The crucial wrong turn of existing liberal contract theories is to associate the phrase "freedom of contract" with negative liberty or personal independence, that is, with the idea that contract law should enforce whatever private deals individuals agree to and otherwise get out of the way. In large measure, this view is the philosophical counterpoint to the Willistonian project – and indeed Williston himself advocated such a stance.[16] If contract centrally concerns sophisticated business dealings, then a negative liberty view is neither surprising nor entirely unjustifiable.

But this narrow justification has spread beyond the commercial context. It has become a commitment "fundamental in the orthodox understanding of contract law, that the content of a contractual obligation is a matter for the parties, not the law."[17] The strongest version of this claim comes from the legal economist Richard Craswell, who writes that contractual freedom "has very little to do" with contract law and is thus perceived as "largely irrelevant" to its design.[18] In this view, "freedom of contract" more or less devolves into an essentially hands-off stance for the state, a view that misses much of how contract law can, should, and actually does secure freedom.[19]

Existing liberal contract theories may fit well with limited aspects of commercial contracting, but they fail when expanded to cover contract law as a whole. People want, and the law has always offered, much more than just a negative liberty version of contract. Descriptively, then, existing liberal theories miss the texture of why we contract with one another; conceptually, they overlook key features of contractual autonomy; normatively, they slight the diverse goods of contracting.

The conventional liberal view is bad theory. Bad theory is costly, and not just in theory. Together with the Willistonian project, the negative liberty view has helped splinter contract into disparate and noncommunicating fields. For example, many scholars of work and family define their fields as distinct from, and even in opposition to, contract law. In so doing, they are often trying to shield their contract types from what they see as the troublesome implications of the negative liberty view.[20] But they, and we, pay a high price. We all miss the reform payoffs that come from appreciating the autonomy-enhancing potential of contract in employment, labor, and family law and from leveraging insights arising across the whole of contracting practice.

Another cost of the negative liberty view is subtler. After employment law, labor law, family law, and other core fields flee, what's left in contract law today is mostly the law of commercial transactions. Current liberal theories do not have much that is persuasive to say about business law. Even Fried, in his recent work, finds that his liberal theory substantially dissolves into familiar efficiency reforms.[21] To the extent individuals want their sophisticated business contracts to be primarily wealth-maximizing, efficiency analysis should, for the most part, dominate discussion and liberal contract reforms should have little traction.

Conversely, efficiency theorists understand that efficiency cannot be their only metric, even for business law. But adopting any of the current liberal theories – with their muddled conceptual apparatuses and unpersuasive normative programs – would exact too high a price. So, efficiency theorists may say freedom "jumpstarts" contract or plays some other minimal role, but liberal values mostly reside outside their models. The turn by efficiency analysis of contract away from liberal principles is costly and premature, both for their own work and for the law's development.

While existing liberal theories of contractual freedom all fail, that does not mean we have to give up on freedom. The mainstream liberal view of autonomy (as self-determination) remains available, and properly understood, it provides a secure justification for contract law. Choice theory plays nicely with efficiency analysis – it puts freedom back into the equation.

THREE METHODOLOGICAL NOTES

Before we hit the road, three methodological comments are in order regarding the nature of our theory and its precise subject matter and limits. The first concerns interpretation, the second focuses on the difference between categories for deciding and thinking, and the final addresses the path from theory to practice.

1. *On Interpretation*. We view our approach as an interpretation of existing contract law in liberal societies, one that crafts a theoretical framework for its doctrines that presents them in their best light. An "interpretive theory" of law, like ours, is aimed not at discovering the original intentions of lawmakers, nor at analyzing law's historical evolution. It is not intended to uproot existing practices, nor to supplant law with wholly innovative ways of organizing society.

Rather, an interpretative theory is situated between discovery and invention.[22] It builds on existing practices and thus reaffirms much of existing law. But it provides an account of these practices that suggests a new perspective on the law, which inevitably upsets some conventional wisdom. It thus points to possible improvements to the law as well as to new questions that offer a research agenda for future reformers and scholars.

Indeed, as Rawls noted, interpretive theories aim at both understanding an existing practice and directing its evolution. Accordingly, they need to distinguish between "core" features of the practice, which serve as fixed points to which a theory must fit, and other features that can be treated with less deference and are thus reexamined and potentially reformed in light of the theory.[23]

Existing theories of contract law indeed make such distinctions (explicitly or implicitly), treating, for example, the expectation measure of recovery or the consideration requirement as contract's doctrinal core.[24] However, these choices are by no means obvious: consideration, for example, is not even a *necessary*, let alone core, characteristic of contract in most Continental jurisdictions.[25] Furthermore, looking for a rule that runs through the various contract types already presupposes the flattening Willistonian view of contract as a shapeless unified form.

Therefore, our choice of core is different in kind: choice theory focuses exactly on what the now-conventional view obscures – the multiplicity of contract types that typifies actual contract law. We present this multiplicity in its best light by highlighting its autonomy-enhancing function. As with any other interpretive theory, we cannot expect our interpretation to explain every extant feature of the law. But the gaps that choice theory reveals are useful: they help focus attention on whether and why the law doesn't live up to its own (implicit) ideals.[26]

What first appears as a blemish on the law turns out to be the most important takeaway of choice theory – the relative paucity of types in the realms of family, work, and home compared with the sphere of commerce, and the state's obligations in response.

2. *On Deciding and Thinking.* Putting multiplicity front and center raises a second methodological conundrum. If the differences among contract types are as significant as we claim, does that then imply that "contract" is not an important overarching category, which in turn means that there cannot be a general theory of contract law?

No. A general theory is possible if we keep in mind the distinction between categories for *deciding* and categories for *thinking*.[27] Choice theory does imply that the normative concerns underlying contract types are so diverse that simply labeling something as "contract" is not enough to justify any concrete reform consequence. In other words, we cannot justify treating contract as a category for deciding.

Nevertheless, this does not eliminate the significance of contract as a doctrinal category. Quite the contrary. While normative concerns differ among types, there are enough structural similarities that "contract" is still a useful category for thinking. For example, because all contract types must be voluntary – given our fundamental commitment to autonomy as contract's (one) ultimate value – securing voluntariness is a common challenge of otherwise heterogeneous types. Thinking about the proper means for facing this challenge across contract types may be helpful even if we conclude, as we do in Chapter 8, that it is best handled by prescribing distinct doctrinal tools tailored to the normative valences of particular contract types.

Further, the underlying values animating diverse contract types do overlap: they all aim at securing the instrumental and intrinsic goods of contract – primarily utility and community – while securing autonomy, always as the ultimate value and sometimes as a side-constraint (distinctions we set out in Chapters 4 and 7). This overlap ensures that reflecting on the variety of contract types is likely to yield some useful cross-fertilization and that, in turn, justifies studying them together and treating them as the subject matter of unified scholarly analysis.

Finally, appreciating the common function of all contract types in the service of people's autonomy is crucial because it implies that, for every sphere of potential contracting activity, the state should provide a robust menu of choices. It also implies that a liberal state must develop a category of "residual contracting" for people who prefer to reject contract law's favored forms of interaction (a category that may look quite different from the "general" contract law of existing theory).[28] Freedom to choose among types can and does sit comfortably alongside the freedom to dicker over terms.

3. *On Theory and Practice.* As our title indicates and the text will confirm, this is primarily a book in contract law theory. The front half criticizes existing approaches; the back half offers an alternative. Our goal, though, is not just better theory but also better practice.

We advance an innovative conception of contracts because we believe that adopting choice theory and implementing its reform agenda will enhance the self-determination of real people in the real world. Demonstrating a viable path from theory to practice is, therefore, crucial. Otherwise, choice theory is just a happy fantasy. Indeed, we suspect that some readers may become impatient with questions of implementation even in reading this Introduction.

As we see it, these concerns come in two main forms: substantive and institutional. Substantively, critics may worry that our call for multiplicity of contract types will overlook the limits and drawbacks of choice. What if more choice reduces freedom? Institutionally, critics may be concerned that our references to "contract law" doing this or that means we believe that the disembodied "law" is somehow the agent that should offer contract types or facilitate choice within spheres. Are there actual legal institutions sufficiently competent to implement choice theory?

These are legitimate challenges for anyone concerned with putting choice theory into practice. We postpone our reply to Chapter 12, not because the challenges are unimportant, but because a reply requires that we first set out the contours of choice theory. On the substantive side, we identify a range of cognitive, behavioral, structural, and political economy concerns about expanding choice. We offer this list as a research agenda for interdisciplinary scholars interested in implementing choice theory.

Regarding the institutional challenge, we can sketch out some more practical steps. For example, in the sphere of commerce, we often see market demand driving the creation of new business contract types. Sophisticated commercial parties are likely to be the best type-developers in this sphere. They share a wealth-maximizing metric for evaluating terms and they are motivated to do a good design job because they can directly capture much of the surplus they generate.

Challenges arise when the parties' overriding goal moves away from wealth maximization. Then, there is less reason to expect market demand to drive creation of sufficient types. Implementing choice theory thus devolves into a study of comparative institutional competence of actors including state legislatures and judges, the American Law Institute (ALI) and the Uniform Law Commission (NCCUSL), along with public interest groups, law firms, and lobbyists.

One approach is to encourage states to adopt successful types from other states or countries (we give examples of this "comparative" strategy). Another is to encourage them to support rather than squash emerging and utopian types for which there is already some level of demand (the "experimental" strategy). Institutions such as the ALI or NCCUSL may be able to refine innovative types, say for cohabitation, civil unions, "dependent contractors," and so on (the "incremental" strategy). We aren't arguing that any of these institutions should initiate new contract types from scratch. How would they pick? Our thoughts in this section are admittedly preliminary because full answers will inevitably be linked to a particular contract type or a specific state or national institutional design.

Thus, our argument in Chapter 12 about putting choice theory into practice is somewhat modest, but nonetheless crucial. Most important, we rule out the (devastating) possibility that substantive and institutional criticisms are all-encompassing, and show instead that they are local to particular contract types or institutional settings. There is room to implement choice theory such that contract law does a better job than the status quo in enhancing people's self-determination.

A BRIEF ROADMAP

Part I examines the contributions and limits of prior autonomy-based contract theories. We show why Fried's approach to contractual autonomy cannot work and why all the later rights-based versions from promise theory to transfer theory fare no better. Nevertheless, we argue that autonomy, understood as self-determination, is still the ultimate value of contract. Much of the work here is heavy-duty jurisprudence – we aim for brevity while trying to provide enough detail to persuade the specialists.

Part II explores the main goods people seek from contracting. People generally do not enter contracts to become freer, although autonomy does function as an important side-constraint. The main goods of contract are utility and community, as we define the terms. We show why neither good works alone as the ultimate contract value, but both are essential to any complete theory of the field.

Part III sets out choice theory and shows how contract law plays a positive, active, and previously underappreciated autonomy-enhancing role. We start by developing a more tailored view of autonomy for contract and show how that value relates to utility and community. Values in conflict are the toughest challenges, and we show how to resolve them. Then we spell out how those values relate to contract spheres and types – refining choice theory along the way, answering potential objections that it generates, and showing how it resolves many doctrinal puzzles.

Our Conclusion sketches some of the challenges choice theory must face and the research agenda that it generates as we move beyond Williston and Fried. Choice theory shows that contract law matters even more to freedom than has previously been understood.

* * *

Choice theory has several virtues. It offers a normatively attractive view of freedom through contract law. It provides the first conceptually coherent account of core contract values and their interrelationships. And finally, choice theory marks a path for reform that brings contract law closer to widely shared liberal ideals.

PART I

Autonomy as a Contract Value

1

The Challenge of Autonomy

Part I veers into philosophically intricate territory. It can feel a little "in the weeds." Nevertheless, it's important to get this argument right. The stakes are high. Liberal contract theorists today advocate far-reaching doctrinal reforms based primarily on deductions and inferences derived from their philosophical foundations. If the groundwork does not hold together – and it doesn't, as we show – then their advocacy of particular legal reforms becomes unmoored.

In making this argument, we attempt a delicate balance. We aim for brevity and transparency so as not to exhaust the general reader's patience, while recognizing that our account here may not be of sufficient intricacy for liberal contract theory specialists. In most of the book, we keep textual notes to a minimum, while here, we indulge them somewhat to pay fair respect to the intramural concerns of liberal contract theorists. Also, we use multiple quotations from many of the theorists we discuss for a gain in fidelity but perhaps some loss in readability. Part I can be understood in some measure as philosophical stage-setting.

For those inclined to press on toward our positive theory, the takeaway lessons of Part I can be briefly stated:

Chapter 1 starts with Charles Fried's *Contract as Promise* and evaluates its central role in all modern liberal accounts of contract.[1] Fried's work revived debate on the relation of autonomy to contract. This is an enduring contribution. But he failed to resolve his core normative dilemma, that is, how to justify state coercion of contracts. State coercion seems to run counter to individual autonomy as he defines the term.

Chapter 2 then examines the later liberal scholars who have labored to refine and rehabilitate Fried's account. They have struggled to develop a rights-based foundation for contract law that does not rely on its contribution to enhancing individual autonomy. To use philosophical terms, they have aimed at a deontological account of contractual obligation, purged of any teleological foundation. We illustrate this trend by examining contemporary "promise theory," particularly in the work of Seana Shiffrin – with its expansive reformist claims and covert limits. We show that promise theory subtly rests on "transfer theory," which is fine, so long as transfer theory holds up. But does it?

Chapter 3 examines transfer theory. After thirty years of sustained effort, we can now say transfer theory has failed to bridge the gap that criticism of Fried's work made apparent. Transfer theory, and by extension promise theory, cannot justify the state's coercion of contractual obligations. In other words, deontological liberal justifications for contract law all fail in their central task. And, therefore, these theories cannot be used to justify their extensive legal reform proposals – they can't serve as a persuasive counterweight to the ambitious reform programs developed by efficiency analysts of contract.

We round out this part in Chapter 4, which explains why we do not – must not – give up on autonomy as the foundation of contract, even though existing liberal theories fall short. A liberal theory of contract is still possible and appealing if we embrace as its (teleological) foundation a well-tempered conception of autonomy as self-determination, that is, if we return contract theory to its mainstream liberal roots.

FRIED'S CONTRIBUTION

Modern liberal contract theory starts with Charles Fried's *Contract as Promise*, a great, though flawed, work. The first and most enduring contribution of the book is to push back against generations of theorists – from Lon Fuller and William Perdue in the 1930s through Grant Gilmore and Patrick Atiyah in the 1970s[2] – who sought to make contract disappear as a distinct analytic category. More precisely, they tried to fold contract into the fields of tort and restitution.

At a moment when these critics had already announced *The Death of Contract*, Fried offered a powerful moral justification, grounded in Kantian notions of individual autonomy, for continuing to regard contract as a distinct field of study.[3] Contract, as he explained, increases individual autonomy by empowering people to enlist others to their projects. In his words, promise puts "in another man's hands a new power to accomplish his will, through only a moral power: What he sought to do alone he may now expect to do with our promised help."[4] This straightforward intuition of Fried's is reasonable and robust.[5]

The first sentence of *Contract as Promise* presents its main proposition, what Fried calls "the promise principle." He defines it as "that principle by which persons may impose on themselves obligations where none existed before." This is, Fried continues, "the moral basis of contract law."[6]

Fried's argument is rather complex. To see the flow of his rich account, it repays the effort to read the first chapter of his book. Here we just restate the highlights necessary for our later critique. In summary, he argues that the morality of promise-keeping is premised on the trust that a promise invokes regarding the future actions of the promisor.[7] Trust, in turn, is justified by reference to the social convention of promising.

Fried explains that the social convention of promising increases our autonomy by expanding our options in the long run. Promising enables us to achieve objectives that we can succeed in accomplishing only with the cooperation of others, as he writes:

> In order that I be as free as possible, that my will have the greatest range consistent with the similar will of others, it is necessary that there be a way in which I may commit myself. [Therefore, t]he restrictions involved in promising are restrictions undertaken just in order to increase one's options in the long run, and thus are perfectly consistent with the principle of autonomy.[8]

More recently, he captured this point in noting that promise "is a kind of moral invention: ... it allows persons to create obligation where there was none before, and thus it gives free individuals a facility for extending their reach by enlisting the reliable collaboration of other free persons."[9] So far, so good.

But why is the state justified in coercing performance of the promise absent detrimental reliance by the promisee? Why should free individuals not be able to change their minds without legal liability? Fried recognizes the difficulty in closing the gap between the moral value of promise and a state's use of coercion: the social value engendered by trusting promises does not "show why I should not take advantage of it in a particular case and yet fail to keep my promise."[10]

Nonetheless, Fried continues, the individual obligation of promise-keeping is grounded "in respect for individual autonomy and in trust."[11] The promisor intentionally invokes a convention whose function is "to give grounds – moral grounds – for another to expect the promised performance."[12] To renege on a promise is, therefore, to abuse the trust and thus the vulnerability of the promisee, both of which the promisor freely invited; it amounts, in Fried's view, to wrongful exploitation of another individual.

Fried presents his account as the antithesis to a utilitarian understanding of contract. Whereas the utilitarian emphasizes the general importance of enforcing contracts, the "moralist of duty" perceives promising "as a device that free, moral individuals have fashioned on the premise of mutual trust, and which gathers its moral force from that premise."[13] Thus, "the moralist of duty ... posits a general obligation to keep promises, of which the obligation of contract will be only a special case."[14] However, "since a contract is first of all a promise, the contract must be kept because promises must be kept."[15]

This is as far as Fried goes in justifying the morality of contract. It was a big step – arguing that autonomy, albeit of a Kantian sort, is fundamental to contract. Fried's argument revitalized contract theory. He opened the door to many responses and we do not purport to summarize them all.

But two responses – two challenges – are important for our purposes: one questions the justificatory power of abuse of trust; another one doubts the relevance of the morality of promise-keeping to the practices of promise and contract.

THE INTERNAL CHALLENGE

The first challenge is an internal one. It comes most powerfully from Kantian contract theorists operating within the same philosophical tradition as Fried. They argue, contra Fried, that an *ethical* duty not to abuse someone's trust does not justify a *legal* duty for the same, because "hold[ing] a promisor liable for a presently regretted promise" implies that people are obligated to contribute to this "form of good."[16]

As Peter Benson writes, it may be unfortunate that the practice of contract collapses "if everyone felt at liberty to violate it," but this possible consequence cannot "establish an individual's duty to comply with it in a particular instance."[17] Thus, "in Kantian terms, all that Fried has shown is that the promisor's duty to perform is a duty of virtue, not a juridical obligation of right."[18] In other words, abusing a promisee's trust may be ethically problematic, but absent detrimental reliance, that ethical flaw should not give rise to *legal* liability.

Further, Fried's view that contract promotes people's options in the long run (as distinct from their utility) does not render "maximum individual freedom" any more legitimate as a form of "general advantage" which individual people can be forced to serve.[19] By the same token, justifying contract "on the basis that it is wanted by the individuals who are to be bound by it"[20] – holding promisors liable because they voluntarily invoked this practice – cannot work. The reason, Benson claims, is that from a deontological point of view, an account of contract that relies on people's contingent choices provides "no objectively valid standpoint" that can explain why "a present expression of choice should prevail over future choices."[21] In short, if "there is no basis for holding that nonperformance injures anything that belongs to the promisee," then there is "no basis for concluding that the promisor should be made to hand over the equivalent of the promised performance as a matter of compensation."[22]

Jody Kraus, in defense of Fried, argues that the role of the *ex ante* perspective in his account is limited to the background conventions that inform the parties' expectations and is thus compatible with the deontic commitment simply to "vindicate the parties' pre-existing rights."[23] But this point still does not explain why these expectations need to be forcibly enforced. In effect, Kraus has pushed the problem back a level without transforming or resolving it.

The internal challenge shows that, working from within the Kantian rights-based position on freedom that Fried invokes, contract law may impinge on individual autonomy, the opposite of what Fried intends. Fried tries to get around this challenge by relying on the importance of maintaining a social convention, but that's not a rights-based argument, it's a consequentialist (or teleological) one. Not that there's anything wrong with a teleological autonomy-based account of contracts – our theory is built that way from the ground up. But for a deontological approach, the move is fatal.

THE EXTERNAL CHALLENGE

The second challenge is external. It comes not from Kantian critics, but from the other side of the theoretical divide. Richard Craswell, a lawyer-economist, argues that because promise-keeping relies on a plastic or malleable social convention – one that need not take any particular form or have any specific content – it is (almost) irrelevant to contract law.

The promissory convention dictates that the promisor fulfill the obligations prescribed by the combination of the express language she used and the legal background rules that "fill out the details of what it is [she] has to remain faithful to, or what [her] prior commitment is deemed to be."[24] Hence, the value of promise-keeping "cannot guide the legal system in deciding which background rules to adopt in the first place."[25]

Promise-keeping does require that the promised course of conduct is made "nonoptional to some degree."[26] But promise-keeping does *not* dictate any particular degree of nonoptionality, which means that – with the exception of a contract law rule that would render performance totally optional – the value of promise-keeping is neutral in relation to any possible set of such background rules.[27]

The bottom line, then, as Craswell usefully asserts, is that the promise principle has "little or no relevance" to "those [vast] parts of contract law that govern the proper remedies for breach, the conditions under which the promisor is excused from her duty to perform, or the additional obligations (such as implied warranties) imputed to the promisor as an implicit part of her promise."[28]

Craswell's irrelevance thesis is particularly challenging to theorists, like Fried, who insist on a sharp divide between the demands of promise-keeping morality and utilitarian understandings of contract. Why? Because the irrelevance thesis shows how promissory morality works to jumpstart the utilitarian prescriptions.

As Kraus, a friend of autonomy-based theories of contract, explains, "justify[ing] the legal enforcement of the moral obligation to keep a promise" requires the law to "look to the voluntary choice of promisors not only to identify their promissory obligations but to determine their remedial moral duties as well."[29] Kraus continues, noting that, to respect "the positive liberty of individuals to undertake moral obligations as they see fit" implies, in this line of reasoning, the adoption of "majoritarian default terms" so as to refrain from unnecessarily increasing "the costs of exercising the individual liberty to make promises."[30]

Again, Kantian autonomy for contract runs aground: individuals need contract law to determine their moral duties, but promissory morality is irrelevant to shaping most of that law. So, what justifies contract law? And how should it be designed?

* * *

Fried got the ball rolling: autonomy matters to contract. But his argument stalled. He was unable to advance a rights-based account of contractual freedom purged of covert consequentialist moves. Nor was he able to justify any particular reform program. Answering these two challenges to Fried – from the Kantians on one side and the efficiency theorists on the other – has occupied liberal contract theorists for the past three decades. They've made some progress, but have not, as we show next, been able to resolve the apparent puzzle of freedom through contract.

2

Promise Theory

THE STAKES OF PROMISE THEORY

Contemporary promise theory attempts to close the justificatory gap that Fried left open. There are several flavors of this recent work. In this chapter, to make our discussion more concrete, we illustrate promise theory's claim through a close reading of Seana Shiffrin's scholarship. While her account has been arguably the most influential version to date, work by other leading contract theorists, such as David Owens or Daniel Markovits, could serve equally well to illustrate our broader point, so we make reference to their arguments as well.

Promise theorists do not expressly present their accounts as corrective of Fried's, but we believe that reading them as such is revealing. In particular, we show how contemporary promise theory attempts to address the two challenges to Fried we outlined in Chapter 1. This reading highlights contemporary promise theory's continuity with Fried along with its innovative moves – and it provides a basis for evaluating the powerful critique of contract law Shiffrin has launched.

This chapter shows how promise theory operates and why it naturally relies on and converges into transfer theory – a major strand of post-Fried, rights-based theory we discuss in Chapter 3 – which claims that contracting transfers an entitlement in the promisor's future decision-making power to the promisee. We do not assert that promise theory inevitably converges into transfer theory. But we show that it is the most congenial path – one that benefits from a distinguished Kantian pedigree – for theorists who are determined to banish the teleological underpinnings of Fried's account and to rehabilitate the role of promise-keeping as a robust foundational premise for contract law.

By piggybacking covertly on transfer theory, promise theory seems able to accomplish a lot. It can explain the power to create duties, constrain the content of these duties, limit the reasons that may justify noncompliance and set out the consequences of breach. But this seeming success is short-lived. Our next chapter interrogates transfer theory and explains why it is bound to fail – and therefore why promise theory also fails.

THE MORALITY OF PROMISE

Like Fried, Shiffrin founds promise – and thus also contract – on autonomy. But Fried grounds the morality of promise-keeping in the trust that a promise invokes regarding the future actions of the promisor, while Shiffrin takes a different tack.

First, she analyzes "the moral structure of promise" as a "transfer[ ] of decision-making power,"[1] thus conceptualizing breach as conversion. Recall that Fried relies on trust not transfer. And second, Shiffrin argues that – unlike other garden-variety conventions – promise is a convention that we are *obligated* to have if we respect people's autonomy. By contrast, Fried seems to describe promise as a convention *simpliciter* (although he certainly celebrates its virtues). Shiffrin writes,

> For agents such as ourselves, whose embodiment and development must necessarily involve dependent, inter-dependent, and mutually enriching relationships with others, it seems implausible to posit that the right of autonomy must be understood in such a stark individualist way that it would not include the powers necessary to become full agents and to help others become full agents who can recognize and be recognized by others in morally respectful and empowered ways.[2]

To spell out Shiffrin's argument in her voice a little more, she writes that respecting promise is obligatory because "[a]n autonomous life requires the opportunity to engage in meaningful, moral relations with others," which in turn "depend on agents having the ability to make binding promises," and so "the right to autonomy must contain the power to make binding promises."[3] Therefore – and this is the key point for her – "there is a *duty* to establish a convention of promising," which means that "the existence of the convention [of promise is not] optional and its internal structure [is] significantly constrained in light of the moral purpose to which it was being put."[4]

Accepting these refinements, she argues, both provides moral (autonomy-based) grounds for condemning a failure to keep a promise (or a breach of contract) and implies a rather robust set of legal reforms that follow from such condemnation.

PROMISE AND TRANSFER

For promise to serve autonomy along these lines, it needs to take, in Shiffrin's view, a very specific form: the form of transfer. A promise, she writes, creates "a moral obligation to A [the promisor] and the power in B [the promisee] to insist or release A from performance."[5] And she continues, "because the power behind making promises ... involves the transfer of a party's power to change one's mind to another party,"[6] it precludes the development of possible "destructive potentials within the situation," and "works to neutralize aspects of the situation's hazards and to restore an equal standing between A and B in this local domain."[7]

The binary transfer of authority is also significant for Shiffrin because it distinguishes breaking a promise from other abuses of trust. (Note: this is Shiffrin's implicit response to Benson's "internal challenge" to Fried in Chapter 1.) She notes, "[P]romisees must wait to see whether the promisor will act in character as a moral agent or violate the trust."[8] But Shiffrin says, "that aspect – true of many cases in which one is the object of a duty – is not what is distinctive about the status and powers associated with the promissory duty and the relationship. Being a promisee is not a fully passive state; the promisee officially wields power ceded by the promisor."[9] Indeed, Shiffrin's "conception of the ability to promise ... is one on which the promisor has the ability to transfer a right to make a decision to act on certain reasons for another party," an ability which people "must have ... if they are to have the ability to conduct relationships of adequate moral character."[10]

In short, for Shiffrin, the binary transfer of authority explains the "bindingness" of promises and the wrongfulness of breaking a promise: "By promising to φ, the promisor transfers his or her right to act otherwise to the promisee. To not φ, then, is to act in a way the promisor has no right to do, and to φ is to act in a way the promisee has a right that she (the promisor) do."[11]

We have used Shiffrin's complex argument to make a fairly straightforward point: promise theory relies on transfer. It is important to note that Shiffrin is not idiosyncratic on this crucial aspect. David Owens is probably the first contemporary philosopher to present a transfer account of promise, grounded in what he calls the promisee's "authority interest," namely: "the promisee's interest in having authority over the activities of the promisor."[12] (Indeed, Shiffrin's account can be read as an attempt to explain and justify this interest.[13]) Daniel Markovits recently advanced another theory of promise that seeks to provide an alternative, albeit related, justification. He claims that "a promisor intends, within the sphere of the promise, not only to adjust but to

defer to her promisee, to grant him authority over her, and indeed to subordin-
ate her ends to his will."[14]

Interestingly, when they invoke the transfer notion, both Owens and
Markovits – but not Shiffrin – cite Kant's observation on contracts that a
promisee takes "possession" of her promisor's "choice."[15] Modern transfer
theory of contract, which we analyze in some detail in Chapter 3, builds
directly on this Kantian position.

NORMATIVE IMPLICATIONS

Why does all this matter? To return to Shiffrin, her autonomy-based transfer
theory of promise could have practical effect. By understanding promise along
these lines, she intends to show that "the conventionalist view sheds its
association with contingency and comprehensive plasticity,"[16] as Craswell's
"external challenge" from Chapter 1 implies. Instead, "it becomes a view
about a set of practices we are obliged to one another to create and maintain."[17] Specifically, it implies that "[i]n light of this transfer, the promisee
has the right to expect (and often demand) performance and has the concomitant power to use her transferred power or decision to waive or excuse the
promisor's obligation of performance."[18]

Thus, Shiffrin insists that the morality of promise-keeping does not merely
set a limiting principle for contract law, as it does for Kraus (and Craswell).
Rather, it provides the normative backbone of contracts: promise-keeping, for
Shiffrin, is contract law's animating principle, and should guide the interpretation and further development of this vast body of doctrine.[19]

Indeed, Shiffrin argues that the normative teeth of promise-keeping morality
are quite sharp. Whereas "the legal doctrines of contract associate legal
obligations with morally binding promises, the contents of the legal obligations
and the legal significance of their breach do not correspond to the moral
obligations and the moral significance of their breach."[20] This gap is troubling,
Shiffrin claims, both for its own sake and because – given the "strong resem-
blance" between contract and promise – the overly forgiving treatment of
contract law to transgressions is likely to "exert a subtle influence over time on
how seriously the moral agent regarded unilateral promises and how casually
she regarded promissory breach."[21]

To prevent this unhappy consequence for promise-keeping, core contract
doctrines – such as those dealing with consideration, foreseeability, mitigation, specific performance, liquidated damages, and punitive damages – must
be radically reformed. In Shiffrin's view, contractual liability must be both

broader and more rigid, that is, subject to many fewer limitations and backed up by harsher remedies, than it currently is.[22] This is a big claim.

TRANSFER THEORY ROOTS OF PROMISE THEORY REFORMS

The justification for this broad reform program relies squarely on the transfer theory underpinnings of promise theory. They are inseparable. In Shiffrin's account, transfer typically implies that "a promisor is morally expected to keep her promise through performance,"[23] and this obligation applies also to "a unilateral promise [where] nothing is received in exchange" and even if the promisee has not "reasonably relied to her detriment."[24] Only "if, for good reason, what was promised became impossible, or very difficult, to perform" might financial substitutes be appropriate.[25] "Otherwise, intentional, and often even negligent, failure to perform appropriately elicits moral disapprobation."[26] Thus, if promise necessarily functions as a transfer of authority, promissory morality can be satisfied only by "the consent of the promisee," and not by supplying "the financial equivalent of what was promised."[27]

Under this account, when breach occurs, the transfer component of promise theory means that contract law cannot justify "the legal doctrine of mitigation [which] places the burden on the promisee to make positive efforts to find alternative providers instead of presumptively locating that burden fully on the breaching promisor."[28] And because intentional promissory breach is classified as a wrong, it requires not compensation, but specific performance, and may also merit "punitive reactions." Again, this approach stands in sharp contradistinction to actual contract law, here the law's "general prohibition of punitive damages."[29]

Unlike Kraus, Shiffrin is not impressed by the effect of the logic of majoritarian defaults on what may constitute a breach and what should be the proper remedial response. "I doubt," she writes, "that one may alter by declaration or by agreement the moral significance of a broken promise."[30] The reason for this is that "the power to alter the significance and appropriateness of others' reactions to a broken obligation is not within the power of the promisor."[31] As with any other wrong, in responding to another's breach "we have the elective power to forgive, but forgiveness involves, among other things, recognition of a past wrong, not a power to make it the case that the wrong was never a wrong."[32]

For Shiffrin then, contract is species of promise, promise is obligatory because of transfer, and the morality of contract-as-promise-as-transfer requires radically reconstructing contract law.

A DIGRESSION ON THE PHILOSOPHY OF PROMISE

This chapter has been mostly addressed to liberal contract scholars in an effort to explain why recent promise theory fares no better than Fried's original contribution. In the next two pages, we briefly address moral philosophers.

Problems with liberal theories of *contract* go deeper than just their reliance on promise theory. Liberal theories of *promise* are also problematic – and choice theory can help here too. For the purposes of this chapter, we have accepted as true the assumption that contract and promise share the same conceptual structure. But this view is not self-evident.

Some argue that because of its typically informal setting, promise necessarily has a simple binary structure.[33] Indeed, as against the vast heterogeneity of agreements discussed in contract law cases, the philosophical literature on promise typically builds on and works with simple hypotheticals of limited types of voluntary obligations rendered in informal settings. Given this divergence, the simple binary structure of promise need not necessarily constrain other settings where more complicated arrangements may well be preferable.[34]

We take an even stronger view and reject the notion that there is a single binary type of promise. Promise types are as heterogeneous as contract types. Nothing in the literature on promises suggests, let alone establishes, that one specific promise type (the cousin of Williston's commercial contract, if you will) is more basic than the others. The practice of promising often manifests itself in contexts other than the transfer of authority, and this variety of forms is part of the autonomy-enhancing contribution of the practice of promise, rather than an add-on or a blemish to be marginalized or suppressed. Therefore, promise need not and in fact does not always follow the binary logic of transfer, notwithstanding the prevalent philosophical agreement that it does.[35]

Yes, the practice of promising often manifests itself in contexts of binary transfers of authority. But promising (apart from contracting) also arises where, first, the purpose of the promise is to shift future risks and opportunities and, second, the purpose of the promise is to set up a structure for future co-governance of contingencies. These categories of promises deviate from the binary structure Shiffrin and others present as necessary and nonetheless raise none of the "hazards" or "destructive potentials" they are worried about.[36] People make these kinds of promises to achieve utilitarian and communitarian goods potentially available from promising, that is, they promise for the same reasons that they enter contracts (as we discuss in Part II).

We note this parallel to make a bigger point: while most liberal contract theories reason from philosophy to law, the reverse can also be fruitful. Indeed, choice theory can reconstruct theories of *promise* to be more cohesive. Thus, Shiffrin already admits some divergence in the conceptual structure of promise and contract (though the thrust of her work does adhere to the contract-as-species-of-promise idea). For example, she allows that "a promise is not simply transferable" unlike most contracts (excepting personal ones).[37] Also, in discussing "redundant" promises, she highlights the multiple dimensions of variance among types of promises and – even more signifi-cantly – shows that some types of promises imply partial transfers of decision-making power.[38] This last observation diverges from her insistence on the binary form of transfer noted earlier,[39] and can thus arguably allow promising to encompass both the risk-shifting and co-governance promise types we mentioned above.

Reconstructing Shiffrin's views in this way would absolve her work from much of our critique of transfer theory. But understanding promise in this open-ended way that acknowledges built-in qualifications and conditions has a price. It would render promise-as-transfer theory – and thus also contract-as-promise-as-transfer theory – as malleable as Fried's formulation and it would therefore undermine her attempt to respond to Craswell's "external challenge."

Fixing this problem would require a normative framework for promise types. Such a reconstruction of the moral philosophy of promise itself is something that choice theory could provide – but it lies outside the scope of this book. Why? Resolving the debate over the conceptual structure of *promise* is unnecessary for our current purposes – which is to find an appealing account of why autonomy matters to *contract*.

If we are right – that promise types can be as heterogeneous as contract types – then the anti-conversion understanding of the morality of promise-keeping is irrelevant to contract theory. More precisely, each promise type, like each contract type, must be analyzed according to its particular normative concerns. No promise type has the moral primacy necessary to govern the others or to shape contract as a whole. And therefore, there is no reason to share Shiffrin's concern that actual contract law – with its rules for mitigation, expectation damages, and the like – will erode the morality of promise-keeping, because that morality already diverges according to promise type.

On the other hand, even if we are wrong in these preliminary reflections – even if promise is indeed necessarily structured in the binary terms dictated by transfer theory – the promise theory of contract is doomed to collapse given the failure of transfer theory, which we are about to establish in Chapter 3.

This is all somewhat technical. The point is that while promise theory aims high, it rests on shaky foundations – both on the normative/legal contract side and, as it turns out, on the moral/philosophical promise side.

✳ ✳ ✳

Promise theory makes no small claim. Like Fried, Shiffrin argues that the morality of promise-keeping is and should be contract's ultimate justification and should thus guide its interpretation and reform, in ways large and small.

But for the promise theorists' views to stick, they have to answer what we are calling the internal challenge of hidden consequentialism and the external challenge of legal irrelevance. Fried runs aground on the former when he analyzes breach of contract in terms of abuse of trust. Shiffrin and other promise theorists take a step forward when they refrain from invoking trust to explain the wrong of promise-breaking.

Then, to avoid the challenge of legal irrelevance, they attempt to reconstruct promise in binary terms. Thus, they recurrently analyze "the moral structure of promise" (explicitly or implicitly) as a "transfer[ ] of decision-making power."[40] This feature, which has by and large eluded commentators,[41] is significant because it shows that their reconstructed account of promise theory is a version – a sweeping and powerful version – of transfer theory. Indeed, Shiffrin has recently identified herself as a transfer theorist.[42]

While promise theory has been conventionally analyzed as distinct from transfer theory,[43] and contemporary champions of "contract as promise" have paid scarcely any attention to transfer theory, the success of these new theories turns out to depend on the validity of the transfer theory of contract. If transfer theory fails, so does promise theory.

3

Transfer Theory

Following Fried, the core question has remained: what justifies legal coercion of the promisor? The answer is transfer. Rights-based liberal accounts today share this key element: a contract transfers something, some "thing."

Transfer is the Kantian's solution to Fried's dilemma. In this view, law can justifiably enforce contracts – including wholly executory contracts – because the contract itself, as Benson puts it, already transfers from the promisor to the promisee "a legally protected interest."[1] This means that "performance respects those rights whereas breach injures them,"[2] which in turn implies that the transfer justifies the state's intervention to correct this wrong.[3]

If the theory works, it's the transfer that justifies state coercion on rights-based grounds, wholly apart from consequentialist concerns like preserving trust or enhancing autonomy. This is the core move not just for Benson, whose "internal challenge" to Fried we raised in Chapter 1, but also for the promise theorists we discussed in Chapter 2, and for all the other "transfer theorists"[4] we examine here.

WHAT DOES CONTRACT TRANSFER?

Now we can turn away from the promise theorists. While they rely on transfer theory – without it, promise theories collapse – none digs deeply into whether the transfer point is valid. Transfer theorists address this problem head on. Their challenge has been to explain what exactly contracts transfer and how they do so. While transfer theorists vary in nuance,[5] the core propositions remain the same.

Arthur Ripstein, the group's most rigorous neo-Kantian, aptly captures their general orientation regarding transfer. Contract, for Ripstein, is "the legal means through which persons are entitled to make arrangements for them-selves, and so to change their respective rights and duties."[6] The starting point of his analysis of contract – like the premise of his general theory of law – is an individual's right to personal independence. Kantian personal independence is not a good to be promoted but a constraint on the conduct of others, which is exhausted by the requirement that no one gets to tell anyone else what purposes to pursue.[7] Against this background, contract gets its significance by enabling free people to "set and pursue their own purposes interdependently."[8]

For a contract to be binding, both parties must participate in the creation of a new relationship that transfers rights: only if both make use of their "respective moral powers" is the enforcement of such a transfer consistent with their "respective freedom."[9] Consent, in this account, is conceptualized as "two persons uniting their wills to create new rights and duties between them," and thus making "new means available to each other."[10] Unlike the will of either party on his or her own,[11] a united will can justify the transfer of a preexisting right; it can also "create new rights, including rights to things that need not exist as fully determinate antecedent to the transfer."[12] (Notice that, at this point, Ripstein expands the notion of transfer and thus implicitly responds to – or, rather, preempts – some of the critiques launched at transfer theory.[13])

Ripstein's reasoning is complex,[14] but his bottom-line is simple: every individual starts from a position of personal independence, and, then, through a transaction based on a united will, the promisee receives title to compel the promisor's future performance. "By uniting your will with another person's with respect to a particular transaction, you can give that person powers over your person and property in a way that is consistent with your exclusive power to determine how they will be used."[15]

THREE SHARED FEATURES

This brief summary of Ripstein's account barely touches on the complexity and rigor of his work. Nor does it allow comparison with the formulations of other leading transfer theorists. But it does suffice for our purposes, which is to help bring out three characteristic features of transfer theories:

1. *Conceptual View.* As just mentioned, transfer theorists are committed to the conceptual view that the act of contracting transfers an entitlement to the promisee (either an entitlement that pre-exists the contract,[16] or one that the contract itself creates). This point is the basis of their claim that breach must be understood as "an interference with the promisee's ownership interest acquired at contract formation," and thus an injury that the law corrects based on strict adherence to the parties' Kantian independence.[17]

2. *Doctrinal Implication.* Next, transfer theorists converge also on at least one important doctrinal point, that contract law should concern itself with an objective approach to the parties' state of mind. In this, they diverge from, and improve upon, Fried's account. The doctrinal point, which indeed follows a theory grounded in personal independence and clear boundaries between mine and yours, is implicit in Ripstein's account,[18] but emerges explicitly in others. For example, it explicitly engages Randy Barnett,[19] who criticizes Fried for relying on "an inquiry as to the promisor's actual state of mind at the time of agreement" – in contrast to the objective theory that actually dominates existing contract law.[20]

Barnett uses this problem of doctrinal fit to assert a deeper deficiency in Fried's account: its inadequate attention to "the interrelational function of contract law," which, for Barnett, both explains and justifies law's use of "a manifested intention to be legally bound" as the "criterion of enforceability."[21] In a nutshell, for Barnett, "Only a general reliance on objectively ascertainable assertive conduct will enable a system of entitlements to perform its allotted boundary-defining function."[22] This commitment, he argues, explains and justifies why "objective consent generally takes precedence over subjective assent."[23]

There are many steps between Barnett's doctrinal observation and his positive account. We omit them here and raise his work primarily to note that it reflects the uniform view of transfer theorists in endorsing contract doctrine's objective approach, a point to which we return shortly.

3. *Normative Focus.* The final, and most significant, commonality among transfer theorists relates to a shared normative commitment to the idea that freedom means personal independence and not autonomy (or self-determination) – at least insofar as contract is concerned. Thus, for Barnett, the function of contract doctrine is to set clearly "the boundaries of protected domains,"[24] which means that it should "identify the rights of individuals engaged in transferring entitlements, and thereby indicate when physical or legal force may legitimately be used."[25]

Contract law, in this view, is "that part of a system of entitlements that identifies those circumstances in which entitlements are validly transferred from person to person by their consent."[26] And consent is crucial because only by requiring that "others take the interests of the rights holder into account when seeking to obtain the rights she possesses" can contract law properly "facilitate freedom of human action and interaction."[27]

Indeed, consent is so central to Barnett's account that he coins "consent theory" to describe his approach. The significance for Barnett of clear

boundaries emerges from his commitment to an early Nozickian view of
personal independence (the dominant modern libertarian strand of Kantian
thinking), in which individual rights require clear "boundaries within which
individuals may live, act, and pursue happiness free of the forcible interference of others."[28]

Barnett's libertarian account finds a nice echo in Ripstein's Kantian commitment to an individual's right to personal independence. Though the paths
differ, their normative views in this contract law arena largely converge
(Ripstein is eager, however, to distinguish himself from Nozick by, for
example, defending anti-discrimination rules).[29] Both imply that the only
necessary role for contract law – and, for Barnett, the only justified role – is
to enforce the deal to which the parties have mutually consented.

In sum, transfer theory converges along three dimensions. We agree with
the doctrinal point regarding the objective basis of contract law. That point
has been widely accepted,[30] and we endorse it also for reasons that become
clear below. Our critique focuses on the two other shared features of transfer
theory, that is, its conceptual and normative claims.

CONTRACT AND PROPERTY

The conceptual claim of transfer theory fails in two ways. First, contract is not
property. All transfer accounts ground contract in ownership, either a preexisting ownership of one's future actions or of the right the contracting parties
create in such performance. They assume our "sole and despotic dominion"[31]
over these entitlements, and furthermore – and crucially so – that a transfer of
these entitlements (that is: a contract) *necessarily* needs to take the form of a
complete assignment to the promisee of the right to the promisor's future
actions. This assumption, however, just buries contract's moral underpinnings
in a naïve view of property.

Neither the range of transferability, nor even its inclusion within the scope
of an owner's entitlement, is self-defining. Ownership (and property) is open
to competing interpretations and permutations. There is no inevitable content
to the concept – even Blackstone never had a simple Blackstonian vision of
ownership[32] – and no arbitration among the different available conceptions is
possible without pre-commitment to some normative apparatus.[33]

As Felix Cohen demonstrated long ago, every property right involves *some*
power to exclude others from doing something. But this is a rather modest
truism which yields hardly any practical implications, as Cohen already
emphasized.[34] Private property is also always subject to limitations and obligations, and "the real problems we have to deal with are problems of degree,

problems too infinitely intricate for simple panacea solutions."[35] This is not to say that property is just a "laundry list" of substantive rights with a limitless number of possible permutations – but any coherent normative framework for property cannot be stated in the way that transfer theories require.[36]

Thus, transfer theory operates with a big asterisk. It requires that there exists a defensible conception of property as an absolute, unconditional, and unqualified right, which is furthermore securely detached from consequentialist concerns. Neo-Kantians have indeed labored to construct such a view of property. But they have failed, for reasons that go beyond our scope here.[37] No one else has made a persuasive case along these lines either. Transfer theorists cannot indefinitely count on the asterisk of a promised, elusive, non-consequentialist view of property.

Restated, the key conceptual hurdle for transfer theory is the non-self-defining nature of ownership. Contract may transfer some "thing," but what is that thing? The same consequentialist choices we make about autonomy in contract just trace back into consequentialist debates about what we mean by a "thing" in property.[38] By assuming the opposite, transfer theory relies on an implausible view of property.

A move of this sort has been tried before. Remember *The Death of Contract* we noted in Chapter 1? That book was part of the reliance theorists' attempt to assimilate contract into tort and restitution – a project that prompted Fried to argue for contract as a distinct practice, rooted in its own morality. Analyzing contract as if it were property works no better today than did assimilating it to tort and restitution some generations ago. Contract needs to be understood as a distinctive legal category. Choice theory shows how to accomplish this task.

DUTY AND POWER

The second conceptual problem with transfer theory, even more crucial for our current purposes, is its problematic understanding of contract law itself. In line with Fried's notion that contracts must be kept because promises must be kept, transfer theorists' accounts require that contract be viewed as fundamentally *duty-imposing*.[39]

It may make sense to analyze tort law doctrines dealing with our bodily integrity in these terms – assuming people have such pre-legal and pre-conventional rights, tort law affirms the correlative duties against their violation. But contract law works differently.[40] Rather than vindicating existing rights, contract law is first and foremost *power-conferring*.

We agree that duties not to interfere with people's rights are relevant to contract law, but they are secondary. Rules concerning duress, fraud, and the like, which aim at ensuring that people not be forced into contracts, do impose duties. However, these duty-imposing areas of contract doctrine rely on the same normative commitments that explain and justify law's support for allowing people to self-impose obligations in the first place.[41]

Even more fundamentally, these piggy-backing (duty-imposing) rules – which safeguard contracts' voluntariness – would be meaningless in the absence of (power-conferring) contracts: their role is to protect our ability to apply the powers enabled by contract, and they would be pointless in a world that does not recognize the power to contract. This is exactly why attempts to establish a harm-based, duty-imposing theory that does not piggyback on the normative power to contract are bound to fail: they necessarily assume some notion of reasonable reliance on the contract, which is, in turn, intelligible only in terms of these same normative powers.[42] (The same reasoning applies to the correct, but trivial, observation that contract law is duty-imposing *ex post*, when the promisor is contesting whether she is bound by the promise: this duty is wholly derivative of contract's power-conferring core.)

As a power-conferring body of law, contract law "attaches legal consequences to certain acts" in order "'to enable people to affect norms and their application in such a way if they desire to do so for this purpose.'"[43] This feature captures the empowering role of contract that Fried identified and Kraus later highlights. As Kraus explains, contract is "a particularly valuable means for pursuing ends," because, by recognizing people's power to undertake obligations, it allows individuals to provide credible assurances "to induce promisees to assist them in realizing their ends."[44]

Does the objective theory of contract undermine our conceptual point regarding the power-conferring nature of contract? We think not. Here's the potential difficulty, per Gregory Klass: a purely power-conferring doctrine should be designed to "ensure that a person's acts result in legal change only when it is her purpose to achieve such a change," whereas contract law merely "ensures that a significant proportion of actors ... are likely to have such a purpose."[45]

The objective theory of contract fails to "include mechanisms to prevent inadvertent exercises of the power."[46] Nevertheless, this limit does not undermine our claim. As Kraus argues, "making subjective intent a necessary condition for making a promise" would have frustrated "the point of promising" or at least severely limited its role only to "individuals who make promises to people who already trust them."[47] Therefore, promisors "would choose to make their promises *objectively binding*."[48]

Kraus does acknowledge the downside of objective theory to personal autonomy: it undermines "the negative right of individuals (merely objective promisors) to be free from subjectively unintended obligations."[49] But as Kraus asserts, the law justifiably follows the prescriptions of "personal sovereignty" – the conception of individual autonomy on which promissory morality relies[50] – to "give priority to respect for the positive liberty of faultless individuals" who "choose to undertake objectively binding promises," over the "negative liberty of blameworthy individuals."[51]

In short, contract law cannot be neutral in such a contest, and given the intersubjective context in which it operates, it correctly opts for the objective theory.[52]

NORMATIVE FAILURE IN TRANSFER THEORY

This conclusion not only explains the secure status of objective theory, but also reveals why the resistance of rights-based theorists to considering consequences – even consequences to people's autonomy – cannot work.

Contract is irreducibly concerned with power-conferring rules; even Ripstein begins his account by stating that contract is the "means" that entitles persons "to make arrangements for themselves, and so to change their respective rights and duties."[53] In certain contexts – especially in close-knit groups – these rules may be conventional (social norms enforced notably via the parties' reputational concerns).[54] In many others, contracting heavily relies on the law, so that by subjecting themselves to the potential deployment of "the powerful institutionalized mechanisms" of contract law, people who have no preexisting reason to trust one another can cooperate, and each can rely on the other's rationality as the sole necessary safeguard.[55]

Moreover, even for parties guided by their own social norms, contract law often provides background safeguards, a safety net for a rainy day that can help catalyze trust in their routine, happier interactions.[56] Thus, law (or a law-like social convention) shapes, and does not merely reflect, the interpersonal practice of contracting, and in designing contract law, we necessarily make choices that affect the contours of the parties' bilateral relationship.

The first question for an autonomy-based contract law is not "what *constraints* to people's autonomy are legitimate?" (as it is for many aspects of tort law); rather, it is "how should contract law *enhance* people's autonomy?"[57] The former inquiry is not irrelevant to contracts, of course; but it is meaningless unless we endorse contract, an endorsement that makes sense from an autonomy perspective only if we find contract to be autonomy-enhancing.

This latter inquiry, which is thus more fundamental, necessarily implies an *ex ante* discussion dealing with the ways law can facilitate forms of bilateral voluntary obligations that are conducive to contract's autonomy-enhancing *telos*. This inquiry is not quantitative: it is not about maximizing the amount of autonomy in the world. But it is teleological nonetheless. Contract is not worth keeping in and of itself. Rather, its value derives from its contribution to our autonomy, which is valued for its own sake. So we are looking for the system which is as conducive as possible to people's autonomy, namely: one that generates the most autonomy-friendly implications.

Libertarian contract theorists, like Barnett, may admit that law matters and still endorse a minimalist role for contract law – along the lines of the boundary-crossing principle suitable for Robert Nozick's original version of the night-watchman state in *Anarchy, State, and Utopia*.[58] (As an aside, *pace* Nozick's argument in that famous book, a commitment to his powerful conception of utopia as a framework of utopias requires a much more robust law, including contract law, than the night-watchman state would allow.[59])

The important point here is that there is nothing particular to contract law that justifies or requires Barnett's libertarian account. There is also nothing particularly Nozickian about it – Nozick himself later acknowledged the flaws of his early version of libertarianism and the necessity of a more active role for the state and its laws.[60] However, if a minimalist libertarian view of the state appeals to you, if you believe that would make the world a better place, then Barnett's view could plausibly inform your approach to contract law – but this view is a choice based on consequentialist reasoning, not a requirement derived from deontological principles.

* * *

Notice the tectonic shift in the nature of this last argument: with a power-conferring body of law like contract, the consequences of competing contract systems matter. The door that Fried opened has closed.

We are now seeking a normatively attractive view of individual autonomy to guide the state in shaping its contract law. Contract law confers the power to create new rights which are crucial to people's autonomy, and therefore contract should not be understood in pure conventionalist terms. It is, as Shiffrin correctly implied,[61] a convention that a liberal state is obliged to establish given its obligation to respect people's autonomy irrespective of the instrumental goods (such as aggregate welfare) this practice can also bring about. But because contract is valued for the sake of autonomy, this normative power which the practice confers cannot be defended from an autonomy perspective without engaging with its implications on people's autonomy.

That's indeed quite a different path from the one taken during the rights-based detour, but it's the correct way for contract theory to go. More strongly, it's the only way to go for a liberal theory of contract, and it's where we turn next.

4

Recovering Autonomy

In this chapter, we reconnect contract theory with mainstream liberal concerns by celebrating the teleological underpinnings of Fried's account, that is, we bring forward strands that he and later liberal contract theorists have tried to write out of their accounts. To recover autonomy for contract, we explore three puzzles – independence versus self-determination, intrinsic versus ultimate values, and misfeasance versus nonfeasance. The result is to ready autonomy for its center-stage role in Part III when we present choice theory.

It is time to admit the failure of the ambitious effort to ground liberal contract theory in personal independence and other rights-based incantations. If the proper meaning of autonomy is merely as a constraint, contract is impossible, or rather unjustified. But it is neither.

The way forward is to build a theory of contracts on a conception of autonomy as self-determination or self-authorship. Such an approach answers the classical question of contract theory: on what grounds does the obligation of agreement-keeping arise? The answer, simply, is that having the normative power to bind ourselves is of (instrumental) value.[1]

The value that contract serves is autonomy: law (or any pre-legal convention we should respect) empowers individuals, as Fried argued, to make agreements that facilitate their ability legitimately to enlist one another in pursuing private goals and purposes – and thus contract law enhances our ability to be the authors of our own lives. This seemingly simple statement encapsulates one of the most difficult challenges of contract theory: just as self-authorship requires the ability to write and *rewrite* our life-story, contract law enables us to make credible commitments while safeguarding our ability to start afresh by limiting the types of enforceable commitments we can undertake.[2]

The shift from personal independence (or negative liberty) to autonomy (or self-determination) should be natural to liberals, who generally reject the thin (libertarian) conception of freedom as independence. Self-determination represents a rich conception of freedom; its value is what makes our independence worthwhile: we are all entitled to be free from coercion because this freedom is necessary for each of us if we are to each write by him- or herself the (separate) story of our (separate) lives.

This is why liberals insist that an individual person is free not merely in the formal sense of not being subordinated to the choices of another, but also in the more robust sense of being able to make meaningful choices about how his or her life should go. Free individuals, John Rawls writes, act on their capacity "to have, to revise, and rationally to pursue a conception of the good."[3] A person can be "free" in the formal sense simply because no one else is in a position of domination over her. But this conception is too narrow because it leaves out concerns for the effective realization of that person's ability to form and pursue a conception of the good.

As H.L.A. Hart observed, self-determination is necessary for people to lead the fully human life they are entitled to; while this requires a measure of independence, it "is not something automatically guaranteed by a structure of negative rights."[4]

Substituting independence with self-determination as contract's ultimate value solves many difficulties encountered by previous liberal theories of contract. First, as a power-conferring body of law, contract law is potent means for enhancing our self-determination – an understanding that implies the teleological perspective Fried et al. tried to resist. Also, starting from self-determination means there is nothing mysterious in the duty to perform: this duty, as we explain later in this chapter, nicely follows the obligation of reciprocal respect for self-determination that underlies private law. (This obligation also entails a commitment to relational equality, which we defend in Chapter 8.)

Finally, basing contract theory on self-determination, rather than independence, creates space to address properly the role of utility and community (a task we take up in Part II). These goods do not work as ultimate, freestanding values of contract, but neither are they fully specified by the abstract notion of self-determination. Rather, they are goods that can be components of, or instrumental to, the story of our lives; in other words, they are the reasons why people recruit others through contract.

Note that we are not claiming that contract is the only way for satisfying preferences or engaging in meaningful relationships, just as we do not argue that recruiting others through contract is the only way self-determining individuals can pursue their (utilitarian or communal) goals. But in a world of profound interpersonal interdependence – that is, in our actual world – the ability legitimately to enlist other individuals to these goals is crucial, even if not analytically indispensable.

Putting these ideas together, we conclude that an autonomy-based theory of contract is not about maximizing utility or optimizing community. Instead, it is committed to ensuring a rich repertoire of contract types that empower self-determining individuals to pursue their understanding of utility and community.

INSTRUMENTAL, INTRINSIC, AND ULTIMATE VALUES

Founding the value of contract on self-determination implies, as does any liberal account of contract, that contracts must be *voluntary* undertakings. It also implies that this thin understanding of contract's core is insufficient; that liberals cannot be content with the traditional hands-off posture of freedom of contract. The robust set of doctrines that constitute contract types are not merely optional add-ons that may be nice to have. Rather, as we explain in Chapter 7, taking autonomy seriously requires a proactive law that makes contractual options viable, indeed possible.

This means that a liberal theory of contract law cannot be content simply with guarding our independence. But it does not imply that contract law should dismiss personal independence, a conclusion that would undermine contract law's core commitment to voluntariness.[5]

As we have just hinted, the value of independence lies in its contribution to self-determination – but the former is not merely a means to the latter. We are not arguing that independence is an *instrumental* value – we don't think that the value of independence is fully captured by "the value of its consequences, or [by] the value of the consequences it is likely to have, or . . . can be used to produce."[6] Understanding independence as a means to the end of autonomy implies that our commitment to people's independence must necessarily retreat and give way every time it seems to conflict with the norms that best promote their autonomy,[7] which seems unacceptable.

Indeed, such an easy path to overriding people's independence is exactly the target of Isaiah Berlin's famous warning regarding the *intrinsic* significance of negative liberty. Taking a fully instrumental view of independence might imply (and for some has implied) a carte blanche for ignoring people's "actual wishes," which may be driven by "irrational impulse, uncontrolled desires" and the like, "in the name, and on behalf, of their 'real' selves." The resulting coercion and oppression caused by such views led Berlin to insist that "some portion of human existence must remain independent of the sphere of social control" and that "[t]o invade that preserve, however small, would be despotism."[8]

Such worries about abuse do not necessarily indict thinking about independence in sheer instrumental terms. But the idea that people's actual wishes are mere indicia of what is worthy of respect is objectionable even if there is no abuse, and this objection indicates that such an instrumentalist understanding of independence fails to capture its value. Libertarians may find these problems to be exactly the spur that motivates them to think about independence as law's (or private law's) *ultimate* value. But the choice we face is not binary.

A value can be "intrinsically valuable," that is, "valuable even apart from [its] instrumental value" or its contribution "to producing certain consequences" without being also "of ultimate value." Although a value of this type (think, for example, of the value of art) is either explained or justified by reference to another, ultimate value, or its value lies in being "a constitutive part" or essential ingredient of that ultimate value, its contribution to that value is not fully captured in instrumental terms.[9] The lesson for our purposes is clear: although independence is not an ultimate value, neither is it merely instrumental – rather, it is intrinsically valuable.

As an intrinsic value, independence must be taken very seriously by every decent liberal polity. This prescription entails some implications for contract law, notably its justified commitment to voluntariness. But it does not imply the sole dominion of independence in the contractual domain, as the rights-based theorists would argue.

Treating independence as an intrinsic value, not the ultimate value, is challenging. We need to make sure that independence does not sidestep the ultimate value (self-determination) of which it is a constitutive part or transgress other values constitutive of self-determination. Simultaneously, we must safeguard against its own derogation to a mere means to a superior end. To appreciate the complexity of this task, think of how one who conceives of both healthiness and deliciousness as constitutive of dinner goodness needs to accommodate these potentially conflicting concerns.

This challenge cannot be faced with a magic formula, which is exactly why liberals, like Hart, are unimpressed with the early Nozick's attempt to "lump together, and ban as equally illegitimate, things so different in their impact on individual life as taking some of a man's income to save others from great suffering and killing him or taking one of his vital organs for the same purpose."[10] Whereas the latter is surely unacceptable, the former, Hart insists, is perfectly agreeable since it does *not* "ignore the moral importance of the division of humanity into separate individuals and threaten the proper inviolability of persons."[11]

Hence, Hart focuses us on the significance of the "unexciting but indispensable chore" of distinguishing "between the gravity of the different restrictions on different specific liberties and their importance for the conduct of a meaningful life."[12] Indeed, and in sum, the most fundamental problem with deontological liberal contract theories is their reliance on an impoverished idea of contractual autonomy. They lost touch with the ultimate liberal value of autonomy, which is self-determination, not independence.

AFFIRMATIVE DUTIES IN PRIVATE LAW

Rights-based theorists of contract are unlikely to be satisfied with this position. We have already dealt with several of their objections. Here, we consider a final one concerning our justification for imposing *affirmative* interpersonal duties.

Neo-Kantian private law theorists object to a view that "hold[s] a promisor liable for a presently regretted promise" if it implies that people are obligated to contribute to a "form of good,"[13] or, more precisely, to the extent it imposes on individuals the affirmative obligation of actively supporting the ability of others to self-determine. For them, such an obligation misses the distinction between misfeasance and nonfeasance which they see as the "organizing normative idea"[14] of a liberal private law and thus its signature feature.[15]

We agree that this distinction is indeed relevant to any liberal legal system – and thus to our private law, and more specifically our contract law – but only up to a point. The distinction does not require that we should discard *any* responsibility affirmatively to serve people's self-determination.[16] Private law, like law more generally, is rightly cautious about affirmative interpersonal duties to aid others, in part because they may excessively interfere with people's autonomy[17] (also because, for example, imposing an obligation to rescue may dilute the ethical value of altruism, while pragmatically, it may be difficult to draw lines between easy and hard cases[18]). Placing limits through a negative duty on a person's courses of action is typically less intrusive on that person's autonomy than dictating – through an affirmative duty – what this course of action should be.

This understanding of the intuitive bite of the nonfeasance/misfeasance distinction, defended and demonstrated elsewhere,[19] does *not* imply that people should not bear duties to aid others. Rather, it does imply that, all else being equal, considerations of autonomy can be weightier when deciding on people's moral and legal responsibility to aid others in certain situations or in general. What this constraint means is that affirmative interpersonal duties must take into serious account the self-determination of both parties to an interaction. Indeed, the actual workings of private law manifest the type of unexciting but indispensable judgments we alluded to two pages back in discussing Hart's treatment of intrinsic values.

Thus, private law singles out cases where the responsibility placed on the duty-bearer infringes on her independence but does *not* seriously jeopardize her self-determination. Rather than merely adhering to the thin conception of freedom as independence and thus strictly limiting its role to vindicating each individual's right to independence, private law takes seriously the right to self-determination of all parties to an interaction. And while reciprocal respect for each party's claim to independence can be fully vindicated with strict duties of noninterference, reciprocal respect of our right to self-determination may require some affirmative duties to aid others.

This reasoning nicely explains the canonical restitutionary obligation in mistaken payments cases. Here, the law encumbers the innocent recipient of a mistaken payment, who is "a purely passive beneficiary," with the affirmative task of remedying the consequences of the payor's "unfortunate mistake" – a mistake for which the recipient bears no responsibility.[20] This private law rule imposes on the recipient an affirmative duty not to be oblivious to the mistaken party's circumstances; but this is a modest duty – a trivial burden that neither jeopardizes her self-determination nor seriously undermines her independence.[21]

AFFIRMATIVE DUTIES IN CONTRACT LAW

Now we can circle back to contract law. Conceiving contract in teleological terms implies that promisors do incur some burden in the service of their promisees' right to self-determination. But in the context of contracts – like in the context of mistaken payments – this burden is minimal; as we have seen, it simply requires that people not choose to invoke the power conferred on them by contract law if they do not intend to comply with its rules.[22]

A final thought may help in separating choice theory from all other teleological accounts of contract, notably the economic account of contract as a means for maximizing social welfare. The focus of choice theory on contracts' autonomy-enhancing function easily explains what has always been a puzzle for consequentialists: why does a contract create a duty in the promisor to the promisee specifically? Unlike other teleological theories, our approach gives a straightforward answer: only in this way can contract enable each one of us to enlist *specific* others for our goals.[23] Contract can advance people's autonomy if, but only if, it serves as a device in which specific people can recruit other specific people who can help them in pursuing their goals, and are furthermore empowered with the authority to invoke enforcement proceedings in the case of breach.

Neo-Kantians (and maybe other corrective justice scholars) are still likely to object, saying that our theory violates their concern with private law's correlativity (or bipolarity). It does not, for reasons that go beyond the scope of this book. The answer in short, for the specialist reader, is that correlativity should only require a convergence between a defendant's liability and the plaintiff's entitlement that is premised on law's (*ex ante*) prescription of the ideal interpersonal relations in that area of law.[24]

Here's the big takeaway from this debate: exercising your power to enter a contract (voluntarily and affirmatively) in the service of your own autonomy justifiably entails some obligations (limited and affirmative) to the other party as well. The content of those obligations, and the state's obligations in relation to them, is the crux of choice theory.

✻ ✻ ✻

Contract serves autonomy by enabling people legitimately to enlist others in advancing their own projects, and thus it expands the range of meaningful choices people can make to shape their own lives. That's an important claim, but a preliminary one. To round out the building blocks for a general, liberal theory of contract, the next step is to understand *why* people want to enlist others in their projects.

PART II

The Goods of Contract

5

Utility

What are the main goods we seek when we exercise the power to contract? A general contract theory must identify these goods, explain how they relate to each other, and link them to the ultimate value of autonomy. Only then can we talk about tailoring contract law to meet its normative potential.

In Part II, we show how utility- and community-based theories are best understood as essential building blocks in a robust autonomy-enhancing conception of contract. Note that our nomenclature regarding utility follows the conventional focus on contract's material, economic benefits, though we recognize that the concept of utility can encompass social goods as well. This is also why we are using the terms utility and efficiency interchangeably.

This part is not a comprehensive survey of the pertinent scholarship, nor does it dive deep into the subtle nuances of the accounts we cover. Our mission is more limited and focused: to show, first, how utilitarian and communitarian theories of contract cannot be read as general accounts of contract, and conversely, how they can and should be read as accounts of the goods of contract that an autonomy-based theory must recognize and facilitate. If we put freedom first, what does that mean for utility and community?

INTERNAL AND EXTERNAL VALUES

As a preliminary matter, why are we focusing on utility and community? Aren't there other values fundamental to the texture of contract? Yes. Other "internal" and "external" values may be justified in affecting contract law. But autonomy, utility, and community (as we render them) are different from other values: they participate in law's vision of the ideal interpersonal relationships of the contracting parties.

This framework allows us to analyze other foundational values at the appropriate time – mostly, as it turns out, in Chapter 8, after we lay out the core of choice theory. For example, consider an internal value like "relational equality," conceptualized as reciprocal respect for the parties' right to self-determination. While the commands of relational equality may appear ripe for discussion here, they are better understood as entailments of contract's autonomy-enhancing role, not as independent goods of contract.

Similarly, we can defer discussion of qualitatively distinct "external values," that is, values fundamental for structuring law and society, but ones that arise from outside the contractual relationship itself. For example, we defer consideration of the external value of distributive justice to Chapters 8 and 9.[1] There we discuss two important routes – concerning relational equality and autonomy for vulnerable parties – through which choice theory helps ameliorate the friction between contract law and distributive justice.[2] Distributive justice is an important value, but it is not internal to contract law, as such.

At a more general level, we argue that "internal values" are, and should be, privileged in shaping contract law, though they need not enjoy a strict monopoly as some private law purists claim. This privilege means that "external values" should affect the contours of contract law only if they pass a heightened justificatory bar. Justifying this privilege for internal values in private law theory is a task we take up elsewhere,[3] along with the concomitant issue of how external values may affect or have affected contract law.[4] Now we can turn to utility – an essential building block.

UTILITY AND AUTONOMY

Some economic analyses of contract law conceptualize the field – explicitly or implicitly – as a complex set of incentives. In this view, these incentives should aim at inducing potential transactors to behave so as to maximize aggregate social welfare, where welfare is conventionally defined as preference satisfaction. More specifically, such an account begins with the proposition that "[c]ooperation is productive" and thus "creates value," and concludes that contract law ideally should "induce[ ] optimal performance and reliance at low transaction costs."[5]

This collectivist understanding of contract has much pragmatic strength, but always brings with it an uneasiness regarding the status in contract theory of aggregate utility – a value which is of course external to the parties' contractual relationship. Most contract theorists, even efficiency-oriented ones, won't affirmatively claim utility as contract law's ultimate value. The normative concerns that (explicitly or implicitly) inform this position are familiar: some theorists challenge framing the public good in terms of aggregate preference satisfaction; others question the legitimacy of using private law – of enlisting the interpersonal interactions of private individuals – for such collectivist purposes.[6]

We need not resolve this controversy. Within the domain of contract law, many of the lessons of economic analysis are consistent with a commitment to autonomy as contract law's ultimate value.[7] The reason is straightforward, at least from the point of view of our account of contractual autonomy. Often, maximizing the joint surplus is the good, or at least a good, of the contracting parties themselves. For such contracts, respect for autonomy entails embrace of economic analysis.

Insofar as the efficient reallocation of their respective entitlements is what the parties want, and if (but only if) this good does not undermine the ultimate normative commitment to autonomy, then these theories converge: to respect autonomy, look to efficiency as the measure of ideal law in that type of contracting. (We reserve discussion of values in conflict and of how our account differs from economic analysis for Chapter 8.)

BUSINESS CONTRACTS

To demonstrate the potential usefulness and limits of the economic analysis of contract law to an autonomy-based theory, consider Alan Schwartz and Robert Scott's work on business contracts, that is, contracts between firms.[8] This work exemplifies the best in utilitarian American contract law analysis, and also parallels the driving impetus of a recent welfarist turn in European contract law theory.[9]

For Schwartz and Scott, the central organizing question is, "What contract law would commercial parties want the state to provide?"[10] Their answer is that such law "should restrict itself to the pursuit of efficiency alone."[11] They assume there are no relevant externalities (or rather that such externalities should be specifically targeted by, for example, environmental and antitrust laws). They further set aside concerns of systematic cognitive error because "[f]irms and markets are structured so as to minimize [its] likelihood ... by important decisionmakers within the firm."[12]

For this (externality-free, bias-free, sophisticated-commercial) subset of the contractual universe, Schwartz and Scott sensibly identify the good of contracting as maximizing the parties' joint gains, or the contractual surplus.[13] Given this good, they argue provocatively that much of current business contract law is misguided and should be modified so parties can more easily generate a larger contractual surplus.

To be more concrete, they recommend: (1) reversing some mandatory rules, which "bar enforcement to contract terms that efficiently cope with problems of hidden information and hidden action"[14]; (2) adopting the disfavored textualist approach as the default theory of interpretation[15]; and (3) significantly limiting the domain of state-supplied defaults given the systemic comparative disadvantage of both courts and statutory drafters (vis-à-vis the parties) in supplying efficient defaults and the resulting consequence of these failed attempts of doing so in the form of (costly) opt out by business parties.[16]

This detailed reform program shows the normative power of a thoroughgoing efficiency analysis. But does it fully displace autonomy as contract's ultimate value within the sharply constrained sphere of business contracts? It does not, even for Schwartz and Scott, as a close reading of their work shows.[17] They do assert that business firms are "artificial persons whose autonomy the state need not respect."[18] And they do claim that welfare maximization should solely guide this contracting sphere.[19]

But why privilege utility? For them, it's out of deference to "the parties' objective *ex ante* intentions," a concern they mention as the premise of "The Case for Party Control."[20] Most fundamentally, utility comes first because of concern for "party sovereignty," a term they emphasize and repeatedly use.[21] Their account (along with many other similar ones[22]) seems to stand for the following proposition: given the welfare-maximizing goals typical of the anticipated parties in business contracts, respecting "party sovereignty" requires that the law governing such transactions follow suit.[23]

However, behind the "artificial persons" making business contracts stand real people, and it is the choices those real people are seeking to make that the law ultimately serves. Framed this way, "party sovereignty" devolves to contractual autonomy as we define it – it's a concern best understood as autonomy-regarding, not utility-maximizing. As indirect evidence of this implicit normative framework, consider Liam Murphy's observation that most economic analyses of contract law tend to "take for granted" that an appropriate contract rule would be the one which "is best for each contracting pair" even though there is no guarantee that it is "the one that does best overall, for society at large."[24]

We acknowledge that the significance of party sovereignty can also be grounded in epistemological reasons – in which parties are perceived as carriers of the best information regarding their preferences – so that respecting their choices is just a means for reaching the ultimate goal of aggregate welfare. But the notion that party sovereignty has no freestanding value and is instead subservient to aggregate welfare is just the usual utilitarian move of translating everything to preferences. It fails here for the same reasons as elsewhere: it assumes that all things of value are commensurable and it has no plausible account of the value of preference satisfaction.[25]

Consider the most compelling instance of foundationally utilitarian contracts, those that arise from privatization of public services, where contract law displaces prior public forms of governance specifically to achieve efficient outcomes. In this limited arena, contract law is admittedly "commandeered" for collective purposes, that is, to achieve goals external to contract law. But even here, a liberal polity should resist wholly subsuming autonomy under the aggregate welfare. Instead, we argue, to use contracts *legitimately* in this way, governments must pay an "admission price": at a minimum, these new contract types should comply (as should all others) with the thin, but nonetheless important, constraints implied by contract's autonomy-enhancing underpinnings.

We are challenging the canonical economic view here because it fails to make qualitative distinctions, notably the distinction between autonomy interests and welfarist interests. Taking these distinctions seriously leads to our competing approach along the lines of our interpretation of party sovereignty in Schwartz and Scott's work. This view has the virtue of allowing legal economists to accommodate their (problematic) collectivist welfare-maximizing methodology within an individualist, autonomy-regarding normative framework to which they are typically (if implicitly) committed. In any case, our interpretation is the reason why efficiency analysis of the implications of party sovereignty should matter to contract theorists concerned with freedom.

In our theory, autonomy and utility sit easily beside each other. When people choose to come together in their commercial lives, and to the extent they are then seeking wealth maximization, contract law should facilitate that choice. Thus, enhancing individual autonomy requires that contract law offer various structures for business arrangements – a rich array of corporate, partnership, trust, and commercial contract types. Even regarding a single sphere of wealth-maximizing commercial interactions, autonomy may require multiple types, as we now see with wealth management contract types (discussed in Chapter 9).

With the autonomy imperative satisfied, the inner life of these contract types should facilitate people's welfare goals, to the extent that is what people are seeking. Contract law between such firms, then, should maximize joint surplus, per Schwartz and Scott. This is not because autonomy is irrelevant, but because the concept has already done its work at an earlier stage – in providing the firms an adequate variety of wealth-maximizing contract types and ensuring that none of these types threatens individual autonomy.

LIMITS OF THE BUSINESS CONTRACTS EXAMPLE

There is another lesson we can take from Schwartz and Scott's careful delimitation of their study. Their sharp focus on business contracts helps set out "the theoretical foundations of a law merchant for our time."[26] This is an important task. But it cannot be the basis for a general theory of contract law. Even Schwartz and Scott acknowledge that rules applicable to externality-free, bias-free, and sophisticated-commercial parties may not be suitable for other types of contracts, particularly those involving individuals.[27]

As we move away from their corner case, efficiency analysis remains pertinent – because people so often seek material benefits when they contract – but "party sovereignty" no longer straightforwardly points to maximizing joint economic surplus. Efficiency analysis does not become irrelevant, but its centrality is necessarily diminished as competing values play a larger role.

Legal economic theorists of contract typically struggle when faced with such incommensurable values.[28] They respond usually through one of two flawed strategies. The first, and least convincing approach, is to deny the conflict and instead assert that efficiency analysis can ground normative analysis of contract law as a whole;[29] this is yet another manifestation of the reductionist view, which translates all things of value to preferences. Unsurprisingly, it again fails: when such theorists try to explain areas of contracting that are widely understood to be animated by quite different values – such as marital contracts – the results are uniformly disappointing.[30]

The second, inverse approach redefines and shrinks what constitutes the field of contract law, basically doubling down on the Willistonian project we discussed in the Introduction. Thus, for Schwartz and Scott, contracts between firms are "the main subject of what is commonly called contract law," because other types of contract are governed by other rules, outside of "Article 2 of the Uniform Commercial Code (UCC) and the provisions of the Restatement (Second) of Contracts."[31] As they put it, contracts "between individuals are primarily regulated by family law (antenuptial agreements and divorce settlements) and real property law (home sales and some leases)"; contracts "between a firm as seller and an individual as buyer are primarily regulated by consumer protection law, real property law (most leases), and the securities laws"; and contracts "between an individual as seller and a firm as buyer, commonly involve the sale of a person's labor, and are regulated by laws governing the employment relation."[32]

Radically shrinking the scope of contract law is no more appealing than over-extending economic analysis. Schwartz and Scott's observations may reflect the canonical division of labor of contemporary contract law and the focus of most first-year courses in contract law. This focus on the UCC may have some historical pedigree and may reflect the projects of a specific subset of the bar; or it may have resulted, counter-intuitively, from the otherwise significant *fragmentation* of American contract law at the state and federal level, especially given the extensive legislation covering specific contract types.[33] Be that as it may, none of these contingent facts define the field of state enforcement of voluntary obligations or the autonomy-enhancing functions contract plays (or can play) in people's life. Calling business contracts the core does not make it so.

We do not get closer to a general theory of contract by excluding the vast bulk of contracting that occurs in the spheres of family, home, consumer transactions, and employment.

* * *

Focusing on business contracts has its advantages. As we've seen, efficiency analysis is the right tool when sophisticated parties all seek maximization of joint economic surplus and if (but only if) contract law need not worry about any negative external effects.

However, this focus is misleading for the rest of contract theory. Schwartz and Scott have identified the one limited sphere of contracting in which utility and autonomy concerns mostly seem to converge. Everywhere else, they don't. Their example does not generalize, as they readily acknowledge. Attempts to generalize their approach ignore the other goods of contracting and obscure at least part of the potential of contract as a – maybe *the* – legal means for enhancing our autonomy.

6

Community

THE VALUE OF "COMMUNITY"

People contract not just for economic benefits, but also for the social gains that come from working together, from taking part in a successful collective enterprise. Cooperation, in other words, is at times a good of contracting, in and of itself, in addition to its importance in facilitating economic success. People value interpersonal relationships – not only for instrumental reasons, as a means to some independently specified end.[1] Contract may help in furthering the creation of these intrinsically valuable relationships.[2]

The value of contract law, in this view, lies in enabling "special bonds between people" which "are voluntarily shaped and developed by the choice of participants" and are thus morally desirable.[3] This approach, at least charitably read, does not dismiss or seek to supplant contract's utilitarian goods. Rather, it asserts that, alongside these goods, contract is also a source of freestanding *social* value, which people find to be intrinsically valuable.

Contract provides people an opportunity to enrich and solidify the interpersonal capital that grows from cooperation, support, trust, and mutual responsibility. Theories of contract that bring these interpersonal goods to the fore can be grouped together as "community-based" approaches, in our terminology. They begin with a complaint against traditional theories that, for them, are excessively individualistic and therefore miss the essence of contract. Instead, they premise contract on the interpersonal relations it creates.[4]

At times, these theories become as over-extended as the theories they criticize. To say that all contracts are necessarily relational, and that community is the core, requires marginalizing large swaths of contracting from analysis – it gives results as implausible as those from over-expanding efficiency analysis. This extreme version of a community-based approach is not persuasive. But a more nuanced reading, which celebrates the intrinsic value of the special relationships (some) contracts create and their contribution to our ability to achieve valuable lives,[5] can enrich our autonomy-based theory.

In this brief account, we do not attempt to cover all the literature on contract's interpersonal dimension. In particular, we leave aside the robust law and economics discussion of "relational contracting," that is, the scholarship on the instrumental role trust and solidarity play in long-term, sophisticated contract settings.

At first glance, excluding this comprehensive and vibrant view of contract relations may seem strange. Relational contract scholarship does significantly enrich the utilitarian analysis of contracts. It focuses attention on a diverse set of relational means through which contracting parties can facilitate the good of utility.[6] The issue for us is that, on its own terms, the economic understanding of relations does not add a *distinct* good of contract to the utilitarian one addressed in Chapter 5. As the term has come to be conventionally understood today, the study of "relational contracting" is a subset of the utilitarian analysis of contract.

In contrast, sociologists and (some) philosophers of contract have given more attention to the intrinsic (and not just instrumental) value of the special bonds contract creates. This attention to special bonds was the understanding of "relational contracting" that law and society scholars had in mind when they initially coined the term. And this is the understanding that philosophers bring to the discussion today when they emphasize (in very different terms) the freestanding social significance of contracting.

While philosophers and sociologists are rarely read together in contract law scholarship, doing so is quite enlightening. What unites these two disciplines has been a shared concern for, and focus on, the distinctive, nonutilitarian good of contractual relations. The term that best captures this good is still "relational contracting," but we must leave it aside. It has become so thoroughly bound up with law-and-economics contract theory that using "relational contracting" in the older, sociological sense is just confusing today. Similarly, relatives like "relations contracts" or "community-based contracts" are imperfect.

So, for now, we opt for the awkward term "community" to stand in opposition to the good of "utility" discussed in the previous Chapter. We will argue contract law should support individual freedom to form various types of "communities," just as it should further efficient allocation, when and to the extent this is what the contracting parties seek. "Community"-based values, like their utilitarian counterparts, are necessary building blocks of a general liberal theory of contract. Neither value can be reduced wholly to the other.

Community-based theories can be divided roughly into two groups, what we call thick and thin accounts. Ian Macneil best represents the former camp and is the scholar most associated with the sociological inquiry of relations-based contracts. Macneil's starting point, which we share (along with contract theorists generally today[7]), is that much, if not most, contract practice does not comply with the familiar image of a simple exchange of goods.[8]

Indeed, varied contract types – in marriage, labor and employment, franchising, and other long-term transactions involving asset-specific investments – differ fundamentally from such discrete contracting.[9] Since these long-term contracts are "characterized by complex (*ex ante* unspecifiable) obligations and asset specific (*ex post* noncompensable) investments," they require the parties to "adopt a consciously co-operative attitude."[10] As David Campbell explains, these types of contracts are heavily dependent on relations – they take place in relations, they are a constitutive element of these relations, and they must occur only if and so long as the relations are valued – and are therefore "guided by the relational norms which emphasize preservation of the relation and co-operative adjustment of obligations in order to do so."[11]

Another typical feature of "relations" contracts is the significance of what may be called "contract governance."[12] Although planning the substance of the exchange is still important, "many specific substantive courses of action cannot be planned in advance."[13] Thus, Macneil points out, more emphasis must be placed on the "operating relations" of the parties and on "structures and processes."[14]

While, at times, much of this governance structure is formal and even hierarchical, these contracts necessarily rely also on some measure of trust and solidarity.[15] And in some types of such contracts, the parties "engage in social exchange [and not only in] economic exchange," or at least become highly interdependent, so that their "relations tend to include *both* sharp divisions of benefits and burdens *and* a sharing of them."[16] To give an example, Macneil discusses employment contracts, which are typified by "precise wages and precise work assignments" alongside the sharing of "prosperity ... through bonus schemes, more comfortable working conditions, more overtime, and the like," and of "hard times layoffs [and] smaller profits or even losses."[17]

A utilitarian critic may argue that trust, solidarity, and sharing have no intrinsic value in the context of employment, and are instead merely means for maximizing the contractual surplus. We readily concede the instrumental value, but only up to a point, beyond which lie noninstrumental social values in the sphere of work. We are not sure how to resolve this debate as to employment – and we are not familiar with any study that empirically substantiates one view or the other.

The sphere of intimacy is different. Few people make thoroughgoing instrumental arguments in cases where the contractual community is also part of each spouse's own self-understanding.[18] And those who do make such arguments are not persuasive. Rather, the law governing marital contracts is much better explained by reference to thick community, which typifies what we are calling a "relations"-based contract type. Consistent with our view, marital separation agreements are subject to possible judicial modification for change of circumstances, and premarital agreements are typified by a robust (both *ex ante* and *ex post*) fairness review, for example.[19]

Even more relevant to this debate is the equal division on divorce rule, which has become the most fundamental principle of marital contract law. The best instrumental attempt to analyze this default rule – without reference to the thick community it seeks to sustain – argues that the rule is a means to guard against the incentive to exit the marital community at certain strategically valuable points.[20]

The problem with this fully instrumental account is that it can only justify recovery to the extent of the *opportunity costs* of the nonpropertied spouse, not the rule of equal division that we actually see.[21] When parties enter marriage with substantially differing degrees of market power, as is still often the case given gender inequality, equal division is not necessary to secure the advantages of collective action.

The most compelling (and noncontingent) justification for the equal division rule lies elsewhere: in the ideal of marriage as a "thick community," more specifically, as an egalitarian liberal community. Equal division makes real this noninstrumental ideal of marriage by rejecting any mercenary understanding of the goods of marriage and thus any accounting based on individual desert. Instead, it infuses both costs and benefits with an inter-subjective character. What we are calling "thick community" forms marital contract law around the animating principle of equal sharing, a concern that is not captured in any purely instrumental account of contract goods.[22]

THIN COMMUNITY

Compare this thick account of contractual communities to Daniel Markovits' theory of contract as the epitome of "respectful communities" premised on "the collaborative ideal."[23] This "thin" notion of community is sharply limited: it aims to explain the morality of promise among self-interested strangers.[24] Contracts, like other types of promises, establish for Markovits "a relation of recognition and respect – and indeed a kind of community – among those who participate in them," and it is "the value of this relation" that explains and justifies the morality of promise and the legitimacy of contract law.[25]

This "collaborative" model of contract does not imply any "concern for other persons' interests," but rather "a concern for other persons' intentions and, ultimately, for their points of view."[26] Contract, in this approach, represents the promissory relation among persons whose engagement is rather narrow: "Both the ends that the parties share and the mode of their sharing are circumscribed by the particular terms of their agreement."[27] Thus, contract applies precisely to arm's length agreements between individuals.[28]

Markovits specifically distinguishes his "collaborative ideal" from the thicker, more contextual relations that concern Macneil. Thus, Markovits excludes cooperation which typifies "thicker and more contextual – and therefore more substantively communal" – contractual communities, such as "partnerships or joint ventures [that] create fiduciary relationships among the participants" or "employment contracts" and the like which "supervene on long-term, ongoing relationships that may also present such substantive community."[29]

He also writes out of his theory contracts involving organizations. For Markovits, organizations – being "mere means" – "clearly cannot participate directly in the moral ideals by whose terms the collaborative view explains contractual obligations."[30] He thus admits candidly that the collaborative model cannot account for contracts involving organizations or for those between organizations and individual persons, which "present very different problems – morally and indeed conceptually – from contracts among individuals."[31]

Thus conceived, the morality of contract "identifies and elaborates a form of respect that does not rely on affection."[32] But "in spite of their narrowly formal character," the "collaborative communities" of such contracts "involve genuine respect and remain true communities," because they require each party to "constrain her actions to respect her partner's point of view concerning the collaboration."[33] In this way, "[c]ontracts enable persons who are not intimates nevertheless to cease to be strangers; and breaches do not just reinstate the persons' prior status as strangers but instead leave them actively estranged."[34]

While Markovits admits, as noted, that such arm's length contracts between individuals do not exhaust the world of contracts, he insists that "as a descriptive matter" they "play a fairly prominent role in many individual persons' moral and legal lives."[35] More strongly, Markovits asserts that contracts between strangers "represent the core of contract."[36] Elsewhere, he amplifies this view, writing that "the conceptual core of contract remains the discrete and self-interested exchange, in which contract stands apart from [the] more contextual forms of community that may sometimes accompany contractual activity."[37]

For Markovits, excluding Macneil's thick-community contracts and Schwartz and Scott's business contracts does not "undermine the collaborative view's claim to capture the essence of contract."[38] What is that essence? Markovits says, "[c]ontract law's *primary* purpose" is "to sustain collaborative agreements among individual persons."[39]

LIMITS OF THICK AND THIN THEORIES

We disagree with Markovits' and Macneil's claims to have captured the conceptual core of contract. The reasons parallel our divergence from Schwartz and Scott discussed in Chapter 5. There is no more justification for elevating contracts between individuals than there is to privileging contracts between businesses.[40] For starters, both views have a blind spot for contracts between individuals and organizations, in particular consumer transactions, which play such a large role in modern life. More generally, both approaches try to craft a general theory of contract by excluding too much of our ordinary and most important contracting practices.

And yet, notwithstanding the excesses of community-based contract theories, we find value in these accounts. They are helpful in conceptualizing the decision regarding the goods people are seeking when they decide whether to use, for example, a franchise or commercial agency contract. That choice can be understood, in part, as a decision between creating thin and thick contractual communities. A franchise is "thinner" than a comparable commercial agency contract, because the franchise type lacks the agent's capacity to bind the principal, and it does not have the potential for respondeat superior liability.[41]

Both Macneil and Markovits sometimes capture what people want when they choose to contract. To return to Markovits, his collaborative ideal is indeed a good descriptive fit for the contract types on which he focuses, and it shows one normatively attractive vision of the relationship that contract law can help establish. In some "contracts involving the purchase and sale of personal property," and even more so "of services in many forms, including childcare and elder care, day labor, and services associated with any number of trades and professions,"[42] contract can serve as a "means by which people can "overcom[e] isolation through an intentional pursuit of shared ends," enabling them "to cease to be strangers," by "enter[ing] into respectful relations with each other."[43]

But these values are not the only interpersonal ideals autonomous people can legitimately pursue. Sometimes people seek, and contract law can help provide, the thick communitarian ideal of contractual community envisioned by Macneil. And sometimes people want what we call the "no community" ideal, which we discuss in Chapter 7, on which many other contracts rely, notably consumer contracts.[44] Markovits' claim that the contract *form* implies *recognition* of the other party's intention and point of view may apply even respecting these types of contract. But because this is a very thin requirement, which entails neither *respect* nor *community*, such recognition may be purely instrumental.

* * *

An autonomy-based contract law should facilitate all three alternatives (thick, thin, and no community) and allow people to choose from among these ideals as they shape different spheres of their lives. Accordingly, contract theory should both embrace autonomy as contract's ultimate value (the point we established in Part I) and respect the diverse, sometimes conflicting, substantive goods, material and interpersonal, that people seek from contracting (which we set out here in Part II). The building blocks are all now in place. We are ready to bring them together in choice theory.

PART III

The Choice Theory of Contracts

7

Contractual Freedom

With the building blocks identified, we can now set out the choice theory of contract law. Here's a brief roadmap:

In this chapter, we offer a liberal view of contractual autonomy that links the philosophical grounding from Part I with contract values we set out in Part II. We show that the state's active involvement in contract law can increase human freedom – a claim that may seem counterintuitive, but is not. By supporting multiplicity among types, the state addresses not just material impediments to bargaining, but also social ones rooted in the limits of individual imagination. We illustrate our argument by reference to a number of contract types, consumer transactions mostly, but also employment, suretyship, and business contracts.

Then, Chapter 8 sets out our general theory with a conceptually coherent account of the values and goods of contracting and their interrelationships. There is no single animating principle that captures the quintessence of all contracting practice, but there are intelligible rules that guide conflicts among core values. This chapter also addresses many potential objections and refinements that have accumulated as the book has unfolded.

Chapter 9 engages the descriptive level where we develop a taxonomy that identifies the distinctive subject matter and recurring dilemmas of each contractual sphere. Our view of spheres is instrumental to the goal of ensuring an adequate range of contract types for important human interactions.

Chapter 10 gives a richer account of contract types. We show how local animating principles inform and shape divergent contract types. We define when a type emerges from novel contracting practices and when the state has fulfilled its normative obligation to provide an adequate range of types. We also examine the conditions in which constraining choice within types – by employing mandatory rules or sticky defaults – enhances rather than reduces freedom. Thus, this chapter moves to the prescriptive level while it bridges between contract law and theory.

In Chapter 11, we address the reformist level by considering the market for new contract types, an issue we bracket in Chapter 10. Here, we give examples to show that if contract law is to enhance freedom in each sphere, it must offer a rich menu of types with distinct value balances. Just piggybacking on the will of the parties does not reflect contract law as it is, or as it should be.

Finally, in Chapter 12, we look at limits on choice and examine some institutional challenges to choice theory. We acknowledge that in certain contexts, cognitive, behavioral, structural, and political economy concerns may override choice theory's prescription of multiplicity. Also, in other contexts, concerns about the capacities of legal institutions may counsel against using particular ones to implement multiplicity. We end by sketching a research agenda on institutional pathways and limits for design of contract types.

FROM AUTONOMY TO CHOICE

The key to understanding contractual autonomy is to see it, as Part I demonstrated, as a good that needs to be fostered. But what does that imperative mean in the context of our diverse world of contracting practices? Answering this question is what leads to choice theory. In a sentence, we foster the good of contractual autonomy by ensuring freedom of contracts – that is, by supporting adequate availability of choice among types.

The path from the political philosophy of autonomy to its working out in contract law takes a few steps. Perhaps the simplest and most direct route is by reference to work by Joseph Raz (drawn from his philosophical work, not his contract law theory, which proves to be off the mark). In particular, we develop two points from Raz's political philosophy with particular usefulness for contract theory: (1) to be free, individuals need meaningful choice and (2) states have a necessary role in supporting the availability of valuable options.

Before taking up these points, we offer two important caveats regarding state action. As a preliminary matter, when we reference the state's obligation to enhance choice, we do not mean the state generally must conceive or design innovative contract types. Rather, under conditions and limits we elaborate in Chapters 10 through 12, the state may be obligated to respond favorably to innovations based on minority views or utopian theories, even if there is low market demand initially for these new types, and even if they arise from non-state sources.

More generally, we do not offer a thorough exegesis of Raz's liberalism (though aficionados will note that our reading is closer to Alan Brudner's than Martha Nussbaum's[1]). We need not and do not resolve the most significant critique of Raz's liberalism – the argument that his view amounts to an unjustified form of paternalism.[2] Our discussion later in this chapter demonstrates that, whatever the power of this critique may be regarding Raz's account, it is inapplicable to choice theory which concerns the state's obligation in contract law specifically.

THE IMPERATIVE OF INTRA-SPHERE MULTIPLICITY

With these cautions in mind, we turn to Raz's first point, regarding meaningful choice. We agree with him that freedom requires individuals be able to choose from among options they deem valuable. The idea of autonomy – that people should, to some degree, be the authors of their own lives – requires not only appropriate mental abilities and independence, but also "an adequate range of options."[3] For choice to be effective, for autonomy to be meaningful, there must be (other things being equal) "more valuable options than can be chosen, and they must be significantly different," so that choices involve "tradeoffs, which require relinquishing one good for the sake of another."[4]

Thus, autonomy emphasizes "the value of a large number of greatly differing pursuits among which individuals are free to choose."[5] In turn, a society that pursues this autonomy ideal must ensure that there exists a wide range of social forms that "leave enough room for individual choice."[6]

Consequentialist liberal contract theories – including Raz's own account of contract[7] – miss the crucial role of multiplicity in contract law, perhaps because they, like the deontological liberals we discussed in Part I, constrict their view of contract down to the symmetrical and discrete arm's length exchange. While that arm's length form is one important type of voluntary obligation, it is not an adequate stand-in for contract as a whole. If one takes contract's contribution to autonomy seriously, then contract theory must celebrate the multiplicity of contract types rather than suppress them (as variations on a common theme) or marginalize them (as peripheral exceptions to a robust core).

Multiplicity per se is not enough. Multiplicity *across* contractual spheres helps contract law respond to the various goods contract can help secure, but it is not sufficient to implement what choice theory requires. The availability of numerous contract types for commercial activity, for example, does not add options regarding potential contracting choices with respect to employment, home, or family. In other words, it doesn't enhance freedom if you can choose, for example, either to get married or enter an agency contract.

What is particularly significant to choice, and thus to autonomy, is the multiplicity of alternatives *within* any given sphere of contractual activity, what we term contract law's *intra-sphere* multiplicity. Within each sphere, a liberal contract law must include sufficiently distinct contract types for the diverse social settings and economic functions in which law helps people undertake voluntary obligations. Only such a rich repertoire can enable people to freely choose their own ends, principles, forms of life, and associations.

EMPLOYMENT AND CONSUMERS

Consider a few examples where our theory counsels for more choice among types than the law currently offers:

1. *Employment Types.* First, people should generally be able to choose the type of labor contract they enter. (We say "generally" because in some market structures multiplicity might decrease choice, especially for the most vulnerable workers, an important caveat we develop in Chapter 12; and we limit our discussion to labor *contracts*, as distinct from certain social benefits associated with employment.) Today, the law offers individuals two types: they can work as independent contractors or as employees.

But individuals can't easily pick which type to enter. At present, classifying the parties' relationships as employer/employee or employer/independent contractor is considered a question for the judge or the jury to decide based on the "economic realities," and the parties' characterization of their relationship is not controlling.[8] Formally, the law refers to a long list of nonexhaustive criteria that imply significant ad hoc *ex post* discretion in characterizing the relationship. This discretion seems to preclude, or at least impede, the parties' *ex ante* planning.[9]

But it turns out that the law in action is reasonably predictable such that, with careful planning, well-counseled parties can usually fashion their arrangement so that it will be classified per their mutually desired type.[10] For example, one Silicon Valley startup requires its drivers never wear t-shirts with the company logo because it believes this will help them avoid a later judicial reclassification of what they intend to be an "independent contractor" workforce.[11]

Choice theory's imperative of intra-sphere multiplicity implies that the freedom to choose employment types should be simplified and formalized, so that it becomes meaningfully available and not just to well-counseled parties – with appropriate safeguards so that the most vulnerable workers are not systematically relegated to the most disadvantageous types. These safeguards are *not* external impositions on choice theory, but rather – as we explain in our discussion of relational equality in Chapter 8 – necessary implications of the theory's fundamental normative commitments.

Further, choice theory does not just counsel freer choice among existing types. The nature of work is changing rapidly as we move from an industrial economy to the information and "sharing" economy. It would be surprising to think that the two existing types just discussed would exhaust the typical contractual arrangements that free employers and employees likely prefer. Thus, choice theory also suggests support for new and emerging employment types. (We defer discussion on this point, the "market for new types," until Chapter 11, because it draws on elements of choice theory we have not yet introduced.)

2. *Purchases of Consumer Goods.* As a second example, our approach suggests that people should, in some circumstances, be able to choose between purchasing a good with the protections of consumer transaction law or by using sales law. We recognize that in most jurisdictions consumer protection doctrine applies as a mandatory rule at least to merchant/consumer transactions,[12] so that sales law can govern only cases of nonmerchant sellers (i.e., amateurs) and cases of commercial transactions (i.e., those between businesses). But we are not fully satisfied with such rigid bifurcation.

Insofar as this division derives from public policy concerns – involving possible collective action problems that waivability may trigger[13] – we have no objection (consistent with our allowance in Chapter 5 for "external values" to shape contract law if they meet a sufficiently high threshold). But wherever no such external effects apply, sellers and buyers of consumer goods should have an alternative route, so that the availability of the consumer contract type would indeed add options, rather than just reconfigure an existing one.

For example, we endorse the Massachusetts rule that business purchasers who come within the protection of that state's consumer law may waive their rights even though an individual purchaser could not.[14] Furthermore, we support the allowance made by Texas for written and signed waivers by well-counseled individuals who are "not in a significantly disparate bargaining position."[15]

We could multiply the examples, but we have made the point: diversity of contract types is a necessary condition for contractual autonomy, although it is by no means sufficient (because in many contexts, we need to be concerned with the *quality* of choice as well). The makers of contract law must be alert to opportunities for expanding choice, such as the Texas and Massachusetts provisions, and further explore how these happy possibilities can be made broadly available, rather than remain accessible only to sophisticated parties, as in the employment context.

While previous theories correctly focused on freedom to negotiate terms *within* a particular contract, they have missed the role freedom plays *across* contract types.

THE STATE'S OBLIGATION TO ENHANCE CHOICE

As we mentioned, Raz's own account of contract, like the accounts of other autonomy-based contract theorists, missed the generative role of law in offering choices.[16] But a new take on his rightly celebrated insight in political philosophy – regarding the state's responsibility for ensuring choice – can help remedy this flaw and highlight the crucial role of law for contract.

Raz starts by noting the diversity of valuable human goods from which autonomous people should be able to choose and the distinct constitutive values of those goods. Given that diversity, he argues, the state must recognize a sufficiently diverse set of robust frameworks for people to organize their lives.[17] But the state's obligation to foster diversity and multiplicity cannot be properly accomplished through a hands-off or passive approach to the law. Why? Because such an attitude "would undermine the chances of survival of many cherished aspects of our culture."[18] A commitment to personal autonomy thus requires that a liberal state, through its laws, work more actively to "enable individuals to pursue valid conceptions of the good" by providing them a multiplicity of options.[19]

This important obligation is relevant to contract law. As Stephen Smith notes, contract law plays a crucial role in the practice of undertaking voluntary obligations by expanding "the range of options available to individuals" and thus increasing "the possibility of autonomous action."[20] And while it is difficult to define "what constitutes an 'adequate range of options'" (we'll discuss this in Chapter 10), it seems plausible that, at a minimum, "the range of options that exist in a society without contract law will sometimes be inadequate" and that "contract law makes available options that would otherwise be unavailable."[21]

LAW'S INDISPENSABLE ROLE

To be more concrete, this indispensable role of law in making contractual options possible can be demonstrated across a wide spectrum of contract types, ranging all the way from purely instrumental deals with strangers – what we call "no-community" contracts – to thick communitarian contract types.

1. *Consumer Transactions*. Consumer transactions are a useful type of "no-community" contract for us as they illustrate a number of distinctive features of choice theory. Dori Kimel's account of contract implicitly puts consumer transactions at the core of contract law. While we reject this (and any other) essentializing strategy, we agree these deals are a big category worthy of attention. (Because of their centrality to our theory, we touch on consumer transactions here, and return to them later in this chapter and again in Chapter 8.)

Kimel argues that the intrinsic value of contracts lies in "the value of personal detachment," that is, of "doing certain things with others" both "outside the context of already-existing relationships" and "without a commitment to the future prospect of such relationships."[22] As he explains, detachment is valuable "as an alternative to dependence on (pre-existing, future) personal relations. And contracts are valuable as a practice that, with regard to a certain range of activities, facilitates this very option."[23]

Though overstated, Kimel's focus on detachment helpfully demonstrates the requirement of active legal support of contracts. Law is indeed crucial for the very possibility of consumer transactions – the paradigmatic contract type that responds, in our view, to Kimel's account of detachment-based, autonomy-enhancing contracts. (Note that our reference here to "law" in general rather than to "contract law" is intentional: while contract law can play a significant role in making consumer transactions a viable autonomy-enhancing alternative, other bodies of law that are regulatory in nature are also important for this task.[24])

2. *Commercial Contracts*. Beyond enabling consumer transactions, which are a significant subset of the anonymous side of contracting, an active approach to contract law (more than just the passive enforcement of the parties' deal) is crucial in supporting contracts even in the commercial context.

As Schwartz and Scott acknowledge, legal facilitation is indispensable for certain of the business contracts they address, although they are purely instrumental deals between firms. Law is crucial in these business contracts in two nontrivial types of cases: first, "in volatile markets, when a party's failure to perform could threaten its contract partner's survival"; and second, "when contractual surplus would be maximized if one or both parties made relation-specific investments."[25]

3. *"Relation"-Based Contracts*. Active contract law is no less significant in Macneil's "relations" contracts as well, where it helps facilitate trust-based interpersonal relationships. Though social norms, moral commitments, and

reputational concerns drive much party behavior, a hands-off policy and a minimalist (libertarian) attitude to freedom of contract can hardly suffice to overcome endemic difficulties to long-term cooperation.

Various impediments to contract are pervasive in all these settings – information costs (symmetric and asymmetric), cognitive biases, bilateral monopolies, heightened risks of opportunistic behavior, and other transactions costs (in the broad sense).[26] Merely enforcing the parties' expressed intentions would not be sufficient to overcome the inherent risks of such endeavors. Contract law provides the background reassurances that help catalyze the trust so crucial for success. Even where law is rarely invoked – as in the context of "thick community" contracts – its active engagement is likely to be the *sine qua non* that makes viable these challenging types of interpersonal relationships.[27]

Across a range of contracting spheres, the liberal commitment to contractual autonomy requires active engagement by the law. The impediments to secure contracting often depend on the specific features of the particular contract type and therefore each type requires its own legal facilitation. People can, by and large, further customize their contracts to their particular needs and circumstances. But in most cases these refinements build on an off-the-shelf legal edifice that already addresses many of the difficulties they might otherwise have to face.

In short, many valuable forms of interpersonal interaction only become available thanks to the prior, active support of law. Before applying their freedom *within* a particular contract, people need to rely on law's support for freedom *across* contract types.

CONTRACT TYPES AND CULTURE

We have just discussed how the diverse contract types that law facilitates help to overcome various bargaining obstacles. But alongside this material effect, law's inventory of contract types affects our contracting practices in an even more profound, albeit subtler, fashion.

To appreciate this effect, consider the difficulties facing parties who seek to shape their contract as, say, one of bailment, suretyship, or fiduciary in an environment in which these notions have not been coined. Setting up terms that would duplicate our conventional design of these contract types is surely complex, so transaction costs along the lines discussed earlier would inhibit such contracts in many cases.

But this material aspect does not fully capture the difficulty such parties face. For us, the concepts of bailee, surety, or fiduciary have core conventional meanings that make them culturally available as possible modes of contracting. Without such salient meanings, which are by and large (at least in modern times) legally constructed, these parties may not even reach the stage of confronting bargaining obstacles, because they may face a preliminary impediment, an obstacle of the imagination.

By contrast, once the "character" of a contract type or its raison d'être gains broad social and cultural recognition, most people know roughly what they are getting into when they, for example, engage a surety, buy insurance, enter a consumer transaction, lease an apartment, or start a new job.[28] When we say "roughly" above, we are acknowledging that the correspondence between contract law and its popular understanding is far from perfect. There are cases where these gaps go to core features of a contract type (a problem we take up in Chapter 11). But most of the time, the gaps relate to details and thus pose no real challenge to our claim.

Once chosen, the salient categories contract law employs then affect people's preferences respecting constitutive categories of their own relationships.[29] In explaining this phenomenon more generally, one commentator argues, "[f]reedom of the individual today consists less in a freedom of role creation than in a freedom" to "choose among positions and behavioral standards, created and safeguarded by the state."[30] And once a role has been chosen, its "role expectations" affects the choosing individual "through two means: first, through the psychological act of internalization of its behavioral expectations, which are then considered right and just; second, through a system of positive or negative sanctions."[31]

Old-fashioned "freedom of contract" does not acknowledge these roles. Freedom to tailor-make terms, while important, does not consolidate expectations or express shared normative ideals regarding our basic categories of interpersonal relationships.

Consider the example of suretyship. Suretyship is a complex contract type, the subject matter of a full-blown Restatement.[32] A surety is a product of inescapably legal construction distinct from, say, a fiduciary or bailee. But the concept of a surety – someone who undertakes an obligation to substitute another's duty to pay (or perform) if that other person fails to do so[33] – is widely recognized. Many people know (vaguely, to be sure) what it means; at times they even know some of its basic rules, such as the right of a surety who was required to pay or perform to recover from the primary obligor.[34]

From the perspective of the existing Willistonian paradigm of contract theories, rules such as these are defects in the "general" law or oddities to be rationalized or eliminated.[35] Choice theory offers a different perspective: such rules should be seen as tools that each contract type uses to reflect, and help further inculcate, widely shared understandings of ideal party relationships – in this case, suretyship relationships.

People can thus invoke this contract type as a means for facilitating transactions that would have been too risky otherwise because the primary obligor's ability to perform is in doubt.[36] Indeed, exactly because contract types – like our private law categories more generally – tend to blend into our natural environment, they help structure our daily interactions.[37] So when contract law offers us multiple contract types, it participates in the ongoing social production of stable categories of human interaction by consolidating people's expectations of themselves and others. In this, law enlarges the range of valuable options available to us.

Note that contract law cannot possibly serve this expressive and cultural role as to every idiosyncratic arrangement that parties may pursue. There are surely other, at times even more pressing, obligations a liberal regime committed to people's self-determination must face, including the provision of multiplicity of choices in other (noncontractual) aspects of their lives and of the minimal social and economic conditions (or capabilities) needed to enable individuals to make autonomous choices. So, we do not prioritize the constitutive obligation of contract law over all other state obligations.

Rather, we argue that insofar as the state invests in contract law – as it surely does – it must do so with an eye to its core choice-enhancing obligations, including the constitutive role it can play by offering valuable contract types. Indeed, law can, should, and to some extent already does perform this function respecting a limited number of core types of interpersonal arrangements.

CONTRACT TYPES AND REGULATION

In this chapter, we have argued that contract law, by constructing a rich variety of types, performs an indispensable autonomy-enhancing role – it facilitates our ability legitimately to enlist others to various projects, both utilitarian and communitarian. But none of what we have said (or will say) implies that contract law can always do, or even typically does, this work on its own. Indeed, for them to flourish, many of the contract types we discuss in these pages require some regulatory support.

Note that, by "regulation," we do not intend an expansive definition that would sweep in all products of legislative or administrative bodies. Such an expansive view would imply that contract law is, by definition, only "judge-made." This is not our view. Contract law can be made by judges, legislators, or administrators. Which state body creates contract law is wholly contingent, and varies drastically across legal systems and through time. In many European (and other) countries contract law is part of a Civil Code. Today, in the United States, much of contract law is no longer made by judges (recall the ascent of the Uniform Commercial Code). So when we refer to "regulation," we mean something more limited: that the state provides some administrative apparatus aimed at facilitating the primary rules of contract law (whether judge-made or otherwise) that directly govern the parties' relationship.

Consider the case of insurance contracts. Courts tried to develop a set of rules that would attend to the distinctive features of insurance contracts. They might have developed a new contract type by building on the *contra profer-entem* rule and a tailored inquiry into "reasonable expectations" of policy-holders.[38] But the process ended up as a regime "in disarray," typified by "unpredictable decisions" and sheer "judicial error."[39] Ronald Gilson, Charles Sabel, and Robert Scott attribute this disappointing failure to the institutional limitations of generalist courts which had to face this complex market.[40] Accordingly, they convincingly argue that courts could employ a more fruitful strategy of using "their power of administrative review to induce regulators to seek clarification of insurance terms and policies."[41]

Indeed, the complexity of many areas of contemporary contracting often requires a hybrid of private law and regulatory measures. Let's return again to consumer transactions. Most of us avail ourselves of this contract type on a daily basis in our ordinary lives. The law of consumer contracts includes a specific set of rules dealing with issues like disclosure, cancellation, and warranty.[42] These distinctive features of the type play a crucial role in making consumer contracts viable. But consumer protection law includes not only the contract rules that apply directly to the interacting parties. It also contains a thick additional layer of regulatory measures administered at both state and federal levels and varying across different national systems.

For example, in America, states' "Unfair and Deceptive Practices Acts" or similar legislation regulate various types of misleading statements and repre-sentations as well as other deceptive acts and practices.[43] In addition to establishing a private right of action, such laws entrust government officials – typically the state attorney general's office, but in some cases, also consumer protection offices at the city and county level – with the authority to adminis-ter and enforce these rules.[44]

Likewise, the Federal Trade Commission is quite active in regulating consumer transactions, taking action in areas like misleading advertising, coercive or deceptive sales techniques, and marketing campaigns that prey on the credulity of the young, the elderly, or the infirm.[45] And there are additional federal agencies (and sometimes state counterparts), such as the Food and Drug Administration and the recently formed Consumer Financial

Protection Bureau,[46] which similarly regulate specific industries in ways that are also crucial for consumers.

These and many other administrative institutions – think antitrust, securities regulation, and regulation of credit and debt collection[47] – seek to target systemic market failures that can hardly be addressed on the transactional level.[48] They also provide (when they work well) the infrastructure for a secure marketplace within which effective choices can be made.[49] In this way, these administrative devices comply with the state's responsibility to facilitate our private interactions.

Significant as they are, these regulatory regimes complement and supplement, rather than supplant, the contract rules of consumer transactions. As with consumer transactions, other core areas of voluntary obligation combine the private law of contract types with public regulatory support.

*   *   *

"Freedom of contracts" stands for contract law's participation in the cultural production of diverse contract types among which people may choose. Diversity of contract types, then, is not an artifact to be harmonized into "general" contract law nor explained away by reference to some general contract principle. The array of contract types constructed by law affirmatively supports people's ability to seek their conception of the good in a way that they might not bargain for – at times, might not even consider – if they were defaulted into a prototypical commercial contract.[50]

For example, by contrast to the saliency of suretyship, consider the cultural invisibility of the "dependent contractor," an employment type that does not (yet) exist in the United States but could occupy the space between independent contractor and employee.[51] Courts, legislators, and scholars are starting to explore this missing contract type. But for now, millions of people who already occupy this interstitial role in the new economy remain stuck in employment contracts that don't fit their needs.

In sum, ensuring sufficient diversity of valuable contract types is a core feature, benefit, and indeed *obligation* of a contract law regime committed to human freedom.

8

How Contract Values Relate

A legal theory that relies on multiple values must address how they interrelate. Because the values we invoke – autonomy, utility, and community – are oftentimes treated as rivals, our theory carries a heavy burden in this arena. The primary task of this chapter is to show that the choice theory of contract dissipates some of these apparent conflicts and provides important guidelines to the resolution of the others.

Additionally, this chapter answers a number of conceptual challenges that we have deferred as they have cropped up along the way. We now have in place enough elements of choice theory to address issues of horizontal coexistence among values, vertical implications (including the role of voluntariness as a contract value, the residual category of freestanding contracting, how autonomy functions as a side constraint, and relational equality), the challenge of neutrality, and last but not least, the implications of choice theory for economic analysis.

HORIZONTAL COEXISTENCE

The key to resolving the conflicts among core values is to assign each value its proper role. Autonomy, as we explained in Chapter 4, is contract's ultimate value and the source of the state's obligation to provide meaningful diversity of contract types. But autonomy is not why individuals make contracts, so it cannot be its sole value. Utility and community are contract's instrumental values. Community may even be intrinsically valuable to the extent it is constitutive of the autonomy-enhancing potential of certain contract types.

Often utility and community are mutually reinforcing. This is because interpersonal capital facilitates trust, which, in turn, gives rise to economic success, and economic success tends to strengthen trust and mutual responsibility.[1] But sometimes contract's potential goods push in different directions. Utility and community can be in conflict. What then?

Contract law cannot always help people obtain competing goods. It is not the job of autonomy-friendly contract law to decide which value trumps or how they should be balanced. Rather, contract law should support multiple contract types, each of which offers a distinct balance of goods, so that parties can choose their own favorite balance.[2] In this regard, choice theory supports "horizontal coexistence," the obligation that contract law *amplify*, not *arbitrate*, choice.

Consumer contracts, thick community contracts, business contracts – all of these support equally fundamental types of human activity; yet each responds to different values autonomous people may seek. This means that the proper place for utility and community is not at the level of animating contract law as a whole. Rather, they are components of distinct contract types that support people's diverse pursuits and interests, whether it's their interpersonal relationships, the maximization of their joint material surplus, or the many permutations between these poles. Only a sufficiently rich repertoire of contract types properly facilitates people's ability to choose and revise their various endeavors and interactions.

If contract law is to live up to its promise of enhancing autonomy, it must facilitate people's ability to pursue the utilitarian and communitarian goods that contracts can bring about. So our division of labor does *not* imply that utility and community are unimportant to contract. If much of the value of contract comes from freedom to choose among types, and if the most important values that should shape these types are utility and community, then these values are nothing short of crucial to contract law.

And yet we argued that the value of utility and community in contract is neither fundamental nor freestanding, but rather derives from the way that they serve the parties' autonomous pursuit of their goals. Therefore, in the next section we illustrate the "horizontal coexistence" we have just discussed, and then in the following four sections, we examine the "vertical implications" of our claim that autonomy is contract's ultimate value, while utility and community are the goods an autonomy-based contract law usually helps to secure.

REVISITING CONSUMER TRANSACTIONS

Situating utility and community under autonomy's rule helps explain where previous totalizing contract theories have gone astray. At times, people may prefer not to obtain certain goods that in other contexts seem fundamental.

When that is the case, an autonomy-enhancing contract law will meet them where they are. Consider the good of community.

Macneil is right to highlight the prevalence and significance of diverse contracts in which interpersonal cooperation is of the essence. But there are equally important contracting spheres for which the communitarian goods he celebrates are beside the point, at least for most parties. For example, recall the thin communities Markovits discusses or the inter-organizational contracts Schwartz and Scott address.

More pointedly, consider a consumer transaction for a relatively inexpensive good or service primarily intended for personal use. In that significant sphere of contracting, the consumer is (typically) uninterested in personal relations with the merchant and does not want to dicker over terms, or take the effort to become even minimally acquainted with the terms of the contract. Indeed, individual autonomy is enhanced insofar as law helps people make such transactions quickly, anonymously, and securely so they can focus their time and attention instead on other – more valuable (for them)[3] – projects.[4]

This "no-community" commitment can explain and justify some of the most conspicuous features of consumer contract law, notably the rules which afford consumers certain rights to cancellation and warranty that go far beyond the protective measures anticipated by "classical" contract law.[5] Lawyer-economists have investigated (and debated) the desirability of these asymmetrical rules via the lens of behavioral economics.[6] Our perspective is different.

We focus on the distinctive roles these transactions play in the lives of the typical parties. More specifically, for one party only (the consumer) they are like errands whose friction needs to be minimized if contract is to be loyal to its ultimate normative commitment to autonomy as self-determination. Entrenching this "errands conception" of consumer contracts would help detach its cultural meaning from that of "negotiated deals." This would be an important achievement. First, it would help rationalize the attendant rights that people have when they act as consumers. Second, it would have the happy side-effect of preventing firms from (ab)using consumers' misconceptions of being morally bound to comply with, rather than challenge, unfavorable conditions that "stand on shaky legal ground" just by virtue of being a party to what looks like a formal contract.[7]

This account builds on the importance of investigating *the way* in which consumers' preference-satisfaction contributes to their autonomy, which in turn requires situating it in their life stories (thus revealing the transactions' typical, errand-like character). In taking this step, we depart from economic analyses of consumer contracts, a departure that piggybacks on our general critique of poorly delimited efficiency theories.[8] In sharp contrast to these theories, ours finds preference-satisfaction (here for consumers, but also true more generally) important, not for its own sake, but rather for its contribution to our autonomy.

Our innovative account of consumer contracts is determinedly ahistorical, consistent with our interpretative methodology as discussed in the Introduction. A historical account would track how this type largely resulted from paternalistic regulation that limited classical freedom of contract.[9] Nonetheless, viewed in its best light, we can say that this contract type enhances freedom overall because it likely expands buyer autonomy more than it reduces autonomy for sellers (which are typically organizations with no claim to autonomy).[10]

But there exists a range of cases where the autonomy-reducing effect of consumer protection rules may dominate: some people may find some consumer transactions to be self-fulfilling experiences in and of themselves – they just love to shop. That's why we advocated in Chapter 7 that consumer contract law should make available alternative types in settings where consumer transactions do not impose costly external effects.[11] If alternatives are available – like the Massachusetts and Texas options we noted – then the consumer contract type adds an option, rather than just limiting an existing one. Consumers can then make their own (individual) choices between the "souk" or "bazaar" model of "as is" contracting and the "errands" model of consumer protection law.

We move now from horizontal coexistence to the vertical implications of choice theory. In turn, we consider (1) voluntariness, (2) residual contracting, (3) side constraints, and (4) relational equality. We start with voluntariness.

VOLUNTARINESS AS COMMON DENOMINATOR

Choice theory's ultimate commitment to self-determination implies that law should be responsible for, as Raz says, "creating the conditions for autonomous life, primarily by guaranteeing that an adequate range of diverse and valuable options shall be available to all."[12] But because autonomy is emphatically "incompatible with any vision of morality being thrust down people's throats," it must stop there and "leave individuals free to make their lives what they will."[13] This premise implies that contract is – and should remain – a voluntary obligation. People may not be forcibly pushed to seek contract's potential utility or community goods.

To be sure, voluntariness may be *contingently* conducive to efficiency and to community. But there may be (categories of) cases in which this contingent link does not apply. Insisting on voluntariness (even) in these cases testifies to the privileged position of autonomy. It means, for example, that party sovereignty is *not* simply an instrument for securing the efficient allocation of resources in society.[14]

This proposition of voluntariness, which underlies the liberal commitment to "freedom *from* contract,"[15] constitutes the common denominator of the otherwise heterogeneous realm of contract law. While the commitment is uniform, the doctrinal means to ensure voluntariness vary tremendously: in addition to doctrines like offer and acceptance and duress, think about the familiar common law resort to formalities like consideration or writing[16] or about the civil law requirement of intent-to-contract.[17] Different liberal legal systems pick and choose among this inventory or tailor-make other tools.

Oftentimes the choice among many of these tools would be better handled if conducted at the level of contract types, rather than at the wholesale level of "general" contract law – a move that would allow voluntariness to be informed by the type's animating principle. (This point applies beyond voluntariness to other "general" contract doctrines such as fraud and unconscionability whose application varies depending on the context.[18]) Choice theory counsels that we ensure vindication of general principles by implementing them locally.

Choice theory also suggests going another level in thinking about voluntariness: the concept itself may even take on different meanings in different contract spheres. For example, scholars have proposed, and choice theory would support, that the parol evidence rule should be relaxed in more interpersonal contexts, while it should be imposed strictly in high-value corporate transactions where the parties gain more from *ex ante* certainty and are more likely to ensure the contract is the full expression of their intentions.[19] Or, we could vary default rules regarding parties' intent to be bound in different situations, such as preliminary contracting or spousal promises.[20] Finally, our "errands" conception of consumer contracts implies that, in this context, voluntariness is secured by ensuring that the nonbargained terms correspond to (or exceed) consumers' typical expectations (in which case attributing consent to the consumer is no more objectionable than attributing consent to a buyer of a car who lacks knowledge of its mechanical features).

Despite this value in tailoring at the level of types, a common overarching commitment to autonomy implies a trans-substantive concern for voluntariness (a view that converges with Ripstein's account of a "united will"[21]), especially given the challenge that the objective theory of contract poses for this value.[22]

A RESIDUAL CATEGORY OF FREESTANDING CONTRACTING

A choice theory of contracts must not be content just with offering a rich variety of contract types. Alongside this menu, it must offer a residual category of freestanding contracting, which allows individuals to reject the state's favored forms of interaction and decide for themselves how to mold their interpersonal interactions.[23]

This point is properly acknowledged in most Continental legal systems, in which contract types – or "nominate" contracts as they are called – play a relatively important role (as we claim they should). Although courts tend to begin the legal analysis of contracts by seeking to classify them into the existing categorization of contract types, they are careful *not* to treat this list as comprehensive and thus acknowledge both "mixed contracts" (that cut across contract types) and "innominate" or atypical contracts.[24]

It seems indispensable to freedom that people be able to "invent" their own private forms of contracting outside of any familiar contract type (a freedom that distinguishes contract from property[25]). The law governing such residual contracting should be shaped with this purpose in mind, rather than piggyback on the commercial contract that the Willistonian project imagined as the default.

Indeed, a residual contract law that can serve as such a liberating device is likely to be very different from what is currently termed "general" contract law.[26] Our thoughts here are necessarily preliminary and speculative. It seems to us such residual contract law should be as open as possible to idiosyncratic choices, and thus arguably "emptier."

The obligation to take idiosyncrasy seriously probably means that, rather than setting up majoritarian defaults, residual contract law should be guided by an effort to set aside such conventional preconceptions and should thus perhaps offer checklists, allowing people to check an option or write in their own. Such careful tailoring is, no doubt, cumbersome, and thus may indeed be unappealing in many (or even most) cases. But it has its virtues. In addition to its significance from an autonomy-enhancing perspective, a residual contract type that requires the parties to reach explicit agreement on all (or most) aspects of their transaction likely tends to strengthen their commitment to the contract irrespective of the monetary consequences.[27]

AUTONOMY AS SIDE CONSTRAINT

While autonomy often recruits community and utility to shape the multiple contract types that self-determination requires, these values do not always dovetail. Within any particular type, autonomy's role as the ultimate commitment of contract implies that it should generally trump contract's other values when they conflict. Thus, in addition to the enabling role of autonomy in our theory, it also occupies an independent, protective role, when autonomy functions as a "side constraint."[28]

Usually, promoting contract's other values – utility, community, or a blend of the two – does not clash with, and indeed enhances the ultimate value of autonomy. But there are cases when promoting the goods of contract might undermine its autonomy raison d'être. For example, communitarian demands of loyalty that pose excessive limitations on contractual parties' exit – that is, on promisors' freedom to change their mind – might collide with party autonomy.[29] Similarly, value conflict may arise in efficient contracts between consumers and organizations, given that organizations, unlike consumers, have no independent claim to autonomy.[30] In many such conflicts, contract's commitments to community and utility should give way to rules that best promote contract's ultimate value.

Thus, the notion of autonomy as a side constraint may be the most coherent justification for a number of otherwise puzzling contract law doctrines. For example, it justifies some restrictions on enforceability of employee non-compete agreements[31] and limits on the advance sale of future wages.[32] And it helps explain the *unilateral* right of termination of long-term contracts, which is semi-inalienable at least regarding certain contract types.[33]

We do not imply that autonomy straightforwardly and necessarily trumps utility or community. Rather, our approach may require exploring (at least) two alternative responses. Thus, it may imply that we first try to resolve such conflicts by looking more closely at the meaning of the utility or community value for people's autonomy.[34] Just as your garden-variety contract limits one's future options in the service of self-authorship, the vibrancy of certain utility- or community-oriented contract types may require curtailing certain future choices; and insofar as a (complicated, to be sure) analysis of the overall effects of such limitations on people's self-determination shows that they are positive, the incommensurably higher status of autonomy poses no real difficulty.

Other conflicts, however, are real and fundamental and may even require a (seemingly impossible) tradeoff. Then, we turn to the second response. In most of these cases, autonomy should take priority. But we recognize the possibility that (in rather rare cases, we assume) this presumption may be overridden if, and only if, its costs to the utility or the community goods of contract pass a sufficiently high threshold.[35] We cannot hope fully to address here these challenges of value incommensurability, so for now we just flag the concern, and note that its implications for liberal contract theory seem no more intractable than for legal theory in general.[36]

RELATIONAL EQUALITY

The fourth and final implication of the status of autonomy as contract's ultimate value is also quite intricate and can only be addressed here tentatively.

1. *Substantive versus Formal Equality*. The point can be stated succinctly: contract law – like private law more generally – should be guided by *substantive*, rather than *formal*, equality.[37] If contract is to serve people's self-determination, and not only their (Kantian) independence, contract law cannot rely, as it is conventionally portrayed, on a formal conception of equality that seeks to abstract away the particular features distinguishing one person from another.

To sharpen the point, respecting each other's independence does not require any consideration of any individual's features – it merely prescribes a negative duty of noninterference. By contrast, respect for self-determination is hollow without *some* attention to our distinctive features, which make us who we actually are.

Indeed, reciprocal respect for party autonomy requires that we view parties as more than mere bearers of a generic human capacity for choice. In addition, we must accommodate, to some extent, the personal qualities that are necessary for the interacting parties meaningfully to recognize each other as free and equal persons. Such a view of equality is substantive and not just formal.

We acknowledge a significant subset of contract law – including the areas highlighted by Schwartz & Scott and by Markovits – in which formal equality is the all-things-considered best proxy for a state of affairs in which the participants are, more or less, in a relationship of substantive equality. But contract theorists overstate the implications of this observation when they use this congruity to support the claim that formal equality is truly the foundational ideal of contracts in a particular context or in general.[38] The extrapolation does not hold.

Contract law applies any number of doctrines whose basic organizing idea is excluding people whose capacities for contract-making and contract-keeping fall below a certain threshold for participation. Some of these doctrines take a categorical form – for instance, minors do not possess the legal personality to make an enforceable promise.[39] Other doctrines, such as undue influence, are less rigid but, nonetheless, manifest hostility toward some transactions based on the concern that one of the parties is not sufficiently competent to make and accept contractual promises.[40]

The doctrine that exemplifies this concern most dramatically is unconscionability,[41] under which contract law ought to protect the vulnerable party (often, the "poor"[42] or the "weak, the foolish, and the thoughtless"[43]) if: (1) he or she could exercise only formal and not "meaningful" choice and (2) the terms of the contract unreasonably favor the other party.[44]

Furthermore, contract types that are particularly vulnerable to abuses of relational equality – significant subsets of the law governing both employment and real estate transactions – are by now typified by elaborate doctrines of accommodation that specifically address these substantive concerns. Charitably interpreted, these contract types are not merely infused with *external* (constitutional) antidiscrimination concerns, but rather implement the *internal* (contract law) commitment to relational equality.[45]

2. *The Sphere of Employment.* Contract's commitment to relational equality is also the essence of labor law (that is, the law dealing with collective forms of employment). As the introductory section to the Wagner Act makes explicit, the purpose of allowing labor unions to flourish is to address "[t]he inequality of bargaining power between employees who do not possess full freedom of association or actual liberty of contract and employers who are organized in the corporate or other forms of ownership association."[46] Labor law attempts to solve this inequality by giving employees the chance to bargain collectively and thus to place themselves on more equal footing with their employers – with the goal that their resulting contracts embody the voluntariness that is fundamental to choice.[47]

One may worry that the mere possibility of workers' unionization cannot be enough to meet relational equality concerns in employment, and that to distinguish contract from subjugation, individualized contracting should be effectively abolished.[48] But this concern is exaggerated. While current labor law may not be fully successful in equalizing bargaining power between employers and employees, the ability of individual employees – either unionized or not – to bargain in the shadow of labor law makes a real difference.[49] So long as unionization remains a realistic possibility, nonunion employee contracts may fall beneath the protective shadow of labor law.[50]

For labor law to function this way – supporting relational equality of both union and nonunion employees – unions should be able to negotiate so-called "agency shop" contracts that require employees to pay union dues as a condition of employment. To the extent "right to work" laws in some states now prohibit agency shop,[51] these laws *limit* the contractual freedom of both union and nonunion employees. Moreover, and more importantly, agency shop does not meaningfully reduce individual autonomy. It results in an *ex ante* reduction in the amount of money belonging to an employee who has to pay dues, in return for higher wages and benefits and better working conditions.[52] Even assuming that there are employees who are unwilling third-party beneficiaries to agency shop provisions, a sufficient multiplicity of contract types ought to empower employees to seek out employers with desirable union agreements. Mandatory rules are, as we argue in Chapter 10, particularly justified where they are needed in order to sustain the viability of intra-sphere multiplicity.

Indeed, all these doctrines and types – as well as other, more covert means courts use[53] – constrain the permitted gap between the (required) commitment to substantive equality and the (pragmatic) use of formal equality as an imperfect proxy.[54] Admittedly, courts and legislatures often apply overly restrictive understandings of these protective doctrines and types – perhaps because they have not fully internalized the relational equality view necessary for contractual autonomy. The significance of these buffers is, however, structural: they protect against the excesses of treating contracting parties as formally equal. In other words, they create the opening for the carriers of contract law to turn what would otherwise be a *freestanding* ideal of formal equality into one that is *conditional* on its (loose) compatibility with substantive equality.[55]

This closes our discussion of vertical implications – what it means to take seriously the idea that autonomy is the ultimate value of contract such that other values must (usually) give way. But we are not quite done with the problem of values in conflict.

THE CHALLENGE OF NEUTRALITY

Some readers may worry that choice theory actually betrays our liberal commitments rather than serving them. Our approach, according to this argument, violates "the precept of state neutrality" both in its endorsement of self-determination as contract's ultimate value and in privileging a limited, albeit not insignificant, number of contract types. This critique blends reference both to concrete neutrality ("neutrality as a first-order principle of justice") and to neutrality of grounds ("neutrality as a second-order principle of justification").[56]

Consider first the challenge of concrete neutrality. Wouldn't a more neutral regime – one that equally supports all possible arrangements that people might want to take up – be superior for the task of facilitating people's ability to choose and revise their various endeavors and relationships? And doesn't focusing on contract types obscure the value of "a vibrant general contract law" – valuable both because it offers legislative (or reporting or teaching) economy and because it allows, or maybe even encourages, parties to set up their own terms of interaction?[57]

Let's start with this last point. Because we believe that contract types all do share a commitment to voluntariness, we do not call for eradicating all general contract doctrines, and agree that some doctrinal implications of this commitment take a trans-substantive form.[58] But voluntariness, as we argued earlier in this chapter, can be better (and more neutrally) protected by recognizing divergences in the meaning of voluntariness across different types, and by deploying different doctrinal tools better suited to protecting that value within each type.

To go a step further, our commitment to voluntariness should not require parties to contract explicitly about their relationship through "general" law. Such a forced contracting system would be quite burdensome, rendering certain types of interpersonal relationships too costly to enter into, at least for some. In many contexts it would also still miss the "authentic," substantively neutral position, because all contracting schemes ratify the parties' contingent background expectations and power imbalances. What may seem an innocent equilibrium generated by neutral market processes is oftentimes a path dependent contingency that, as such, should not necessarily be privileged.[59]

Even if, or to the extent that, choice theory may entail a "crowding out" effect, this effect seems to be offset by the greater range of options provided by contract types. These options would cease to exist, or become available only in rather circumscribed settings – or only to those who can afford to engage in extensive negotiation of their contract conditions[60] – were it not for the support of the law. Note also that choosing a type is the beginning, not the end of contractual choice. People can bargain over most terms within most types, so that they have greater choice-making capability overall by operating within the legally facilitated range of types.

Finally, whatever detrimental effects law's active facilitation may entail is likely to be remedied if, first, contract law takes seriously our proposal to reinforce minoritarian and utopian contract forms (discussed in Chapter 11) and, second, if it properly structures the "residual category of freestanding contracting" along the lines we have just briefly articulated.

In sum, our approach seems to score quite high on the neutrality test. To see why, realize that contract law cannot practically give equal support to all the possible arrangements people may want to make; further, it should not even try to offer such support because having too many options may curtail choice just as much as having too few (the "paradox of choice" point we reference in Chapter 12). Because law's support makes a difference – very few contract types would have looked as they do, and would have worked as well as they do, without the active support of law – contract law necessarily prefers certain types of arrangements over others.

Furthermore, even respecting each contract type, law cannot be strictly neutral because every choice of a set of legal rules governing a particular contract type facilitates and entrenches one ideal vision of the good in that particular context. But the obligation to provide a diverse menu of contract types imposes less than its alternative, namely: the one-type-fits-all of traditional contract theories with their global, overarching principles.

Finally, we consider if maybe there is some other neutral principle, besides choice theory, that could serve as contract's ultimate value. For example, as a thought experiment, imagine democracy fills that role.[61] Could contract law safely and solely rely on whatever choices our elected representatives entrench in their legislated products? Democracy is surely relevant insofar as it is invoked to highlight the broad leeway choice theory gives to liberal polities to offer their own distinctive menus of contract types. These menus can and should vary based on local histories, local needs, local preferences, and local utopian experiments.

But democracy cannot substitute for choice theory in providing the normative underpinning of liberal contract law. Considering democracy as the foundational value conflates the search for substantive moral truth with that of institutional legitimacy. It also overstates the comparative advantage – in terms of either competence or legitimacy – of legislatures vis-à-vis courts in private law matters.[62] By whichever path we take concerning concrete neutrality, we return to choice theory.

The remaining challenge may concern "neutrality of grounds," a challenge that contests our endorsement of self-determination as contract's ultimate value. We have already set out our response in detail in Chapter 3, and need just restate it here: because contract is a power-conferring body of law – which people can but need not invoke or use in pursuing their objectives – it is hard to think of any intelligible, let alone neutral, alternative to autonomy as self-determination as contract's ultimate value.[63]

THE PRICE OF FREEDOM FOR EFFICIENCY ANALYSTS

We have one final matter to address before we conclude this chapter. Because our choice theory of contracts designates a significant role to utility and thus to the economic analysis of contract law, and given the contemporary predominance of lawyer economists in the academic discourse on contracts, it may be helpful to summarize briefly how our view differs from theirs. We see five distinctions:

1. Most basically, whereas the economic canon seeks to facilitate preference satisfaction so as to maximize social welfare, we argue that such facilitation

is important only because, and therefore only to the extent that, it is conducive to people's self-determination. What makes our theory liberal is that it places the importance of enhancing individual self-determination ahead of maximizing collective welfare.

This fundamental difference implies several further distinctions:

2. Preferences that undermine self-determination should be, in our account, generally overridden. This imperative comes up in a limited, but non-trivial set of circumstances, such as cases refusing enforcement of employee non-compete agreements, limiting advance sale of future wages, and upholding the semi-inalienable unilateral right of termination of certain long-term contracts, which we noted earlier in this chapter.[64] It may also be triggered by the imperative of relational justice, which (as we explained) is derived from the commitment to autonomy. In these (relatively rare) cases where autonomy acts as a side constraint rather than as an ultimate value, utilitarian preferences must give way.

3. Not all contract goods are amenable to the maximization formula that economic analysis employs. Why? Because the goods of contract sometimes are communitarian in nature, so that part of their point is the process and not just the outcome. Other times, as our account of consumer contracts highlights, people may have autonomy interests that are more fundamental than their welfarist concerns. In other words, in contract types where the contractual relationship has a significant non-welfarist value, contract can no longer be analyzed in the economist's strictly instrumental terms.[65] This is not to say that efficiency analysis has no bite, but that its findings must be tempered in light of the other values at stake – a task that requires reasoning apart from simple utilitarian balancing.

4. Choice theory often offers better descriptive fit with existing contract law, including many doctrines and types we have already explored, and puzzles like mandatory rules and sticky defaults (which we come to in Chapter 10). To give one (small and somewhat technical) example here, choice theory offers a *non-contingent* justification for contracting parties' standing to pursue a breach, to settle, or to sue.[66] These standing rules are implied by contract's role in enhancing individual autonomy, in particular its mission of allowing individuals legitimately to enlist others to their projects. The parties' exclusive standing is neither derivative of, nor is it dependent upon, their comparative competence as private attorneys general. By contrast, for lawyer economists, standing in the parties – and no standing in strangers to the contract or society as a whole – must be based on some *contingent* reason, like comparative competence, if contract is merely a tool for maximizing social welfare.

5. And last but not least, as we will further elaborate below, choice theory implies that facilitating minoritarian and utopian alternatives may be quite important for contract law even if that affirmative state support (with appropriate caveats and qualifications) cannot be fully justified in terms of existing preferences or effective demand – a major departure from the efficiency analysis approach. Autonomy demands an adequate range of choice, even if markets do not supply it and efficiency does not necessarily require it.

As we discussed in the Introduction, freedom has a price, but it's a modest one for efficiency theorists willing to acknowledge some liberal foundation to their project.

∗ ∗ ∗

Why do people contract with each other? To maximize utility, to build community, often to achieve a mix of these goods. An autonomy-regarding contract law amplifies choice by ensuring an adequate diversity of types; it does not arbitrate between the goods people seek – except in the relatively rare cases where autonomy must act as a side constraint. While autonomy, utility, and community are often treated as rivals, choice theory dissipates some apparent conflicts and provides important guidelines to the resolution of the others.

9

Contract Spheres

We have talked about contract values and their interrelations. This is what makes our theory *liberal* and *general*. Now we provide the bridge between choice theory and *contract law as a whole*. To do so, we reject the commercial transaction as contract's core and we offer, in its place, an updated taxonomy of contract types designed to help ensure contract's autonomy-enhancing multiplicity. Our taxonomy groups contracting practices into spheres according to their distinctive subject matter and shared dilemmas.

Like other critics of the Willistonian strategy before us, we reject the commercial contract core as a description of contract law.[1] Our opposition is, we hope, particularly pointed because it relies on a normative commitment to autonomy, the ultimate value Willistonian contract law purports to serve but fails to respect. The commercial contract paradigm does not describe contract law as it actually exists nor does it capture the law's autonomy-enhancing potential. At the same time, the existing framework also generates unnecessary doctrinal confusion for courts. Fixing these doctrinal muddles along the lines we suggest would, in turn, improve contract law's autonomy-enhancing role – a virtuous circle of theory and doctrine.

THREE MOTIVATING EXAMPLES

To motivate our move to contract types and spheres, consider the following three briefly rendered examples:

1. *Bailment.* First, the flattening effect of general contract law seems responsible for much of the doctrinal muddle now troubling bailment law.

According to the conventional paradigm, the prevailing bailment doctrine repudiates the contractual nature of bailments. How so? Because the bailee's responsibility for loss or damage is usually based on a standard of ordinary care in contrast to "general" contract law's typically strict obligation to perform.[2] In this view, bailment is no longer even part of contract law, and the way to bring it back in is to amplify strict liability obligations for bailees. But this universalizing impulse makes no sense for bailment – hence the doctrinal muddle.

Transfer theorists present strict liability as a constitutive feature of promises and contracts.[3] But this proposition is dubious,[4] which is not surprising given the fallacy of the theory on which it relies. Indeed, the question of whether strict liability exceptions threaten to swallow the negligence rule[5] is less important if both the "rule" and its "exceptions" are understood as majoritarian defaults of the bailment contract type.

Rather than decide to treat bailments "as contractual in nature,"[6] and therefore import all of the "general" contract law, reformers should focus on the recurring dilemmas of bailment contracts. The specific rules of bailment are not oddities to be explained away, but rather clues to the normative challenges people seek to solve when they use this contract type.

2. *Liquidated damages.* Another example of the detrimental effects of the commercial contract paradigm comes from the standard debate over liquidated damages. From our perspective, this debate seems frustratingly futile.

Most arguments in favor of the prevailing rule of *ex post* fairness review anticipate contract types in which promisors are vulnerable to making suboptimal choices.[7] That seems a reasonable legal treatment of contracting in such types. By contrast, most of the claims criticizing the rule assume a very different set of contract types, in which sophisticated parties use liquidated damages in anticipation of possibly unverifiable harms of breach.[8] That also seems reasonable, given the goods people seek when they enter this business contract context.

Each argument is right in its own sphere: whereas the former exemplifies contract law's commitment to relational equality, the latter can properly resort to formal equality as a reliable proxy (a distinction highlighted in Chapter 8).[9] Therefore, the rule should likely vary by sphere, rather than be held artificially constant to conform to a misplaced notion of "general" contract law. Interestingly, there are some indications that courts implicitly appreciate this lesson and reduce scrutiny of liquidated damages in cases involving sophisticated parties.[10] This distinction should be made explicit.

3. *Efficient breach.* We see similar confusion and potential distortions generated by the attempt to align intra-family contracts with contracts between

strangers, particularly as regards the theory of efficient breach. Efficient breach runs into its most serious criticism and doctrinal problems when it is applied to promises made in the context of a thick community, most particularly marriage,[11] but also further afield in contract types such as suretyship.[12] Again, the flattening effect of the Willistonian project pushes contract law in the wrong direction. These problems could be avoided if this doctrine were applied selectively to contract types, rather than assuming that once introduced to contract law, it must be applied generally.

THE ROLE OF CONTRACT SPHERES

These brief case studies do not simply reflect the familiar point that, for abstract principles to be properly applied, they need to be carefully adjusted to their context. Rather, the required differences they highlight are best explained by reference to the different animating principles of contract types that have been improperly lumped together. These more fundamental differences may derive from the typical normative commitments of a contract type (as in the intra-family versus business contracts) or from its distinctive subject matter (as in bailment, or, for that matter, suretyship).[13]

Such examples, and numerous others, suggest that in dealing with discrete doctrinal questions we need to examine the normative desirability of competing rules by reference to the animating principles of their specific contract types (an inquiry that requires us to present this principle in its best light possible), and we need some way to understand how types relate to each other, by normative commitment and subject matter.

We are now embarking on the task of linking choice theory with practical contract law reform. This task requires an organizing framework for contract types. But we cannot and should not return to the pre-Williston taxonomy of contract categories. That list was an atheoretical mishmash which threatened the rationality and integrity, and thus also the legitimacy, of contract law. Hugh Collins – a commentator who appreciates the efficiency benefits of allowing "greater differentiation" in the rules of contract – notes, "[i]f the rules differ according to the category of contract, then private law requires principles which can provide a rational explanation for the categorization and the reasons for differential regulation."[14]

Choice theory offers these missing principles that can legitimately require us to replace the old abstractions of the orthodox "freedom of contract" model with a theory-driven and descriptively well-formed taxonomy for "freedom of contracts."

FOUR SPHERES OF CONTRACTING

An autonomy-regarding theory requires a taxonomy that reflects the typical contexts in which people enter contracts and responds to the distinctive dilemmas that arise in those interactions. There are many ways such a taxonomy could be constructed. Here we offer one that collects contract types into spheres. Our cautious language in the material that follows derives not only from the fact that this is a preliminary effort, but also from a commitment to a functional and dynamic mode of taxonomic work.[15]

The *subject matter* of a contract is bound to make a difference regarding the ideals that law can plausibly embrace and hope to further. One salient dimension along which we can readily distinguish among contracts is whether the subject matter primarily concerns "people" or "things." This distinction is neither exhaustive nor stable. But the division has some appeal: it reflects real distinctions in how contract law operates, and it has the virtue (perhaps) of historical pedigree. Blackstone divided contract in part between "rights of persons" and "rights of things."[16]

Our second dimension concerns whether the *locus* of contracting is in some sense "private" or "public." This axis is even less stable than the former (and it has been subject to much justified criticism). As we construe it, this dimension looks at whether contracting practices are oriented toward the internal, domestic, or personal versus those that are relatively more external.

These two axes yield four salient spheres of contracting: family, home, employment, and commerce (see Figure 1).

Each sphere then includes a range of types. For example, (1) *family*: we might see prenuptial, civil union, and cohabitation contracts, along with marriage contracts; (2) *home*: real estate purchase and lease contracts, co-living and other "intentional community" contracts; (3) *employment*: at-will, for cause, and independent contractor contracts; and (4) *commerce*: sales, consumer, insurance, and derivative contracts.

We can now see that labor law (alongside certain mandatory rules of employment law) not only helps to secure relational equality – as we explained in

		Subject matter	
		People	Things
Locus	*Private*	1. Family	2. Home
	Public	3. Employment	4. Commerce

FIGURE 1: Four Spheres of Contracting

Chapter 8 – but it also adds a type: an employee can work in either a union or nonunion environment. Indeed, labor law's nonuniversal coverage is what enables it to perform both tasks: it can perform a multiplicity-enhancing role only if it is not mandatory. But neither can the union type be vanishingly scarce or it would undermine labor law's ability to address relational equality concerns for employees generally. Collective employment contract types help ensure the voluntariness component even in nonunion employment contract types.[17]

TWO INSTRUMENTAL ROLES FOR SPHERES

Nothing fundamental to choice theory depends on the particular labels we are adopting. One can easily imagine other ways to divide the contractual universe. Thus, we have no commitment to these axes or labels. Nor are we committed to a two-by-two matrix, nor even to the idea of spheres. There are valid normative reasons to group contract types along many different dimensions. Some of the reasons for adopting our particular framework turn on its intuitive appeal and manageability, how it nicely reflects long-standing divisions and debates in contract law, and even its aesthetic virtues (as we see them). But the more fundamental reasons for structuring our taxonomy in this way lie in its important instrumental roles for choice theory.

1. *Substitutes.* The first and main reason is that this taxonomy is conducive to understanding choice theory's requirement of intra-sphere multiplicity. It highlights the obligation of liberal contract law to support choice within each familiar category of human activity, such that, within each sphere, we see contract types that are *partial functional substitutes* for each other. They need to be substitutes because choice is not enhanced with alternatives that are orthogonal to each other; and their substitutability should not be too complete because types that are too similar also do not offer meaningful choice.

This means our taxonomy of spheres does *not* imply that new types are valuable only insofar as they nicely fit it. Rather, we acknowledge that other types that may challenge this (we think conventional) division of spheres may be just as (or maybe more) valuable. Indeed, our division of the contracting universe to spheres is thoroughly instrumental to the commitment to secure real choice. It is a heuristic device that can help us see whether law supplies sufficient alternatives that can credibly function as substitutes; and thus, it is a means to the goal of enhancing freedom.

2. *New Types.* The instrumental role of our taxonomy also helps address the question of when new contract elements become a new type. In other words,

how can we decide whether some shift (addition, omission, or revision) in the current terms of a given type indeed generates a new type?

As should be apparent by now, choice theory implies that different contract types should be guided by distinct (and robust) animating principles, which thus serve as the "normative DNA" of their respective constitutive rules. Now we can refine this proposition by adding that an innovative contractual arrangement becomes a new contract type once its animating principle implies that it can function as a substitute – or at least as a significant additional alternative – to the existing types in that sphere of important human activity.

THE SUB-SPHERES OF COMMERCE

Looking back at Figure 1, it seems intuitive to say that a marriage contract is not a substitute for a sales contract – they are in different spheres. Within the sphere of commerce we noted four types – sales, consumer, insurance, and derivative contracts – but these too reflect quite distinctive contracting prac-tices and are not meaningful substitutes for each other. So, given our defin-ition of spheres, we must say that sales contracts are not properly viewed as being in the same sphere as, for example, insurance contracts.

Another way to say this is that the sphere of commerce comprises a range of sub-spheres of commerce-related contract activity. Within those sub-spheres, contract types do function as substitutes. So, how to break up commerce into sub-spheres? As with the discussion that led to Figure 1, nothing fundamental turns on how we divide commerce. One approach is to look perhaps at the sophistication of the parties along one axis and at the tangibility of the contract's subject along the other axis.

These (admittedly rough and ragged) distinctions suggest a second matrix – with four sub-spheres of commerce. They are: (1) *consumer*: including, for example, ordinary consumer transactions and software licenses; (2) *lending and insurance*: mortgages, credit cards, and health and life insurance; (3) *sales/business*: from commercial sales to partnerships and LLCs; and (4) *finance/risk*: derivatives, guarantees (Figure 2). Again, we do not want to get caught up in whether a type belongs in one sub-sphere or another. What choice theory requires is that we ensure availability of a sufficient number of normatively attractive substitute types for any important form of contractual activity.[18]

Why are there so many more contract types within the sphere of commerce than in our other spheres? In part, the answer must lie in the stronger incentives for individual parties to invest in creating new contract types within

		Type of thing	
		Tangible	Intangible
Relative	*Individual*	1. Consumer	2. Lending/Insurance
Sophistication	*Corporation*	3. Sales/Business	4. Finance/Risk

FIGURE 2: *Sub-Spheres of Commerce*

this sphere. Even relatively moderate demand can justify creation of a new type, so long as that type responds to the balance of contract goods that enough people seek. We are constantly seeing new types emerge. To give just one example from the news, consider the recent emergence of the "benefit corporation" – blending profit and social objectives – in about a dozen states.[19] This example could be multiplied dozens of times.

Note that the large number of contract types here, available even to individuals, suggests that people can handle new types without too much danger of confusion. In other words, communication costs – a concern emphasized recently by some private law theorists – does not justify adherence to the Willistonian idea of one "general" contract law. Rather than (over) emphasizing communication costs, private law theorists need to consider the interest of third parties whose concerns are best cast in terms of verification.[20] And they should also pay significant attention to the needs of the parties *inter se*. For these parties to be able to cooperate fruitfully, contract types (and property institutions) in core categories of interpersonal interaction must be relatively stable, so that the types can consolidate the parties' expectations around a discrete coherent animating principle.[21]

THE OBLIGATION TO SUPPORT LOW-DEMAND TYPES

By contrast, there are far fewer contract types in the noncommerce spheres. Why? Perhaps there are weaker incentives to create or demand new types. And even if there is sufficient payoff (as in the spheres of work and home), there may be substantial collective action problems (for employees and home-owners) that lead to pertinent values being left out of new types. But that contingent result does not negate the need for more types.

The autonomy perspective suggests that, where effective demand is weak, the state shoulders a concomitantly greater responsibility to support valuable new types to ensure sufficient choice in important areas of contracting activity. The successful proliferation of types within the commerce sphere suggests that confusion among types is not a significant problem, and should not in itself caution against support for new types in other spheres.

This final lesson – regarding the state's obligation to support low-demand types – may well be the most important practical takeaway of choice theory. To treat the "market for new types" in a unified way and give it the sustained attention it deserves, we make this point the focus of Chapter 11.

A COMMENT ON STATE AND TRANSNATIONAL CONTRACTS

We want to reiterate that our taxonomy is meant to be *indicative* of contracting practices, rather than *exhaustive*. To give one example, our focus leaves out the increasingly large domain of state contracts, transnational contracts, and international contracts. Much contracting in this sphere – say, between individuals or corporations and their own state, or between parties beyond national borders – operates like other familiar types and can be fully analyzed with the tools we develop in this book. But much cannot.

These contract types at both the state and the transnational levels bring their own complexities and are deserving of their own study. Even if we leave aside international treaties, consider government procurement contracts, concession contracts, government employment contracts, design-build and turnkey projects, and sovereign loans. The dramatic fact that one of the parties is a sovereign raises fundamental issues.

When a sovereign party enforces its own contracts, it may, on the one hand, undermine a commitment to relational equality.[22] On the other hand, it may reinforce that commitment, given that sovereignty arguably stands for the self-determination of the nation at large, which in turn connects with the sovereign's authority to rewrite the story of our collective life – premising periodic elections on our right to change our minds.[23]

This broad sphere also raises intricate questions regarding both state representation and the scope of governments' authority to bind their nations.[24] Finally, the international plane brings up interesting institutional complexities. On the one hand, there are innumerable private and semi-public bodies as well as public international organizations that create contract types, building to some extent on lessons from domestic contract regimes.[25] But, on the other hand, there are no authoritative and fully universal international legislative bodies and no authoritative interpreters with general competence.[26] These substantive and institutional challenges deserve careful treatment which we leave for another day (or different authors).

＊ ＊ ＊

We have rejected the faded idea of the commercial transaction as contract's core. In its place, we offer an updated taxonomy of contract types and spheres. This taxonomy is admittedly contingent and contestable in its details. The version we offer is an instrumental tool designed to highlight and help ensure contract's autonomy-enhancing multiplicity. The spheres of contract are the bridge that links choice theory to contract law.

10

Contract Types

The final step in creating a general and liberal theory of contract law is to specify, far more precisely, what we mean by contract types. The term carries substantial weight in choice theory, and raises many plausible questions and objections. What are the links among contract types, contract spheres, and the values people seek? What constitutes an adequate range of types? When does a change in the law create a new type?

This chapter considers these issues. It also addresses contexts in which too much choice within a particular type ("freedom of contract") reduces freedom, for example, by destabilizing the cultural meaning of that type. Here, we show how mandatory rules and sticky defaults which limit choice within a type can surprisingly enhance freedom overall – so long as there exists a sufficient range among types in that important sphere of human activity.

In specifying a theory of contract types, we bracket one issue – the state's obligations to the market for new types – and consider it separately in the following Chapter. Conceptually, it fits here, but it needs a little extra attention because of its role as a major takeaway of choice theory and because it is a magnet for objections to our approach.

LOCAL VALUES IN CONTRACT TYPES

We begin here by noting that there are lots of contract types that become visible once you start looking for them. When you first go outside at night, you just see the occasional light – perhaps the north star of the commercial contract type. After a while, with a new perspective, you can see that it's a starry night, filled with diverse contract types.

This multiplicity of contract types can be disorienting, but it is neither chaotic nor unprincipled. Rather, it can be explained by reference to the recurring dilemmas of the contract spheres and the state's obligation to ensure the availability of meaningful choice within each of these spheres. This means some types within a sphere will foster the good of interpersonal relationships, others the maximization of joint surplus, and others still will be addressed to a complex and shifting mix of these goals.

In other words, other than the ultimate commitment to autonomy, values in contract law are *local* to contract types, not *global* to contract law. We acknowledge that certain contract spheres may be more amenable to particular values. Thus, many contract types, particularly in the sphere of commerce, are mostly about economic gains – maximizing joint surplus by securing efficiencies of specialization and risk allocation – with social benefits being merely a side effect.

Other contract types, say in the family sphere, are more about the intrinsic good of being part of a plural subject, where the raison d'être of the contract refers more to one's identity and interpersonal relationships, while the attendant economic benefits are perceived as helpful byproducts rather than the sole (or at least the primary) motive for cooperation.

While types may cluster around particular values within a sphere, commitment to contractual autonomy nevertheless crucially requires attention to meaningful choice within spheres, not just to diversity among spheres. Within a particular sphere of contracting, contract law should offer a sufficiently diverse range of contract types, each representing a distinct balance of values. The majority may prefer one contract type, but choice theory requires that within each contracting sphere free individuals should be enabled to contract based on a different value balance. Hence the significance of having "relations"-based contract types in the sphere of commerce and of offering more than only thick-community contract types in the sphere of intimacy.

The importance of this last point cannot be overstated. Having stable and normatively attractive forms available to reject makes one's chosen contract type even more of an expression of individual autonomy. Part of the state's obligation to enhance individual autonomy is to ensure the existence of some contract types that most people do not want most of the time. We define ourselves not just by what we choose, but also by the values and goods we leave aside.

TAILORING LAW TO LOCAL ANIMATING PRINCIPLES

Choice theory requires that contract law offer different, but equally valuable and obtainable, frameworks of interpersonal interaction. A mosaic of contract types within a single sphere of contracting activity is valuable – indeed, indispensable – for freedom of contracts and thus for autonomy. How does contract law tailor its rules to the local animating principles of each distinct type? We note three distinct cases, illustrating the spectrum of goods people seek from contract.

1. *Business versus "relations" contracts.* The implicit reform goal of the Schwartz and Scott model of business contracts is to tailor contract law to the animating principle of this sphere. By concentrating on sophisticated organizations seeking the maximization of joint surplus as their ideal-typic contracting parties, they insist that business contract law should be minimal, that is, it should focus on giving the parties wide latitude and enforcing their deal.[1] By reforming existing business contract types in this wealth-maximization direction, contract law would better enhance party autonomy.

Moving away from the business contracting pole, the reform agenda becomes more complex. As contracting parties seek more communal goods, they are increasingly understood, by themselves and others, as active participants in a joint endeavor, that is, as members in a purposive community. As Macneil emphasizes, governance is of the essence regarding many thick "relations" contract types and law should aim at developing governance structures that sustain interdependence and are conducive to long-term trust and solidarity.[2]

2. *Discretionary adjustments versus local refinements.* One path for achieving support for community is through tweaking "general" contract law. The "duty of good faith and fair dealing" is a nice example of a shift in the law that builds a safety net for contracting parties in their contractual community – but maybe takes the law away from what parties to business contracts want and need. Although this general duty is frequently said to inhere in all contracts, in practice it is highly context-dependent, as it should be.[3] Tweaks to the general law are not the best, or even the primary way, for contract law to support community. Such tweaks may lead to even more undesirable ad hoc discretionary adjustments, as the insurance example demonstrates.[4] General law that supports community can make the law less well-adapted for the business context – and vice versa. Local refinements of specific contract types provide better, more tailored means to ensuring an autonomy-enhancing contract law.

Consider, for example, the agency contract type, which structures the agent–principal relationship. A principal is bound by (and may be liable for) her agent's acts.[5] This authority to bind generates vulnerability. Some implications of this vulnerability are straightforward: where an agent binds her principal while acting only in the scope of her apparent authority, the principal has a cause of action for breach of fiduciary duty.[6] Other consequences are subtler; they imply intricate governance rules[7] dealing with topics such as disclosure,[8] consultation,[9] and adjustments.[10] Because these governance rules are not easily amenable to any form of maximization function, agency and other "relations" contract types are qualitatively different from contracts for the sole pursuit of efficiency gains,[11] yet equally indispensable for human flourishing. Such rules make the agency type effective, but don't and shouldn't generalize to "general" contract law.

3. *Intimate contracts.* Finally, we reach the most intimate, social pole of contracting – say in the context of marriage contracts in the family sphere or perhaps old-fashioned law firm partnership contracts in the business setting (we come to this type just below when we discuss what constitutes an "adequate" range of types). As the "plural identity" of the contractual community becomes a more constitutive element of each individual's identity, applying responses from wealth-maximizing contract types threatens to undermine, rather than advance, the goods these contract types aim to encourage. It is indeed not surprising that marital contracts are governed by a unique set of rules, which derive – as we have discussed in Chapter 6 – more from the typical characteristics of this contract type than from any general principle of contract as a whole.

MID-GAME AND END-GAME DRAMAS

As these examples demonstrate, our distinction between utility and community is not about whether the contracting activity is economic in some absolute sense. After all, we are dealing with contracts that always have economic implications, especially at the "end-game" when the contractual community breaks down and people may move from cooperation to breach. But colorful dramas at breach should not obscure the daily – and ultimately more germane – mid-game life of contract types.[12] Hence, we focus on the role of contract types as forums for various sorts of interpersonal relationships – with thick, thin, or no community, and we argue that the predominant character of each contract type along this spectrum affects (or at least should affect) its doctrinal architecture.

Even rules about end-game breach can be analyzed from this perspective because they can, and often do, serve as background norms to channel and shape participants' expectations in the varying contract types at stake.[13] In other words, mid-game purposes dealing with the daily and the mundane should inform end-game rules dealing with failures and pathologies. Once we understand the distinctions among the normative principles that animate contract types, and the varied roles they can play in mid-game and end-game relations, then we can begin to design concrete areas for contract law reform.

For example, in community-based contracts, perhaps we should require the parties to share the efficiency gains secured by the promisor's alternative transaction after breach, *contra* the general law that disallows such recovery. The general law rule is derived from wealth-maximizing contract types and is the proper approach when that is what people seek – but not for the "relations" context.[14]

We have shown how to identify the animating normative principle of a contract type, and how the values of that type are local to a particular sphere. But what happens when people want a contract type with a different animating principle within that same sphere? How do we know if contract law is providing an adequate range of types? When should we split types? When does a change in contracting practice amount to creation of a new type? We turn now to these problems of multiplicity.

AN ADEQUATE RANGE OF TYPES

What constitutes a normatively adequate range of existing contract types within an important contracting sphere? This question raises two interrelated concerns. As Ori Aronson puts it: (1) "what is the 'pluralistically optimal' *amount* of alternatives a state is required to (strive to) provide," and (2) "what is the 'optimal' degree of *variance* the state should seek to maintain among the given alternatives."[15]

1. *N and Δ*. Addressing these questions – which Aronson terms "the N question" and "the Δ question"[16] – across the spheres of contracting requires complex judgments. Our formulation of the obligation for intra-sphere multiplicity indicates that, for choice to be meaningful, N should not be too small. Conversely, as we discuss below, if N gets too big, choice can actually be curtailed for cognitive, behavioral, structural, and political economy reasons.[17] Similar issues arise for the Δ question – too small (and maybe also too much) variation among types means individuals have insufficient choice among contract goods. An important part of the research agenda for choice theory is to investigate these conditions that justify different design choices.

Additionally, we have said nothing about the actual determinants of these variables. Addressing this crucial question requires, as Aronson indicates, "to take account of our knowledge of how people choose and how choice mechanisms can be tweaked ... through strategic design of the supply side."[18] It should be, in other words, a major focus of behavioral and institutional economics studies of contract law (a point we take up briefly in Chapter 12).

Identifying the optimal N and Δ for a sphere of contracting is not the end of this line of inquiry: reformers would still need to decide *which* innovative contract types law should facilitate. This is another topic we haven't addressed (though we offer some preliminary thoughts in the next Chapters). Aronson is again helpful, indicating that because both "the needs and beliefs of people" and our "social conditions" keep evolving, these decisions are likely to be dynamic and maybe even experimental.[19]

2. *Delaware Corporate Law*. Probably the best example of a first approximation of adequacy comes from the world of long-term business arrangements, where contract law (in the appropriate, broad sense of the word) offers more than one set of defaults, so as to facilitate multiple types of interpersonal interaction. These range from agency contracts, through partnership contracts (notably LLCs and LLPs), to forms of corporate contracts (from closely-held to public corporations).[20] Each of these contract types is characterized by its own governance structure and set of solutions to the typical difficulties (notably agency costs) that would probably have inhibited such business activities but for their legal facilitation.[21]

Delaware law provides a good example: it enhances autonomy by creating a "menu" of available options – with mandatory restrictions for corporations but not for partnerships or limited liability companies – so firms can easily "brand" themselves according to their preferred normative orientation.[22] Another example comes from small firm context, where the choice between partnership and the corporate form depends in part on the type of relationship the parties seek to create, ranging from closely knit "unitary" relationships to arm's length "adversary" relationships.[23]

3. *Partnership Law*. Another example of what may constitute an "adequate" range concerns contracts among law firm partners. They have available a sufficient range of contract types to enable them to change their minds about their preferred normative balance within their contractual relationship – an important aspect of what constitutes adequacy.

The shifting relations among lawyers in firms illustrate the point. As one article notes, "For those lawyers who entered the legal profession 20 to 30 years ago, becoming a partner at a major law firm was like entering a marriage."[24] Now, many of these firms have reorganized as limited liability partnerships to maximize revenue, facilitate entry and exit of lateral partners, and shield individuals from liability. The choice of contract type can go the other way too. In many cases, lawyers are leaving corporation-like law firms for marriage-like partnerships. As one lawyer said, describing such a move, "The biggest cultural aspect of our firm is that it is based on the old-fashioned partnership. We're partners first and business colleagues second."[25]

This easy ability to tailor contractual relations to one's desired normative balance, and shift back and forth among attractive types, indicates that contract law has provided an adequate multiplicity of types in this sphere – at least for well-counseled counsel.

TWO WRINKLES ON MULTIPLICITY

Whereas the choice theory prescription of multiplicity of types is straightforward, its implementation is not always simple.

1. *Splitting Types.* As a first rule of thumb, for a contract type to do its autonomy-enhancing work, it should be guided by one robust animating principle that can effectively consolidate expectations and clearly express coherent normative ideals. This rule implies that each contract type should be rather narrow, but that many should be offered. Thus, a contract type should be split if it addresses too-divergent values.

To give a contemporary example, consider what has happened with the leasehold contract. There, a single type has been largely bifurcated: the residential type is now replete with "non-waivable rights and obligations [that] may have little to do with the history of lease concepts," while the commercial leasing type lacks any such "wholesale substitution."[26]

2. *Single-Value Multiplicity.* Furthermore, at times the prescription of multiplicity is autonomy-enhancing even where no significantly divergent values are at stake.

Consider the contracts we enter into for investing our money. Such contracts enable us to enlist the superior skills, knowledge, and experience of others for an important task that affects significant aspects of our welfarist interests. Facilitating such delegation is autonomy-enhancing. The alternative of self-management is daunting because of the resources in time and expertise that investment management nowadays requires. Being able safely to delegate this task to others removes these burdens so that we can focus on projects we may view as more intrinsically valuable – a move that enhances our autonomy.[27]

Contemporary law is not content with one framework for this task of investment management, but rather offers two major contract-based alternatives.

First, people can contract with *financial fiduciaries*, in which case the fiduciaries are obliged to follow the investment policies the individuals would have adopted if they had the expertise to manage their own passive investments. This version, drawing on trust law principles, requires fiduciaries to diversify their holdings, an approach that mimics what a prudent investor normally does with a self-managed portfolio.[28] Second, and alternatively, people can invest in corporations. Corporate managers are expected to take a very different approach from financial fiduciaries: they may stick to a single area of expertise and take on risky, nondiversified ventures.[29]

So, individuals seeking investment services can choose between at least two distinct contractual alternatives, both primarily wealth maximizing but geared toward investors with different levels of wealth, sophistication, and risk tolerance.

In sum, more choice among types usually enhances freedom. Much less often, but in a nontrivial set of cases, we think multiplicity cuts the other way. Pinning down the appropriate limits on choice among types constitutes an important part of the research agenda we briefly address in Chapter 12 and hand over to those interested in implementing the choice theory approach in contract law.

Having discussed the value of limiting choice *among* types, we now turn to a distinct concern, limiting choice *within* a type. This is already a familiar issue in contract theory, unsurprisingly difficult given its focus on a single contract type. We offer the distinct perspective that emerges from choice theory.

MANDATORY RULES AND STICKY DEFAULTS

A recurring challenge in designing the specifics of diverse contract types is the choice between mandatory (or immutable) rules and default rules. The fundamental commitment of choice theory to voluntariness[30] implies that people should generally be able to choose not only among various contract types, but also terms within each. Such choice ensures that contractual relations best serve each of our conceptions of the good and the proper means for realizing it, given our particular needs and circumstances.

As a first cut, our analysis tracks the conventional view's preference for sticky defaults. However, there are times when mandatory rules are the only credible solution.[31] Mandatory rules may be necessary to safeguard against third-party negative externalities. They may also be needed to vindicate contract law's commitment to relational equality, which is an aspect of private law's normative baseline of just relationships, as discussed in Chapter 8.

But, where no externalities are at stake and where relational equality is secured, mandatory rules are troublesome because they do not accommodate heterogeneity, let alone idiosyncrasy. So, in these cases, contract law should not mandate its rules; rather, people should be able to modify them at will, tailoring their arrangements in accordance with how they prefer to cast their interpersonal relationships. In certain contexts, however, law may legitimately regulate and at times even strictly scrutinize such opt-outs to guarantee that they indeed reflect people's informed choices.[32]

To the extent possible, then, contract law should try overcoming problems of information asymmetry, cognitive biases, and strategic behavior – as well as engaging in the cultural production of stable expectations regarding contract types – by prescribing sticky defaults, rather than curtailing choice by using mandatory rules.[33] So far, our view converges with the traditional "freedom of contract" analysis.

But choice theory can make a contribution to the debate here by suggesting two additional (and novel) explanations for at least some of the mandatory rules and sticky defaults that are so prevalent throughout contract's diverse domain. We call these the "viability" and "expressive" justifications for mandatory rules.

1. *Viability*. The first justification emerges in response to the misplaced ambition of the classical freedom of contract paradigm. That model examines the impediments to informed cooperation through just one prototypical contract form, that is, the commercial transaction. Blind to the role of contract types, conventional analysis struggles to justify the diverse settings in which regulation is warranted.

By contrast, choice theory already anticipates a multiplicity of such regulations corresponding to the multiplicity of contract types. It is no stretch for us to claim that contract law must fine-tune its devices to address quite diverse challenges. Thus, in our model, we can justify regulating opt outs in part to ensure that contract types are viable, notwithstanding the systemic difficulties they would otherwise encounter.

2. *Expressive*. Our second refinement reflects concern that too-easy adjustment may undermine the cultural function of particular contract types. To give an example from fiduciary law, the "general" contract law rhetoric of gap-filling and optionality may signal indifference toward fiduciaries' duty of loyalty. But such indifference may dilute the expressive function of fiduciary law.[34] Insofar as these effects threaten the social norms that seem crucial to sustaining the fiduciary form, they may also pose a valid concern for liberal

contract law. Attention to the expressive function of a contract type can also justify mandatory rules, up to a point.

On its face, respecting the viability and expressive justifications may seem to be in tension with the commitment to autonomy. But it is not.

An autonomy-based theory of contract surely rejects any form of "strong" paternalism. It does not sanction overriding people's choices for what the state perceives to be their own good. But the classical justifications for limiting opt-outs are different. Where they do not resort to the external concerns of market structure and political economy, these limitations rely on "weak" paternalism – grounded in cognitive failures, ignorance, or extreme pressure – and can thus be justified by reference to what fully rational individuals would accept (maybe even endorse).[35]

Choice theory, in which self-determination and not independence is contract's ultimate value, follows suit, endorsing these (autonomy-based) justifications for securing contractors' informed consent. But it adds two sets of (again autonomy-based) concerns that also justify immutability: (1) safeguarding the parties' relational equality and (2) ensuring the viability of contract types and their distinct expressive effects. Together, these elements suggest a new, principled approach to evaluating mandatory rules and sticky defaults that is better reflective of actual practice.

Assuring compliance with relational equality is a trans-substantive concern of contract law that implicates all contract types. By contrast, considerations of viability and expressive effect can justify immutability only in more circum-scribed conditions. More specifically, according to choice theory, mandatory rules are justified even absent externalities or a threat to relational equality if and only if three conditions obtain: (1) the regulation is indispensable to the viability of that contract type, so that without it people would have *fewer* options regarding a given activity; (2) people are able to engage in that activity using an alternative, less-regulated contract type (so invoking the regulated contract type reflects an exercise of meaningful choice); and finally (3) the regulation entails the minimal interference with people's choice necessary to overcome the relevant material or expressive concerns.

1. *Enabling Choice.* The first condition highlights the possible autonomy-enhancing role of mandatory rules in facilitating, at times even enabling, contract types. A prime example for a contract type that would be meaningless

without extensive regulation is consumer contracts. As we have discussed, the key feature of this "no-community" type is that it allows people to make quick, anonymous, and secure transactions, which frees them up to engage in their other, more valuable projects.[36]

This choice-enabling feature of consumer contracts also refines one particularly troubling aspect of the recent (quite uniquely American[37]) trend of broad enforcement of mandatory arbitration and no-class-action clauses in consumer contracts. From the perspective of our "errands" conception of this contract type, consumers should not be faulted for the poor "readability scores" of these clauses. Indeed, choice theory implies that their inclusion in consumer contracts should *not* be able to upset consumers' background expectation of relatively unimpeded access to courts or to reasonably equivalent procedures for dispute resolution.[38]

2. *Adequate Alternatives.* The second condition is more demanding. It requires that there be sufficient intra-sphere multiplicity regarding the activity and that people indeed make informed choices when invoking the more regulated contract type. People who do not want to enter into what they perceive as an overly or misregulated contract type should not be deprived of an area of self-determination.

As an example, recall that we endorse giving individuals the ability to opt-out of judicial *ex post* characterization of their employment type. The heavily regulated employee contract type does not impede autonomy so long as individuals retain the ability to become independent contractors. By providing a viable alternative, we enhance the autonomy of people who find the mandatory rules and sticky defaults that typify employee contracts objectionable. (Providing additional alternative types, like "dependent contractor," "job sharing," or nonunion collaborative structures may further enhance autonomy in the sphere of work, an issue we return to in Chapters 11 and 12). Even if people choose the employee type, they are freer if they had the opportunity to consider and reject attractive alternatives.

The point carries over beyond employment law to any area where only one heavily regulated type exists. Again, as we've noted, choice theory endorses offering people the ability to engage in an arm's length purchase through sales law (with the caveats discussed earlier) if they object to the constraints that constitute consumer contracts and if they prefer the "souk" model of "as is" contracting over the "errands" conception of consumer contracts.[39] (Recall that even if they indeed opt for this model, their contract is still subject to the requirements of relational equality, which justify at least some degree of immutability of products liability law.)

3. *Minimal Interference*. Finally, the third condition highlights the significance of sticky defaults of various kinds as a preferred alternative to mandatory rules. Ian Ayres has recently demonstrated that sticky defaults may be justified on efficiency grounds.[40] Choice theory shows that at times they may serve an important role in enhancing autonomy. Thus, for example, fiduciary law can, and to some extent already does, address the expressive concerns noted above,[41] while avoiding mandatory rules, by employing (to use Ayres' term) "impeding altering rules,"[42] which allow only limited, specific initial waivers of the duty of loyalty. Fiduciary doctrine also incorporates further mechanisms to ensure the informed consent of the beneficiary (or of the benefactor) and maybe even their periodic reconfirmation.[43]

Interrogating the validity of mandatory rules and sticky defaults along these lines may not redeem them all. But this refined analysis of their relationship to autonomy suggests that at least some of these rules may be attractive features, rather than defects, of a liberal, autonomy-enhancing contract law regime.

* * *

Contract types do a lot of work in choice theory. Now, we can see that the multiplicity of types is both ordered and principled. Contract types are the locus for enhancing autonomy because each type can offer a distinctive normative balance that responds to what people seek by contracting. A variety of types in an important sphere of human activity – where such types function as substitutes for each other – ensures that people have meaningful choice among the goods of contracting.

A state committed to enhancing autonomy is obligated to ensure the existence of an adequate range of types in each sphere. In this chapter, we've given content to this core implication of choice theory – in particular we've shown how types carry distinctive balances of values, noted what we mean by an adequate range of types, and explored the limits of choice within contract types. But what if there are too few types?

11

The Market for New Types

The liberal obligation to provide intra-sphere diversity of types implies a major direction for contract law reform and requires some elaboration. In this chapter, we analyze the extent to which choice theory creates affirmative obligations for the state to act in contract law – particularly in the employment, home, and family spheres where market demand alone may not spur creation of sufficiently diverse types. We also make a quick intervention in current debates on harmonization in European contract law. In the next Chapter we discuss an important institutional concern: who should be creating these types?

We have already demonstrated that a purely passive role for the state in contract law is inconsistent with any conceptually coherent and normatively attractive view of freedom. Choice theory requires that the state affirmatively act to ensure individuals have available a range of diverse contract types that can be substitutes for contracting in any important sphere of human interaction.

So, how do we know if there are too few types? If we decide there are too few, what next? Does choice theory obligate the state to initiate new types? How many and which ones? In short, how do we translate the obligation to ensure diversity of types into a workable, plausible, and attractive program of contract law reform? That's the task of this chapter and the next one.

MARKETS COME FIRST

The starting point for this discussion is, and should be, skepticism regarding the state's affirmative role. For the most part, creation of new contract types has arisen from bottom-up, demand-driven strategies, particularly in response to market forces. We agree with efficiency-based contract theories that demand should be an important driver of legal innovation; demand for new contract types generally justifies their legal facilitation (with the caveats we discussed in Chapter 10).[1] A significant accumulation of evidence of people's interest in a given species of voluntary undertaking is usually a sufficient reason for law to recognize, and if needed further facilitate, an emerging contract type.

In the commercial sphere, there are powerful economic forces catalyzing demand – legal entrepreneurs see value from one-off creation of new forms that are then standardized, replicated, and sometimes codified as discrete types – so the task of contract law has been, and likely can continue to be, mostly reactive in this sphere.[2] There is little reason to think that long-standing market failures will prevent the introduction of valuable new forms – though even here path dependency and stickiness in legal norms may still suggest some role for active legal shaping of new forms.[3]

THE STATE'S OBLIGATION TO FACILITATE MULTIPLICITY

While markets come first, they are not the end point for a state concerned with freedom. The choice theory of contract implies, as we have seen in Chapter 7, an obligation – distinct from efficiency theories – on the state to enhance choice. Market-based demand is not a necessary requirement for triggering this obligation. Quite the contrary: this obligation implies that contract law sometimes should respond favorably to emerging innovations even absent significant demand.

Responding to market demand cannot delimit the state's obligations in contract law when the good that people seek moves away from strict maximization of economic surplus, or where collective action problems or other (say, cognitive) difficulties inhibit the translation of people's preferences for new types into market-based demand. Given the range of our contracting values, there is little reason to believe that market-driven contract types necessarily offer us what we need as free individuals. In part, this is because the social benefits of such new contract types are hard for an individual legal entrepreneur to capture. Thus, an autonomy-enhancing contract law should prioritize settings where law's enabling role can best support autonomy through new contracting practices.

It is difficult to expect that legal systems would routinely invent new contract types. Indeed, carrying out the state's obligation to enhance choice in such a top-down fashion is often undesirable given the comparative disadvantage of state institutions vis-à-vis contractual parties in coming up with appropriate innovations. For this reason, at least in typical cases, the carriers of contract law need not (maybe even should not) engage in innovative design.

Rather, they should proactively look out for innovations – such as those based on minority views and utopian theories – that have some traction but would fade if left to people's own devices because of predictable market failures. This is (roughly) the reason why William Eskridge calls for a legislative study commission in celebrating what he describes as the emergence of "a pluralistic family law that relies on 'a utilitarian framework.'"[4] The state should be favorably predisposed to such innovations even absent significant apparent demand insofar as these outliers have the potential to add valuable options for human flourishing that significantly broaden people's choices. This stance fosters what some have called experimentalism – within and across jurisdictions – applied here to contract law reform.[5]

Such experimentalism inevitably relies on either nonlegal underpinnings (such as the social norms of close-knit groups) or the available default generalities. At this point, these generalities follow the Willistonian model, which on its face may suggest that we have marched up the mountain only to march back down again. This concern is overstated, however. First, there do exist nonlegal sources of the experimental strategy; second, there is the comparative strategy, which we discuss in Chapter 12, of relying on suggestive contract types from other legal systems. Third, and most fundamentally, there is no inevitability to the currently available default generalities.

Choice theory addresses this point. While acknowledging that thin voluntariness is a common denominator of all contract types, our approach counsels that we replace what is currently termed "general" contract law with a true residual category of freestanding contracting, a category that is properly designed for the task of fostering idiosyncratic choices.[6] Thus, choice theory plays an instrumental role in facilitating its own most important reform project.

The obligation to provide new contract types may be (almost) irrelevant to the commercial sphere, given the robust market-driven push for these types. But it entails quite significant implications in the other three broad spheres of contracting – contingent always on the set of limitations and the institutional concerns we take up in Chapter 12. We briefly sketch now some of the "next step" questions about how choice theory should affect the direction of contract law.

INNOVATIVE EMPLOYMENT FORMS

Choice theory suggests reforming the sphere of employment, not just to allow more choice between employee and independent contractor status, as we proposed earlier,[7] but also by supporting the emergence of innovative new contract types. It is unlikely that the old, forced binary choice of employment contract types – developed for an earlier industrial-based economy – fits well with what people seek from the far more diverse world of work they encounter today.

1. *At Will/For Cause Choice.* Empirical studies have shown that most employees incorrectly believe their employment can be terminated only for cause, yet about 85% of nonunion employees can be fired at will.[8] Employment-at-will is the default employment contract type in all American states (except, oddly, for Montana), for employees who do not have a contract for a fixed term.[9] Making that default more explicit and visible may clarify employers' obligations to employees in a way that formal law so far has been unable to achieve. One simple way of doing that is for a state to offer both types of employment contracts and require its employers to register as offering either employment "at will" or "for cause" and, in a conspicuous way, notify employees of that choice. Such a regime would provide employees with a salient indication of this fundamental feature of the employment relationships each firm offers.

We could go a step further. States vary in how they define "at will" along three major dimensions: Is there a public policy exception? Is there an implied contract exception? And is a covenant of good faith and fair dealing implied? Some states recognize all three – putting them closer to the "for cause" type – most states are in the middle, some recognize none.[10] As an employee, you get one state-chosen combination. Perhaps a state could define and make available an additional "at will" type that offers a distinct cluster of exceptions corresponding to a different normative balance.

2. *Dependent Contractors.* Demand for a new, intermediate type – variously labeled as "dependent contractor" or "independent worker" – appears to be growing rapidly, with support across the political spectrum and across labor and business groups.[11] Versions of this novel employment type have already emerged in Canada, Germany, and Sweden.[12] Like independent contractors, workers of this intermediate category provide their own equipment and control their own hours, but, like employees, many of them are economically dependent on a particular company and vulnerable to the costs of termination without notice or severance.

While the so-called "sharing economy" has created powerful demand for some version of this new type, existing law currently blocks its emergence in the United States. As U.S. District Judge Vince Chhabria recently wrote regarding this constrained choice in an ongoing dispute: "[T]he jury in this case will be handed a square peg and asked to choose between two round holes. The test the California courts have developed over the 20th Century for classifying workers isn't very helpful in addressing this 21st Century problem. ... [P]erhaps Lyft drivers should be considered a new category of worker altogether, requiring a different set of protections."[13]

Why continue to force workers into the existing boxes when there is strong evidence that both workers and businesses want something different? This is a great area for state-by-state experimentation. Designing this new employment type will not be easy: the law must face squarely the challenges of regulatory arbitrage and boundary disputes that we discuss in Chapter 12.[14] Also, any new type must meet the minimal, but mandatory, baseline suggested by relational justice concerns. But if these concerns are satisfied, race-to-the-bottom reasons for limiting choice do not seem acute here. A state committed to enhancing autonomy should not stand in the way of emergence of new employment types that give people what they want in this sphere.

3. *Job-Sharing.* There are additional possibilities that diverge even further from the prevailing binary structure of employment contracts. Job-sharing – not to be confused with work-sharing[15] – has emerged as a particularly attractive form of flexible work arrangement.[16] It allows employers to retain new parents, older employees not yet ready for retirement, and others who want less work in their work/life balance.

In America, job-sharing first became popular in the legal profession when attorneys sought to work shorter hours but were restricted by workload demands and personnel budgets.[17] Then it spread to large companies in America, half of which now offer some type of job-sharing arrangement, usually informally negotiated.[18] The Federal government has also been proactive in facilitating creation of public sector workplaces with job-sharing opportunities.[19]

There is no reason to think, however, that the current versions of job-sharing exhaust the potential of this contract type. Law can be instrumental in expanding its availability outside the Federal government and beyond the lawyer and large firm contexts. Eliminating legal obstacles to the growth of job-sharing arrangements is a first, necessary step.[20] Other countries, such as Italy, have gone even further, proactively facilitating job-sharing by defining it as a distinct contract type.[21] This last step renders job-sharing more culturally salient and makes it more economically viable by stabilizing contractual defaults regarding responsibility, attribution, decision-making mechanisms, time division, sharing space and equipment, and availability on off days.

4. *Innovative Contract Types in Labor Law.* So far, we have focused on contract type multiplicity in (individual) employment law. But our argument extends equally to the (collective) labor law context. Since the passage of the Wagner Act in 1935, unions have been the centerpiece of American labor law,

the main pathway to ensure relational equality for workers as they negotiate with employers.[22] But beyond unions are worker cooperatives, employment stock option plans (ESOPs), and nonunion collaborative structures – that is, a spectrum of contract types for collective employment.

Although worker cooperatives have existed for over a century,[23] it wasn't until 1982 that Massachusetts became the first state to pass a law specifically supporting worker cooperatives as a corporate form.[24] Since then, eleven more states have passed worker cooperative acts[25] that help solidify the contract type in the public consciousness and provide a framework to support the survival and growth of worker cooperatives.[26] For example, California's recently passed Worker Cooperative Act makes it easier for worker-owned businesses to raise capital and to scale up hiring of workers.[27]

Similarly, ESOPs have emerged as an alternative to unions.[28] Under an ESOP, employees are paid partly in company stock, thus aligning the interests of the company and its employees.[29] The growth of ESOPs was spurred initially by legislative support in the 1970s that created a series of tax subsidies.[30] By 1990, ESOPs were employed by over 10,000 companies.[31] As union membership has shrunk, ESOPs have emerged as a viable, alternative contract type for collective employment, a type that helps inculcate its own distinct form of labor relations.[32]

Conspicuously absent from the American labor landscape has been the use of nonunion collaborative structures – for example, joint labor-management councils, participatory teams, and representative councils. Although these mechanisms are popular in advanced economies like Japan,[33] they remain outlawed in the United States, an artifact of the eighty-year-old ban on "company unions" under the Wagner Act.[34] If this outmoded ban were repealed,[35] and workers were given the choice, say by majority vote, whether to adopt nonunion collaborative structures, such structures could provide an alternative labor contract type of value to both labor and employers.[36]

These suggestions are by no means exhaustive of what choice theory requires. Conversely, these preliminary reflections are not aimed at establishing that any one of these reforms is necessarily required. What choice theory counsels is adequate multiplicity – a prescription that American employment and labor law does not yet fulfill.[37]

ASPIRING FAMILIES

Choice theory celebrates the development of alternatives to conventional contract types in family settings. This approach is relevant both to the "vertical" dimension of parenthood – think adoption and surrogacy – and to the "horizontal" dimension of alternatives to conventional marriage – such as cohabitation, civil unions, and covenant marriage.

1. *Parenthood*. Choice theory supports a far wider array of alternative contract types for family formation than currently exists. We have already seen the slow increase of contract types for adoption, which today includes, for example, "closed" and "open" types. Surrogacy is now coming to the fore, given the increasing sophistication of assistive reproductive technology, delays in onset of childbearing and decreases in fertility, and the legalization of same-sex marriage.[38]

There is wide variation among states and countries regarding the surrogacy practices, if any, they allow (some places criminalize the practice). We need not enter those heated debates.[39] For states that choose to allow "gestational" surrogacy (where the egg does not come from the surrogate), then choice theory suggests the state should ensure availability of a range of types. Actual surrogacy contracts reflect quite varied goods that surrogates and the intended parents are seeking. Some want a thick community, including ongoing relationships after the child's birth; others want no contact. Some want their contract to reflect an altruistic exchange with limited payments for direct medical care; others want a more commercial exchange with payment for services, including lost income.

There are multiple challenges today for surrogates and intended parents – medical costs; fees paid for surrogates, eggs, and sperm; and travel costs to states where surrogacy is legal.[40] An important cost, though, is that each surrogacy contract is an expensive, heavily negotiated event because of the uncertainty around enforcement and the high stakes of the contract.[41] The lack of standardized contract types limits access to surrogacy to wealthier parties who can afford the heavy up-front legal costs of dickering over terms (though the emergence of a specialized bar may mitigate this cost[42]). This is freedom of contract, not "freedom of contracts."

Choice theory suggests that states like California, which endorse gestational surrogacy and enforce a broad range of surrogacy contracts, have an additional role to play. They should offer at least two contract types – "altruistic" and "commercial" – reflecting the diverse goods people seek and the contracting practices that are already emerging.[43] And there are probably more than just two attractive types that can be offered. As with consumer and employment contracts, these autonomy-enhancing surrogacy contract types should be situated within a regulatory envelope that addresses internal values, notably exploitation and commodification, as well as other, external public concerns.

2. *Alternatives to Marriage.* We turn now to marriage and its alternatives. People today seek, and contract law should support, a wider range of intimate family arrangements than the old division of married or single – the familiar checkboxes that appear on every official application from passports to hospital admissions. For example, we support the approach – that by and large reflects existing doctrine – in which cohabitation law should not mimic marital law, but should instead be shaped as a distinct contract type characterized by a different level of spousal commitment.[44] This understanding of cohabitation law helps in making cohabitation a viable alternative to marriage. It also helps justify the immutable elements of marital contracts – notably *ex post* fairness review and the judicial authority to modify based on change of circumstances.[45] As we noted in Chapter 10, having an adequate alternative (like cohabitation) to a contract type (like marriage) is an important component of a liberal justification of mandatory rules.

This example generalizes: the variety of contract types available for families should reflect increasingly diverse practices of what constitutes "family" in the first instance. Thus, choice theory is also helpful in addressing a recent debate as to the legitimacy of civil marriage itself. Opponents argue that institutionalizing marriage violates fundamental liberal precepts by endorsing a controversial comprehensive conception of the good.[46] In response, Ralph Wedgwood recently argued that institutionalizing civil marriage is justified – at least as to its core features dealing with the spouses' mutual obligations (the only ones that interest us here). He claims that marriage is necessary to satisfy the most fundamental aspirations of many people in life, and, further, it does not harm others who do not share these aspirations – so long as the state does not actively promote marriage in a way that implicitly stigmatizes other ways of life.[47]

But what about nondyadic relationships? Wedgwood offers three arguments against advocates for these relationships: (1) nondyadic parties can tailor-make a contractual arrangement, (2) replacing marriage with their favored arrangement may make sense if and only if most people come to favor these types of relationship, and (3) supporting polyamorous relationships is likely to recreate "some of the harms that historically accompanied polygamy."[48]

Choice theory suggests that the first two prongs of this response are inadequate: the first obscures the significance for autonomy of the availability of a contract type; the second unjustifiably sanctions the hegemony of one contract type in the family sphere. Indeed, given the significance of law's facilitation of conventional dyadic relationships and the importance of our family arrangements to our chosen conceptions of the good, our theory implies that law should *not* just be content with supporting marriage, even with – or maybe especially given – its widespread use. Also, the law should seek to facilitate alternative arrangements. In this context, one that is simultaneously core to individual self-determination and fraught with societal hostility, the state's obligation especially includes attention to minoritarian or utopian ones.

The obligation of multiplicity does not imply that law should support harmful arrangements. This limit to law's obligation to facilitate – based both on relational equality and on values external to contract law – may mean that a polygamy contract type should not be certified given its "sordid and familiar recent history."[49] We are in no position here to pass judgment on this front, which is in any event unnecessary for our purposes. Whatever may be the case regarding polygamy, there are other possible avenues to diversify the state's inventory of family contract types – notably, by facilitating "non-conjugal aspiring families," such as multigenerational groups and voluntary kin groups – which do not seem harmful and can thus safely serve as viable alternatives.[50]

INNOVATIVE MODELS OF HOMEOWNERSHIP

Private law – more specifically, property law – already offers a rich menu of homeownership models. In addition to traditional forms, such as of the fee simple, leasehold, and installment sales arrangements, we now have an increasing array of shared-interest residential developments including condominiums and cooperatives (co-ops). There is still room, however, for an autonomy-enhancing contract law that makes valuable contributions in the sphere of home.

We note here just two of the promising directions for innovative types that are currently in the contract law literature – home equity insurance and shared equity homeownership. So far, both have been advanced in response to *public* concerns. The first type was mostly triggered by the lessons of the subprime mortgage crisis and is pertinent mostly to middle-income families; the second comes up in discussions of affordable housing for lower-income households. While the public macro-concerns are important, we argue that even if they were set aside, there is a good case from *within* the autonomy-enhancing values of contract to support such proposals.

1. *Home Equity Insurance.* Home equity insurance is a promising innovative contract type that would allow homeowners to share or offload the major undiversified risk that arises from homeownership – the danger that home value will decrease due to changes in the neighborhood or the local housing

market. By adopting this contract type, owners enter into a different relationship with their home. They remain responsible for onsite influences on home value that derive from changes within the physical bounds of the property and which they are in a good position to control or prevent. But they are (relatively) immunized from risks deriving from factors beyond their direct control.[51]

While insurance and financial products already available on the market partially provide this alternative type,[52] they are flawed and not widely used.[53] The two main types are "capped equity insurance programs" and "equity hedges." The first entitles homeowners to compensation based on fluctuation in the housing market but is capped at a maximum value and is exercisable at a specified future date. The second version pays out a percentage of loss in home value attributable to specified offsite causes.[54]

Neither existing form is free from difficulties. The availability of equity insurance, for instance, raises the moral hazard concern that homeowners will be less motivated to keep their homes in good repair or to negotiate aggressively for a good price at resale – if they believe the program will compensate their losses. (One pilot program, currently operating in Syracuse, New York, seeks to address these concerns with use of a formula, based on average pricing changes within a home's ZIP code area, to determine a fixed insurance payout.) Home value hedges, meanwhile, require sophisticated design to account for strategic behavior, inflation, uncertainties in how long the homeowner will wait to sell, and other market features.[55]

Moreover, both existing forms fail, at least in part because they have not yet coalesced into coherent and stable contract types. As Lee Anne Fennell argues, making such alternative types more viable, and possibly even prevalent, probably requires a "user-friendly risk management interface," namely, "off-the-rack" contractual arrangements that would form the basis for bargaining around onsite and offsite risks.[56]

It requires, in other words, the creation of new contract types that invite individual buyers and sellers to customize the degree of risk to which the new owner will be exposed – akin to the creation of traditional mortgage form (which was itself a creature of federal government contract type creation).[57] A new contract type along these lines should be attractive to many middle-class families, as it would offer them a home-owning experience free from the financial roller-coaster ride of the past decade.

2. *Shared Equity Types.* For lower-income households who cannot afford to buy in the first instance, equity insurance does not offer a viable alternative to renting. Complying with choice theory's prescription of multiplicity for

people of modest means is challenging. It can arguably be achieved using unconventional models of tenure, such as community land trusts, shared and limited equity cooperatives, and deed-restricted homes. Additional approaches include mutual housing associations and shared appreciation mortgages.[58] These models of shared equity homeownership "restructure[ ] the 'owner's interest' [by] introducing a stewardship regime that … prevents the loss of affordably priced homes."[59] But they often raise (among others) quite difficult monitoring problems and typically rely on some public (or public-spirited) sponsorship.[60]

We cannot offer here any easy (or other) solutions to these challenges, which – as with some other contract types[61] – may well require not only innovative contractual arrangements but also a supportive public, regulatory infrastructure. Our goal in conceptualizing these programs of affordable housing as subspecies of a contract type that can serve as an alternative to leaseholds is more modest: to demonstrate the potential reformist implications of the choice theory of contract.

Providing adequate alternatives to widespread access-to-housing problems should not be regarded only as part of the policy agenda of advocates of low-income households. Similarly, helping middle-income households separate house-as-home from house-as-investment is not just a job for private insurance markets. These are also, we argue, urgent items for a contract law agenda informed by the autonomy-enhancing promise of choice theory.

EUROPEAN PLURALISM

We turn for a moment from the market for missing types in the American context to a related issue in European contract law. Does the creation of a single "European" law mean that there will be fewer contract types? Contract law is undergoing substantial development in Europe. A disparate group of national legal systems is gradually transforming into a community and now a union. This transformation deserves separate treatment by real experts, which neither of us purports to be. Our intervention here is quite modest, though useful perhaps as a way to reconcile views that have, until now, been perceived as intrinsically opposed.

One of the important debates concerning contract law in Europe relates to the normative value of "harmonization." The pushback against the creation of one unified European contract law has taken many forms, most of which are irrelevant to our account. However, one objection is pertinent here. This view celebrates the plurality of existing national contract laws because it allows citizens of any member state to opt out of a legal tradition "they dislike and opt *in* to the one they prefer."[62] In reply, harmonization advocates argue that situating legal pluralism at the inter-jurisdictional level may generate undesirable fragmentation[63] and it may promote regulatory competition that leads to a "race to the bottom."[64]

We are in no position to arbitrate this debate, but our freedom of contracts perspective may offer an attractive path forward. If European contract law is formulated along the lines of our proposed choice paradigm, it may be able both to secure the benefits of harmonization and to preserve the liberating choice-based potential of multiplicity.[65]

From the choice theory perspective, both of these values sit comfortably together. Thus, if there is to be a single European contract law, it should be the choice theory version – a single law that offers individuals multiple contract types that correspond to the actual diversity of goods that people seek. Instead of choosing German law *or* French law, choice theory suggests offering people German law *and* French law *and* other contract types necessary to ensure meaningful autonomy to contracting parties across Europe. As such, a European contract law can ensure to its users no less freedom of choice than is already available from the diversity of the underlying national contract law systems.

To put the point even more strongly, a freedom-enhancing European law may be obligated to support even more contract types than the sum of those already available at the national level in the core spheres of human interaction, and further ensure that they are sufficiently distinct so as to comply with the prescriptions of choice theory.

* * *

Part of the value of investing in minoritarian or utopian contract types is precisely that most people would *not* choose them. Autonomy requires that people have the ability to choose from among meaningful, distinct options. We are freer people, we are more confident in being the authors of our lives, not just through the contract types we choose, but also through those we affirmatively reject. Therefore, even if there is no significant market demand (yet) for certain new contract types, even if they might appeal to only a small subset of potential contracting parties, contract law should ensure availability of some such types.

While liberal contract law has an obligation to support new contract types, there are limits. At a certain point, the marginal value from adding another type is likely to be nominal in terms of autonomy gains. When the state's obligation to enhance autonomy is satisfied, then contract law has offered enough types. Those who still want something more than or different from "freedom of contracts" can use the residual type of freestanding contracting to custom craft their own contract – that is, they retain (an upgraded version of) the classical freedom of contract.

12

Choice Theory in Practice

We have now set out choice theory and shown how it dominates existing approaches, whether grounded in autonomy, utility, or community. But offering better theory is not our only goal. We believe implementing the reform agenda of choice theory in practice, scholarship, and teaching will help enhance the self-determination of real people in the real world. The path from theory to practice is therefore of first-order importance.

At every step throughout the book, we have made concrete reform recommendations. These are not sufficient to constitute a restatement of contract law, but they are enough perhaps to demonstrate that choice theory is not a utopian manifesto or happy fantasy. We intend these examples to guide the makers of contract law in their daily work of applying and interpreting diverse contractual doctrines. But who are these makers of contract law to whom we direct our reform proposals? Are they competent to implement choice theory? What are the limits of choice?

Our theory must attend not just to the autonomy-enhancing potential of multiplicity, but also to its limits. Likewise, we must consider what institutions – if any! – are up to the reformist task. In short, choice theory raises tough substantive and institutional problems. Addressing these concerns is the task of this chapter.

In brief, we believe an unqualified call for multiplicity should be rejected. Sometimes, cognitive, behavioral, structural, and political economy reasons imply that more choice may actually reduce freedom. But those circumstances will be local to certain contract types or market structures, not universal to contract as a whole. Frankly, we just don't know in which contexts the probable effects of these concerns are significant enough to justify limiting multiplicity. This is not too surprising given that, for over a century, we've hidden these questions from view under the influence of the flattening and universalizing Willistonian approach. So, concretely, what choice theory generates now is an expansive research agenda. The first part of this chapter touches on these substantive questions. We are opening a door and hoping others will walk through.

There's also the question of who implements choice theory. We have talked throughout the book about what a "liberal polity" requires and how "contract law should" do this or that. That's risky language. It may suggest that we think the "law" is somehow an agent that acts of its own accord. We don't. Law is a set of coercive normative institutions, so legal theory must always attend to the institutional dimension. The question here is whether there are actual institutions competent to make the tradeoffs implied by choice theory.

The brief answer is that implementing choice theory is a matter of comparative institutional competence. For example, in the commercial sphere, we expect private parties to dominate contract type creation, while in the family and employment spheres, other, more public actors may take the lead. The latter part of the Chapter explores these institutional issues.

SUBSTANTIVE LIMITS ON MULTIPLICITY

Thus far, we argued that multiplicity of types is conducive to autonomy. Other things being equal, this is indeed the case. But other things are not always equal and multiplicity is not cost-free. Sometimes, too much choice *among* types ("freedom of contracts") ends up reducing freedom, rather than enhancing it, if, for example, multiplicity induces a race to the bottom – a spiral in which vulnerable parties systematically default into a disadvantageous type. We see four main concerns that may require actively limiting multiplicity or at least guarding against its potential pitfalls:

1. *Cognitive Constraints*. If there are too many distinct types, then multiplicity itself may curtail people's effective choice – a "paradox" that cognitive psychologists have well documented.[1] We are heartened that people seem to manage the wide diversity of contract types in the commercial sphere without too much difficulty and suspect that, by analogy, there is room to add types in the other spheres before hitting a cognitive ceiling. But addressing such cognitive limits is a delicate challenge for contract law design, important to flag here and otherwise beyond our scope. (One point that may be worth mentioning, though, is that we are concerned with cognitive constraints that hamper choice, and not with the sheer dis-utilities that the experience of choice sometimes generates.[2])

2. *Boundary Disputes*. Multiplicity may also trigger boundary disputes arising from *ex post* opportunistic maneuvering.[3] This difficulty does not negate the value of contract type diversity, partly because having in mind a salient model (or a few salient models) of the intended transaction likely reduces the probability of *ex post* misunderstandings – at least by comparison with the alternative of contracting through the necessarily vague "general" contract law.

But boundary disputes nonetheless pose a challenge for legal architects. This is an area where a comparative law approach may be fruitful – there is deep European civil law experience with contract law types and therefore, necessarily, with managing border disputes.[4] Their cost is probably reduced to the extent that law successfully conveys the animating principles of the various contract types.[5] We hope our call to reinvigorate the significance of types in contract law scholarship and education makes a modest contribution in this direction. We recognize, though, that this hortatory effect may not be enough.

So we acknowledge that boundary arbitrage concerns may justify heightened formalities for entry – and such formalities should be refined with an eye to ensuring that both parties have the same contract type in mind.[6] To preempt an objection, we think such "entry rules" should be shaped so that they could not be fairly treated as significant impediments to people's freedom of action. An alternative strategy to formalities on entry, which we generally disfavor, is one of *ex post* equitable inquiry.

3. *Vulnerable Parties*. Offering a few alternative, standardized types for the same activity typically opens options for weaker parties just as competition over prices increases consumers' choice. As a general matter, choice enhances freedom. But this is not always the case.

Contract law reformers who subscribe to our approach need to be cautious *not* to add types and at times even not to provide multiple types where doing so likely undermines autonomy. The former case may come up where the additional type is likely to trigger *ex post* arbitrage – of the kind we have just discussed – by the party with greater leverage. In that case, adding the new type might result in bypassing the normative baseline prescribed by relational equality as it applies to these parties.

The latter category is even more dramatic. Here we think of market structures where multiplicity might undermine the autonomy of weak parties rather than, as usual, augmenting it. Indeed, there exist asymmetric scenarios – say, markets for unskilled workers in times of nonnegligible unemployment – that result in employers having significantly greater bargaining power than employees. Such "frictions" in the labor market can give rise to monopsony in which multiplicity may generate a race to the bottom that would systematically curtail autonomy.[7]

4. *Political Economy*. Certain contract types may be particularly vulnerable to the risk of interest-group rent seeking.[8] When the autonomy-reducing consequences of such rent seeking likely outweigh the autonomy benefits from an additional contract type, reformers should again not support the new type.

These four concerns are the main reasons we can see why contract law sometimes must limit rather than expand types. There are other possible concerns, but these seem to us to entail a lower level of risk. For example, disaggregating contract law to distinct types may hinder cross-fertilization and learning, but this risk only materializes if we lose sight of the common denominators of various contract types, exactly what choice theory counteracts. Indeed, reintegrating contract types from the spheres of work, home, and intimacy into the category of contract helps preserve the common vocabulary that is required for it to serve as a category of thinking.

In sum, more choice among types usually enhances freedom. Probably less often, in a nontrivial set of cases, we think multiplicity cuts the other way. Pinning down limits on choice among types constitutes an important part of the research agenda for choice theory. We hand these puzzles over to those with the appropriate skill sets to investigate further.

INSTITUTIONAL CONCERNS: WHO MAKES TYPES?

Our reference to contract law throughout this book deliberately brackets one significant implementation issue, namely, identifying the proper institutional agent(s) for these tasks. Can courts or legislatures – the ordinary contract lawmakers in liberal societies – perform the role choice theory requires, that is, can they secure contract type multiplicity? How about private law-creating bodies like the American Law Institute (ALI) and the Uniform Law Commission (NCCUSL)? What is the role of public interest groups, private law firms, and lobbyists?

These are fundamental questions. Unlike other types of social norms, law is always expressed institutionally and its institutional form is often consequential. Thus, in deciding how – and maybe even whether – to advance any of the new types we noted in Chapter 11, it is not enough to ask just the substantive questions we discussed thus far. We cannot avoid asking the institutional questions. Are the relevant legal actors competent to implement choice theory?

1. *The Business Contract Challenge.* To appreciate the challenge here, consider Schwartz and Scott's argument in Chapter 5 regarding business contracts. There, they advocate that legislatures and courts generally retreat from crafting contract law rules and types. Even the best private institutions, like the ALI and NCCUSL, should not, in their view, be making business contract law and should instead take a minimalist and reactive stance. All these institutions, they argue, have intractable structural weaknesses that disable them from being good rule (or standard) creators.[9] There are just too many subtle contracting contexts and too many ways to maximize. Sophisticated contracting parties will, at some nontrivial cost, substitute parameter-specific rules for any default that outside institutions create.

Schwartz and Scott's work argues that sophisticated commercial parties are more competent at providing business law rules than are competing legal institutions. The key to their argument is that private commercial parties share a wealth maximizing metric for evaluating contract terms. Also, they are motivated to do a good design job because they capture much of the surplus they generate from each case (or series of cases, for repeat players).

Here's the challenge for choice theory. If writing efficient defaults for business contracts is too complex for courts, legislatures, or even the ALI, then why do we think any lawmaking institution can implement choice theory? Perhaps, we should just leave contract type creation to market players.

This conclusion comes too quickly. Extrapolating from the sophisticated business contract context to contracting as a whole is a mistake. Even if we assume that drafting wealth-maximizing terms in the commercial setting is relatively simple (which it's not), institutional inquiries always turn on the comparative competence of the possible actors.[10] What happens when the parties' overriding goal moves away from wealth maximization? What if the parties cannot capture the gains from developing new types directly? Then there is less reason to expect market demand and private actors to drive creation of sufficient types.

Shifting away from the business contract setting does not suddenly make legal institutions absolutely more competent, but it may make them comparatively more so. Outside the profit-maximizing context, typical parties suffer from constraints (notably collective action problems) that likely make them less competent at creating contract types than courts, legislatures (public or private), or other agencies or civil society groups. Even if a legal institution may not be perfect for the task, it may still be better suited than the contracting parties. Thus, the Schwartz and Scott view regarding business contract types does not apply universally. In particular, their challenge does not apply to the contracting spheres that the Willistonian paradigm marginalizes and choice theory emphasizes.

2. *Recognizing New Types.* The best answer to the institutional skeptic is the significant compliance (though imperfect and insufficient) of evolving contract law with the obligation to support multiplicity. There is already a significant fit between what choice theory requires and the path of new types emerging across contract law jurisdictions.

Consider, for example, "cohabitation," which is a set of judicially created mutual inter-spousal obligations that differ from marriage contracts.[11] Where it exists, this doctrine ensures restitution if there are significant asymmetric contributions by one cohabiter – if the asymmetry arises either through "a substantial equity investment in real estate or personal property titled in the other partner's name" or via services that go beyond "the ordinary give-and-take of a shared life."[12] This judicially created doctrine goes some way to structuring cohabitation as a distinct contract type which helps stabilize relationships of long-term informal intimacy between marriage and, say, roommates.[13]

The failure of cohabitants to gain legislative recognition may be best explained by a collective action and political economy story.[14] Whatever the cause, this outcome is unfortunate from an autonomy-enhancing perspective. Giving couples a choice between cohabitation and marriage is superior to a one-size-fits-all type – even though marriage allows contracting around most of its rules. Dickering over terms is costly. Asking the parties to create their own arrangements is especially difficult in this intimate sphere.

For contract lawmaking institutions to enhance self-determination of real-world parties, the type suppliers needs some evidence of how actual people will respond to, or be affected by, the contract type they design. Here, courts did just that. They picked up an emerging – albeit minoritarian – innovation and then recruited contract law to ensure its viability. Going forward, there is no reason to think legislatures (or private contract lawmaking bodies like the ALI) are incompetent to tinker with and consolidate this emerging type. In time, legislative recognition could stabilize it and help reinforce its culturally distinctive meanings (subject to caveats on the costs of multiplicity noted above).

3. *Incremental Expansions of Choice.* Concern for modesty regarding institutional competence has further implications for choice theory. Judges and legislatures (and the ALI and NCCUSL and similar bodies) probably

shouldn't be making up types from scratch. How would they decide in the absence of comparative experience from other jurisdictions or expressed demand locally?

That said, the minimal obligation of choice theory is that there exists more than one salient contract type for a given contract sphere so people are not channeled to a sole law-sponsored option. This minimal obligation does not necessarily require contract lawmakers to specify a new type. It may be enough simply to make a marginal option more salient and then offer some procedure by which parties can manage the systemic coordination (or other) problems typically raised by new arrangements.

For example, in the employment context, creating full-blown new contract types may be difficult. But there are the more modest steps we discussed in Chapter 11. A state could require employers to register as offering at-will or for-cause employment. Creating choice among already-existing types is not an overly demanding task for legal institutions; whatever systemic difficulties they face, it is hard to see why they likely fail in implementing such straightforward choice-enhancing reforms.

A more ambitious approach is required for creating new employment contract types like "job-sharing." On the one hand, it seems unlikely that market forces will generate stable and robust forms of this sort. On the other, the specific solutions currently offered (noted in Chapter 11) may also be suboptimal. What's the balance? In our view, the quality of particular types on offer seems secondary to the value of the imaginative work of any such scheme. Rendering the idea of job-sharing viable is a crucial step even if there is much room for later tinkering in markets, and refinement by judges and legislatures.

A final, and perhaps the most powerful, institutional mechanism for introducing new contract types is through a comparative method that learns from successful experiments in other jurisdictions. As we noted in Chapter 11, a state could offer a new employment type simply by selecting a distinctive cluster of the three major at-will exceptions already in force in another state. Or states can look to the experience of other countries. For example, creating a dependent-contractor type does not require imagining the type from scratch – Canada, Germany, and Sweden have already created templates, as we've discussed.[15]

As these comments suggest, inserting an institutional dimension into choice theory is complex. It requires attention to the features of the contractual sphere (or maybe type), to the typical characteristics of the relevant legal actors, and to the particular institutional setup of diverse jurisdictions (by subnational unit or across countries). It may benefit from comparative studies and from legal history that provide case studies of evolving (and declining) contract types. A serious effort here may require access to a diverse set of interdisciplinary tools that we lack.

*   *   *

Our task in this chapter is limited. Most importantly, we have ruled out the (devastating) possibility that substantive and institutional criticisms are all-encompassing. Instead, we have shown that the challenges of putting choice theory into practice are reasonably tractable. They are likely local to particular contract types and institutional settings. And they are, in principle, amenable to research and experimentation.

Conclusion

We have now set out choice theory, a general and liberal theory of contract law. We cannot hope to explore in this concise book all the possible challenges the choice theory of contract must face or the opportunities it may open up. But we have tried to point out a few along the way.

For example, choice theory can (1) cabin Schwartz and Scott's work to settings where the parties seek solely to maximize the contractual surplus[1]; (2) reconceptualize consumer transactions as "no-community" (or "errands") interactions and thus highlight the autonomy-reducing effects of arbitration and no-class-action clauses[2]; (3) argue (cautiously) that wherever no external effects are applicable, sales law should be an available alternative to consumer contract law[3]; (4) highlight the cultural significance of contract types such as suretyship and fiduciary law[4]; (5) offer an autonomy rationale for semi-inalienable rights of termination in long-term contracts and limited enforcement of noncompete clauses in employment contracts[5]; (6) reconcile the doctrinal puzzles of bailment law[6]; (7) recast the liquidated damages debate and address the confusion around efficient breach[7]; (8) suggest that promisees in "relations"-oriented contracts get a share of the profits captured by their promisors through their efficient breach[8]; (9) add a new twist to the debate over mandatory rules and sticky defaults[9]; and most importantly, (10) channel the efforts of contract law makers and reformers to identifying contract spheres that do not offer a sufficiently diverse menu of contract types.[10]

This list is just a start. We expect that evaluating contract law doctrines through the prism of choice theory would point to many other, similarly helpful, local reforms.

Choice theory creates a wide-open research agenda for contract scholars. For example, implementing intra-sphere multiplicity – that is, taking seriously the most important finding of choice theory – requires investigating the cognitive, behavioral, structural, and political economy factors that should guide development of types and may limit their expansion in particular areas. Similar difficulties await those who take up the challenge of devising a residual category of freestanding contracting that facilitates choice outside any legally sponsored contract type and does not simply piggyback on the commercial contract law. Also, we have not spelled out how choice theory operates in additional spheres of contracting, like the broad domain of state and transnational contracts; nor, conversely, have we pinned down how incorporating those spheres would require adjusting choice theory itself. Finally, we have bracketed institutional concerns for implementing choice – a task that requires careful attention to particular state and national structures for contract law reform.

We hope that by now we have convinced you that choice theory – with its close attention to contract types and to contractual freedom – provides both a credible description of contract law's heterogeneous terrain and a promising normative foundation that explains many of its otherwise puzzling features.

Over the past century, scholarship on contract law has moved from the common law's *unprincipled multiplicity* to Williston's *unprincipled uniformity*, and from there to Fried's *principled uniformity*. Choice theory aims to shift the field finally to *principled multiplicity*. To get there, we have moved beyond Williston's answer to the question "what is contract?" and Fried's take on "what is freedom?"

MOVING BEYOND WILLISTON

The most important overarching point is that contract law should move away from the universalizing tendency advocated by the Willistonian project. The notion of a "general" contract law, with doctrines meaning the same thing across different contexts, was part of a particular historical moment in classical legal theory, a moment that has passed, leaving in its wake much doctrinal confusion.

Choice theory now offers a liberal perspective on how to clear up much of the mess. Little in contract law should be "general." Even "voluntariness," the most trans-substantive concern, should be safeguarded with divergent and better-tailored doctrinal tools that vary among contract types and spheres. Similarly, the "duty of good faith and fair dealing" – perhaps the duty most universally implied in contracts today – should *not* apply uniformly across the board, as we've argued. The same goes for application of many other familiar doctrines.

The thread that links these points is that the values of contract law types are local, and the doctrinal tools to achieve those values should be local too. The key lesson of choice theory is to use the animating principle of the particular contract type, rather than any global principle of "general" contract law, as the benchmark for evaluating the doctrine and prescribing guidelines for its proper evolution.[11] Once released from the straightjacket of classical contract theory – with its search for a unifying principle as its common core – contract law proves to be fertile ground for autonomy-enhancing legal reform.

Choice theory also offers lessons for contract law teaching. There is nothing necessarily wrong in focusing on the *questions* that contract types all share. But students should come to understand how the *answers* vary according to type. Even a basic contracts law course should devote some time to holistic study of a few contract types that function as substitutes in any one sphere.

This approach would engage students in considering the divergent normative concerns that animate types and get them thinking about the particular doctrinal features of those types beyond just reaching for relatively empty categories such as "public policy" or "equity." It should not be a stretch for students to understand that the range of available types affects contractual freedom no less than the scope of permitted tinkering within a type.

MOVING BEYOND FRIED

Liberal contract law cannot be content with following the parties' will or protecting an individual's independence in the way that Fried and his followers have taught. Rather, contract law must proactively enhance people's autonomy, with autonomy as defined in the mainstream liberal sense of self-determination.

In an increasingly interdependent world, self-determination often requires people to undertake voluntary obligations that can be mutually beneficial. But we face numerous material and cultural impediments. At first sight, the inventory of contract law doctrines embedded in an array of contract types may seem confusing, almost chaotic. Choice theory brings focus to the doctrinal muddle and shows that the law's varied solutions to recurring bargaining dilemmas are not random. They respond to the spheres of activity in which people contract, and to the different contractual values people seek, whether utility, community, or a mix of these goods.

Choice theory also shows the way forward: the state is obligated to ensure the availability of diverse, normatively attractive contract types in each important sphere of human interaction. Only in this way can contract law comply with its most fundamental imperative, enabling people to make their lives meaningfully their own by legitimately enlisting others to their most important projects. This is how freedom matters to contract.

Acknowledgments

This project has relied on the support and forbearance of so many people as it has evolved from lunchtime conversation to essay, to article, and then to book.

First, we thank Charles Fried, Alan Schwartz, and Robert Scott. We learned contract law through the prism of their scholarship and fellowship, and we are especially grateful for their often critical, always useful comments on this book.

This book represents a moment in an ongoing conversation with them and with the other leading contract law theorists whose work we discuss in the text, including Peter Benson, Greg Klass, Jody Kraus, Daniel Markovits, Joseph Raz, Arthur Ripstein, and Seana Shiffrin. We've tried to present their views with care; they've pointed out where our arguments fall short; and we've revised in reply. This back-and-forth is what makes scholarship exhilarating.

In addition, we benefitted enormously from careful readers at all stages of the writing process, including Julian Arato, Aditi Bagchi, Oren Bar-Gill, Mark Barenberg, Shmulik Becher, Itzik Benbaji, Eyal Benvenisti, Leora Bilsky, Brian Bix, Ora Bloom, Sam Bray, Nili Cohen, Guido Comparato, Guy Davidov, Nestor Davidson, Deborah DeMott, Irina Domurath, Avihay Dorfman, Ariela Dubler, Liz Emens, David Enoch, Chris Essert, Robert Ferguson, Tali Fisher, Andrew Gold, John Goldberg, Victor Goldberg, Thomas Gutmann, Bernard Harcourt, Alon Harel, Ron Harris, Martijn Hesselink, Clare Huntington, Felipe Jiménez, Kate Judge, Avery Katz, Larissa Katz, Amalia Kessler, Russell Korobkin, Shelly Kreiczer-Levy, Roy Kreitner, Shai Lavi, Jae Lee, Tom Lee, Ethan Leib, Ronit Levine-Schnur, Shahar Lifshitz, Bertram Lomfeld, Irina Manta, Menny Mautner, Gillian Metzger, Hans Micklitz, Guy Mundlak, Russ Pearce, Katharina Pistor, Ariel Porat, David Pozen, Amit Pundik, Florian Rödl, Nick Sage, Chris Serkin, Hila Shamir, Jed Shugerman, Henry Smith, Steve Smith, Rebecca Stone, Steve Thel, Ernest Weinrib, Tess Wilkinson-Ryan, Katrina Wyman, and Ben Zipursky. We have tried to address comments by each of these readers – even when, as often happens, reactions by one directly contradict those of another.

We also thank workshop participants at the Cambridge University Faculty of Law, the Centre for the Study of European Contract Law, Columbia Law School, the European University Institute, Fordham Law School, Harvard Law School, Tel-Aviv University Faculty of Law, UC Irvine School of Law, UCLA School of Law, University of Connecticut School of Law, and the 2013 Conference of the Israeli Private Law Association, and six anonymous reviewers for Cambridge University Press.

Zack Bannon, John Briggs, Swift Edgar, Inbar Gal, Ahuva Goldstand, Samuel Roth, and Alex Weiss provided superb research assistance; Kate Garber helped design the cover and ably assisted with the book's production. Thanks also to the Marc and Eva Stern Faculty Research Fund at Columbia Law School for its generous support.

Finally, warm thanks to our editor Matt Gallaway for shepherding this project from proposal to publication.

Notes

INTRODUCTION

1 Peter Benson, *Contract, in* A COMPANION TO PHILOSOPHY OF LAW AND LEGAL THEORY 24, 29 (Dennis Patterson ed., 2d ed. 2010).

2 *Cf.* Mark Pettit Jr., *Freedom, Freedom of Contract, and the "Rise and Fall"*, 79 B.U. L. REV. 263 (1999). *See also* Friedrich Kessler, *Contracts of Adhesion – Some Thoughts about Freedom of Contract*, 43 COLUM. L. REV. 629, 641–42 (1943) ("freedom of contract must mean different things for different types of contract").

3 *Cf.* ROBIN WEST, NORMATIVE JURISPRUDENCE: AN INTRODUCTION 201–03 (2011) (emphasizing "the pathologies that follow from law's absence").

4 *Cf.* Ronald J. Gilson, Charles F. Sabel, & Robert E. Scott, *Text* and *Context: Contract Interpretation as Contract Design*, 100 CORNELL L. REV. 23, 82–83 (2014) (noting the dangers of generalist courts interpreting contract law in specialized areas, here insurance law).

5 CHRISTOPHER MCCRUDDEN, BUYING SOCIAL JUSTICE: EQUALITY, GOVERN-MENT PROCUREMENT, & LEGAL CHANGE 529 (2007) (noting also that in the civil law approach to contracts, "central to [ ] understanding the subject matter of [any] particular contract will have been an earlier choice made on what *general* type of contract is involved [so that the] initial classification process is a vital part of the process of understanding what will be considered by the courts to be central when assessing the subject matter of the contract.").

6 *See* Tony Weir, *Contracts in Rome and England*, 66 TULANE L. REV. 1615, 1638–39, 1647 (1992).

7 "Nominate" contract types came first, followed later in the Justinian (Byzantine) period by recognition of "innominate" contracts, that is, contracts that do not belong to any recognized, "nominate," contract type – a reform driven perhaps by the difficulties of a "contract-types-only" regime or maybe by the desire for freestanding contracting. *See* REINHARDT ZIMMERMAN, THE LAW OF OBLIGATIONS: ROMAN FOUNDATIONS OF THE CIVIL TRADITION 534–35 (1990); *see also* J.A.C. THOMAS, TEXTBOOK OF ROMAN LAW 311 (1976) ("The 'innominate' contracts constitute the

nearest approach that Roman Law made to a generalized system of contract"); *but see* Alan Watson, *The Evolution of Law: The Roman System of Contracts*, 2 LAW & HIST. REV. 1, 19 (1984).

8 The classification of types can be found in all the main commentaries to the German Civil Law Code § 311 (which establishes a general freedom of contract). *See, e.g.,* VOLKER EMMERICH, MÜNCHENER KOMMENTAR ZUM BÜRGERLI-CHEN GESETZBUCH § 311 (7th ed. 2016); BARBARA VOR GRÜNEBERG, PALANDTS KOMMENTAR ZUM BÜRGERLICHEN GESETZBUCH, prologue to § 311 (75th ed. 2016); MANFRED LÖWISCH & CORNELIA FELDMANN, STAUDIN-GERS KOMMENTAR ZUM BÜRGERLICHEN GESETZBUCH § 311 (2012). Dozens of "typical" contract types are named, described, and regulated in the Code (such as contracts for purchase, § 433 BGB, loan, § 488 BGB, services, § 611 BGB, partnership, § 705 BGB, and marriage, § 1405 BGB) or in another statute (such as commission contracts, § 383 HGB, or insurance contracts, VVG). When contracts mix elements, German law has two main ways (the "absorption" and "combination" methods) to shunt analysis of "hybrid" or "mixed" contracts through the distinctive law of underlying "typical" types. *See infra* Chapter 12, note 4 (noting when each method applies). "Atypical" types, such as guarantees (RGZ 146, 123; 165, 47; BGH 14.10.1982, III ZR 14/82, WM 1982, 1324) or swap agreements (OLG Stuttgart 14. 12. 2011, 9 U 11/11) have their own method of analysis. Finally, German law has mechanisms for dealing with "mixed" or "atypical" types that, through long usage, become firmly established (such as franchising contracts, OLG Düsseldorf, NJW-RR 1987, 631). Courts may recognize them as distinctive "customary" types, GRÜNEBERG, *supra*, prologue to § 311 para 12 (citing cases), or as "new" types, MICHAEL MARTINEK, MODERNE VERTRAGSTYPEN (1991–1993); alternatively, they may be codified into the BGB (such as payment services contracts, § 675f BGB). Thanks to Bertram Lomfeld for clarifying the German approach to types.

9 *See* SAMUEL WILLISTON, THE LAW OF CONTRACTS (1st ed. 1920); RESTATE-MENT (FIRST) OF CONTRACTS (1932).

10 *Cf.* BRIAN H. BIX, CONTRACT LAW: RULES, THEORY, AND CONTEXT 159–60 (2012) (emphasizing the significance of the differences among contract types).

11 *See respectively, e.g.,* Karl N. Llewellyn, *The First Struggle to Unhorse Sales*, 52 HARV. L. REV. 872, 880, 904 (1939); Robert E. Scott, *The Promise and the Peril of Relational Contract Theory*, in REVISITING THE CONTRACT SCHOLARSHIP OF STEWART MACAULAY: ON THE EMPIRICAL AND THE LYRICAL 105, 108 (Jean Braucher et al., eds., 2013).

12 We examined RANDY BARNETT, CONTRACTS: CASES AND DOCTRINES (5th ed. 2012), JOHN DAWSON, ET AL., CONTRACTS: CASES AND COMMENT (10th ed. 2013), E. ALLEN FARNSWORTH, ET AL., CONTRACTS: CASES AND MATER-IALS (8th ed. 2013), TRACEY E. GEORGE & RUSSELL KOROBKIN, K: A COMMON LAW APPROACH TO CONTRACTS (12th ed. 2012), CHARLES L. KNAPP, ET AL., PROBLEMS IN CONTRACT LAW: CASES AND MATERIALS (7th ed. 2012), and ROBERT E. SCOTT & JODY S. KRAUS, CONTRACT LAW AND THEORY (5th

ed. 2013). *See also* LAWRENCE J. FRIEDMAN, CONTRACT LAW IN AMERICA 25 (1965); *but see* MACAULAY ET AL., CONTRACTS: LAW IN ACTION (3d ed. 2011) (a rare contracts casebook still organized around types).

13 Of 1255 excerpted cases overall, 728 are commercial, 197 employment, 155 home, and 75 family. FARNSWORTH, ET AL. – the dominant casebook with over half the market – has 120 commercial, 27 employment, 23 home, and 13 family cases. We counted mixed sales of goods and services (say, in construction contracts) as employment cases, but they fit perhaps better as commercial cases. Also, many family cases arose in promissory estoppel settings, and maybe should not be counted as contracts at all. So, the ratio of commercial cases to other cases is, if anything, higher than we report.

14 Lawrence Friedman wrote, back in 1965, that contract law teaching is like "a zoology course which confined its study to dodos and unicorns." FRIEDMAN, *supra* note 12, at 20.

15 For example, in the notes of an undue influence case, FARNSWORTH, ET AL., *supra* note 12, at 385, remarks that, "[a]lthough the court found that no confidential relationship existed between Odorizzi and his employers, such a finding is often central to avoiding a contract on the basis of overreaching." Thus, the tightness of the contracting community sometimes matters, but the book does not pin down when. SCOTT & KRAUS, *supra* note 12, at 860–61, note thirteenth amendment concerns that keep specific performance from being available in contracts for services. But they don't explore the extent to which autonomy concerns should limit contracting parties' ability to bind themselves to deliver services. KNAPP ET AL., *supra* note 12, at 599–635, illustrates how unconscionability doctrine applies in consumer contracts, but does not help sort through what makes this contract type distinctive.

16 *See* Samuel Williston, *Freedom of Contract*, 6 CORNELL L.Q. 365, 368–69, 373 (1921) (developing an early incarnation of this view).

17 STEPHEN A. SMITH, CONTRACT THEORY 59, 139 (2004).

18 Richard Craswell, *Freedom of Contract, in* CHICAGO LECTURES IN LAW AND ECONOMICS 81 (Eric A. Posner ed., 2000); *but cf.* Randy E. Barnett, *The Sound of Silence: Default Rules and Contractual Consent*, 78 VA. L. REV. 821 (1992).

19 *See generally* HANS-W. MICKLITZ, ON THE INTELLECTUAL HISTORY OF FREEDOM OF CONTRACT AND REGULATION (2015) (offering a nuanced comparison of the meanings of "freedom of contract" in the United Kingdom, France, Germany, and the European Union and their respective intellectual histories).

20 *See, e.g.*, Martha Field, *Compensated Surrogacy*, 89 WASH. L. REV. 1155, 1173 (2014) (noting "a possible objection to surrogacy is that it inserts contract into what has traditionally been an intimate realm").

21 *See* Charles Fried, *The Ambitions of* Contract as Promise *Thirty Years On, in* PHILOSOPHICAL FOUNDATIONS OF CONTRACT 17, 23 (Gregory Klass et al., eds., 2014).

22 On the distinction between invention, discovery, and interpretation, see MICHAEL WALZER, INTERPRETATION AND SOCIAL CRITICISM 1–32 (1987).

23 *See* John Rawls, A Theory of Justice 19–20, 48–49 (rev. ed. 1999).

24 *See, e.g.,* Robin Bradley Kar, Contract as Empowerment II: Harmonizing the Case Law, *available at* http://papers.ssrn.com/sol3/papers.cfm?abstract_id=2476759.

25 *See, e.g.,* Konrad Zweigert & Hein Kötz, An Introduction to Comparative Law 159 (Tony Weir trans., 2d ed. 1987); Gerhard Dannemann & Stefan Vogenauer, The Common European Sales Law in Context: Interactions with English and German Law 263 (2013).

26 *See* Ronald Dworkin, Taking Rights Seriously 118–23 (1977).

27 *See* Hanoch Dagan, *Doctrinal Categories, Legal Realism, and the Rule of Law*, 164 U. Pa. L. Rev. 1889, 1910, 1915–16 (2015).

28 *See infra* Chapter 8, text accompanying notes 23–27.

CHAPTER 1

1 Charles Fried, Contract as Promise: A Theory of Contractual Obligation (1981). *See generally Symposium, Contract as Promise at 30: The Future of Contract Theory*, 45 Suffolk L. Rev. 601 (2012).

2 *See generally* L. L. Fuller & William R. Perdue, Jr., *The Reliance Interest in Contract Damages*, 46 Yale L.J. 52 (1936); Grant Gilmore, The Death of Contract (1974); P. S. Atiyah, The Rise and Fall of Freedom of Contract (1979).

3 *See* Fried, *supra* note 1, at 17 (justifying obligation to keep promises in "basic Kantian principles of trust and respect").

4 *Id.* at 8.

5 *See* Thomas Gutmann, *Some Preliminary Remarks on a Liberal Theory of Contract*, 76 Law & Contemp. Probs. 39, 52 (2013) (arguing "the notion of contract is inherently founded on the idea of two or more persons realizing individual self-determination by means of voluntarily entering legally binding agreements").

6 *See* Fried, *supra* note 1, at 1.

7 *Id.* at 9.

8 *Id.* at 13–14.

9 Charles Fried, *The Ambitions of* Contract as Promise *Thirty Years On*, in Philosophical Foundations of Contract, 17 20 (Gregory Klass et al., eds., 2014).

10 Fried, *supra* note 1, at 14.

11 *Id.* at 16.

12 *Id.*

13 *Id.* at 17.

14 *Id.*

15 *Id.*

16 Peter Benson, *Contract, in* A Companion to Philosophy of Law and Legal Theory 24, 41, 43–44 (Dennis Patterson ed., 2d ed. 2010).

17 Peter Benson, *Abstract Right and the Possibility of a Nondistributive Conception of Contract: Hegel and Contemporary Contract Theory*, 10 CARDOZO L. REV. 1077, 1100 (1989).

18 Peter Benson, *Contract as Transfer of Ownership*, 48 WM. & MARY L. REV. 1673, 1682 (2007).

19 Benson, *supra* note 17, at 1111.

20 *Id.*

21 *Id.* at 1112.

22 Benson, *supra* note 18, at 1683.

23 Jody S. Kraus, *Philosophy of Contract Law*, *in* THE OXFORD HANDBOOK OF JURISPRUDENCE AND PHILOSOPHY OF LAW 687, 728–29 (Jules Coleman & Scott Shapiro eds., 2002).

24 Richard Craswell, *Contract Law, Default Rules, and the Philosophy of Promising*, 88 MICH. L. REV. 489, 490 (1989).

25 *Id.*

26 *Id.* at 518.

27 *Id.* at 515–16.

28 *Id.* at 489.

29 Jody S. Kraus, *The Correspondence of Contract and Promise*, 109 COLUM. L. REV. 1603, 1630 (2009).

30 *Id.* at 1633.

CHAPTER 2

1 Seana Valentine Shiffrin, *Are Contracts Promises?*, *in* THE ROUTLEDGE COMPANION TO PHILOSOPHY OF LAW 241, 242–43 (Andrei Marmor ed., 2012).

2 Seana Valentine Shiffrin, *Promising, Intimate Relationships, and Conventionalism*, 117 PHIL. REV. 481, 520 (2008).

3 *Id.*, at 502.

4 *Id.* at 522.

5 *Id.* at 507.

6 *Id.* at 516.

7 *Id.* at 507–08.

8 *Id.* at 510.

9 *Id.*

10 *Id.* at 517.

11 *Id.*

12 David Owens, *A Simple Theory of Promising*, 115 PHIL. REV. 51, 73 (2006).

13 In the meantime, Owens himself disassociated his account from transfer theory. *See* David Owens, *Does a Promise Transfer a Right?*, *in* PHILOSOPHICAL FOUNDATIONS OF CONTRACT 78, 91–95 (Gregory Klass et al., eds., 2014).

14 Daniel Markovits, Promise Made Pure 26 (unpublished manuscript). This grant of authority is essential in his view because the power to promise is grounded in "human

sociability – in the promisor's interest in promissory *solidarity*, secured by establishing the promisee as an authority over her." *Id.* at 17. In other words, Markovits argues that sociability requires not only the ability to act "*in support* of [others'] ends," but also to "be always open to one another's *authority*." *Id.* at 13, 15. This is why, like Shiffrin, Markovits insists that breaching a "pure promissory obligation" is wrongful: "the wrong of breach turns exclusively on its involving a denial of the promisee's authority; and it thus arises entirely apart from the promisee's reliance or subjective expectations concerning the promisor's conduct." *Id.* at 31. Markovits' theory of *contract* shares the communitarian foundation of his promise theory, but does not rely so heavily on the idea of transfer and is thus immune from many of the implications of our critique of transfer theory (although not from all of them). We discuss and criticize Markovits' communitarian contract theory in Chapter 6, *infra*.

15 *See* Owens, *supra* note 12, at 71; Markovits, *supra* note 14, at 26.
16 Shiffrin, *supra* note 2, at 523.
17 *Id.*
18 Shiffrin, *supra* note 1, at 244.
19 *Id.* at 241.
20 *See* Seana Valentine Shiffrin, *The Divergence of Contract and Promise*, 120 HARV. L. REV. 708, 709 (2007).
21 *Id.* at 742. *See also* Shiffrin, *supra* note 1, at 254.
22 *See* Shiffrin, *supra* note 20, at 722–27.
23 *Id.* at 722.
24 *Id.* at 710.
25 *Id.* at 722.
26 *Id.*
27 *Id.*
28 *Id.* at 710.
29 *Id.*
30 *Id.* at 729. For more on this front, which we do not address here, see Seana Valentine Shiffrin, *Must I Mean What You Think I Should Have Said*, 98 VA. L. REV. 159, 167–68, 175 (2012); Daniel Markovits & Alan Schwartz, *The Expectation Interest Revisited*, 98 VA. L. REV. 1093, 1097–99 (2012).
31 Shiffrin, *supra* note 20, at 729.
32 *Id.*
33 *See* Liam Murphy, *Contract and Promise*, 120 HARV. L. REV. F. 10, 15–16 (2006).
34 *See* T.M. SCANLON, WHAT WE OWE TO EACH OTHER 302–03, 31–12 (1998). *See also* Gregory Klass, *Promise Etc.*, 45 SUFFOLK U.L. REV. 965 (2012). For two other strategies for dissociating promises and contracts, Michael G. Pratt, *Contract: Not Promise*, 35 FLA. ST. U.L. REV. 801 (2008); Aditi Bagchi, *Separating Contract and Promise*, 38 FLA. ST. U.L. REV. 707 (2011). For Shiffrin's responses, see Shiffrin, *supra* note 1, at 245–50, 252–54.
35 *See, e.g.*, Stephen Darwall, *Demystifying Promises, in* PROMISES AND AGREEMENTS: PHILOSOPHICAL ESSAYS 255, 273 (Hanoch Sheinman ed., 2011).

36 *See supra* text accompanying notes 6–7.

37 Seana Valentine Shiffrin, *Immoral, Conflicting, and Redundant Promises, in* REASON AND RECOGNITION: ESSAYS ON THE PHILOSOPHY OF T. M. SCANLON 155, 164 & 177 n. 34 (R. Jay Wallance et al., eds., 2011).

38 *Id.* at 170–71.

39 *See supra* notes 5–11 and accompanying text.

40 Shiffrin, *supra* note 1, at 242–43.

41 *But see* J. E. Penner, *Promises, Agreements, and Contracts, in* PHILOSOPHICAL FOUNDATIONS OF CONTRACT, *supra* note 13, at 116; Owens, *supra* note 13. Both Owens and Penner criticize Shiffrin's transfer conception of promise on very different grounds from ours.

42 *See generally* Shiffrin, *supra* note 37.

43 *See, e.g.,* Liam Murphy, *The Practice of Promise and Contract, in* PHILOSOPHICAL FOUNDATIONS OF CONTRACT, *supra* note 13, at 151, 153 (mentioning these accounts – which he entitles "moralistic" and "corrective justice" – as two of the three main "camps" in contract theory, with the third being what he calls "instrumentalism").

CHAPTER 3

1 Peter Benson, *Contract as Transfer of Ownership*, 48 WM. & MARY L. REV. 1673, 1683 (2007).

2 *Id.* at 1674.

3 *Id.* at 1707.

4 This term was coined by Stephen Smith, *see* STEPHEN A. SMITH, CONTRACT THEORY 97–99 (2004), but transfer theory relies on a rich natural law pedigree. *See, e.g.,* Helge Dedek, *A Particle of Freedom: Natural Law Thought and the Kantian Theory of Transfer by Contract*, 25 CAN. J.L. & JURISP. 313 (2012).

5 *See, e.g.,* Benson, *supra* note 1, at 1719–31.

6 ARTHUR RIPSTEIN, FORCE AND FREEDOM: KANT'S LEGAL AND POLITICAL PHILOSOPHY 107 (2009).

7 *Id.* at 14, 34, 45.

8 *Id.* at 107.

9 *Id.* at 112, 114–15.

10 *Id.* at 109; *see also id.* at 122–23.

11 *Id.* at 113.

12 *Id.* at 116.

13 *See* David Owens, *Does a Promise Transfer a Right?, in* PHILOSOPHICAL FOUNDATIONS OF CONTRACT 78, 91–95 (Gregory Klass et al., eds., 2014); J.E. Penner, *Promises, Agreements, and Contracts, in* PHILOSOPHICAL FOUNDATIONS OF CONTRACT, *id.* at 116.

14 Ripstein argues, "[W]e [can] create a right on your part and the correlative obligation on mine that I cut your lawn next Wednesday." RIPSTEIN, *supra* note 6, at 116.

A contract, like this simple one, is not simply a favorable disposition towards another person's promised performance; rather, to consent is "to *choose* it by uniting your choice with that person's so as to make that person's act consistent with your purposiveness." *Id.* at 125. Only where there is "both choice and a transaction between the parties," *id.*, do they create an "obligation of right concerning future performance [which] is a title to compel that performance, consistent with the freedom of the obligee." *Id.* at 112.

15 *Id.* at 127. For a similar interpretation of Kant's position, see ERNEST J. WEINRIB, *Punishment and Disgorgement in Contract Remedies, in* CORRECTIVE JUSTICE 148, 153–54 (2012).

16 Some transfer theorists engage in acrobatic exercises to establish that, prior to contracting, the transferred entitlement belonged to the promisee. *See, e.g.,* Benson, *supra* note 1, at 1693–1719; Andrew S. Gold, *A Property Theory of Contract*, 103 NW. U.L. REV. 1, 31–42, 50–53 (2009).

17 Benson, *supra* note 1, at 1707.

18 The closest that Ripstein gets to making the point explicit is in saying that because "[t]he only thing that could count as consent is something that the parties do together … that requires some sort of public act through which their choice can be united." RIPSTEIN, *supra* note 6, at 124, 126. He also mentions that the thoughts any one of the contracting parties may have had are irrelevant. *Id.* at 124.

19 Randy E. Barnett, *A Consent Theory of Contract*, 86 COLUM. L. REV. 269 (1986).

20 *Id.* at 272.

21 *Id.* at 320.

22 *Id.* at 303.

23 *Id.* at 306.

24 *Id.* at 302.

25 *Id.* at 295.

26 *Id.* at 270.

27 *Id.* at 297–98.

28 *Id.* at 291.

29 *See* RIPSTEIN, *supra* note 6, at 292.

30 *See* RESTATEMENT (SECOND) OF CONTRACTS § 2 cmt. b (adopting "external or objective standard for interpreting conduct"); E. ALLAN FARNSWORTH, CONTRACTS § 3.6, at 115 (4th ed. 2004) ("[C]ourts universally accept [the objective theory] today."). *But see* 1 JOSEPH M. PERILLO, CORBIN ON CONTRACTS § 4.12, at 633–34 (rev. ed. 1993) (arguing that contract law upholds parties' reasonable expectations by reference to both objective and subjective factors).

31 WILLIAM BLACKSTONE, 2 COMMENTARIES ON THE LAWS OF ENGLAND *2 (University of Chicago ed., 1979) (1765–69).

32 *See* Carol M. Rose, *Canons of Property Talk, or, Blackstone's Anxieties*, 108 YALE L.J. 601 (1998); David B. Schorr, *How Blackstone Became a Blackstonian*, 10 THEO. INQ. L. 103 (2009).

33 *See generally* Hanoch Dagan, Property: Values and Institutions pt. I (2011).

34 Felix S. Cohen, *Dialogue on Private Property*, 9 Rutgers L. Rev. 357, 362, 370–74, 379 (1954).

35 *Id.*

36 *See generally* Dagan, *supra* note 33, at pt. I.

37 The best neo-Kantian theory of property advances a regime in which the state functions both as a guarantor of people's pre-social and robust property rights against one another, and as the authority responsible for levying taxes in order to fulfill a public duty to support the poor. Strong property rights and a viable welfare state, in this view, cluster as a matter of conceptual necessity. *See* Ripstein, *supra* note 6, at chs. 4 & 9; Weinrib, *supra* note 15, at ch. 8. But such a strict division of labor between a libertarian private law and a robust welfare state wherein the threat of dependence is universally alleviated is quite implausible. As one of us shows elsewhere, the public law of tax and redistribution is unlikely to supplement private law with rules adequately remedying the injustices of a libertarian private law, if not in terms of distribution, at least in terms of interpersonal dependence. *See* Dagan, *supra* note 33, at 63–66.

38 *Cf.* Katrina M. Wyman, The New Essentialism in Property (unpublished manuscript).

39 *See* Gregory Klass, *Three Pictures of Contract: Duty, Power, and Compound Rule*, 83 N.Y.U. L. Rev. 1726, 1726–27 (2008).

40 *See* Jody S. Kraus, *The Correspondence of Contract and Promise*, 109 Colum. L. Rev. 1603, 1608–09, 1614–15 (2009). *See also* Daniel Markovits, *Making and Keeping Promises*, 92 Va. L. Rev. 1325, 1352–66 (2006) (launching an analogous critique of T.M. Scanlon's harm-based theory of promises and contracts which neglects the reasons for making contracts). *But cf.* Curtis Bridgeman & John C.P. Goldberg, *Do Promises Distinguish Contract from Tort?*, 45 Suffolk U.L. Rev. 885, 888 (2012) (arguing that contract is power-conferring and is still "organized around the moral duty to keep promises").

41 *See* Klass, *supra* note 39, at 1765; Kraus, *supra* note 40, at 1619.

42 *See* Markovits, *supra* note 40.

43 Klass, *supra* note 39, at 1739 (citing Joseph Raz, Practical Reason and Norms 102 (1975)).

44 Kraus, *supra* note 40, at 1608–09. *See also* Jody S. Kraus, *Personal Sovereignty and Normative Power Skepticism*, 109 Colum. L. Rev. Sidebar 126, 130–34 (2009).

45 Klass, *supra* note 39, at 1730.

46 *Id.* at 1754.

47 Kraus, *supra* note 40, at 1620–21.

48 *Id.* at 1623–24.

49 *Id.* at 1624.

50 *Id.* at 1609.

51 *Id.* at 1624. As Kraus further argues, "personal sovereignty must carve out an exception for individuals who nonnegligently make objective promises by accident." *Id.* at 1625.

52 By contrast, in unilateral contexts – think about mistaken payments cases with no detrimental reliance – private law (here, restitution) traditionally does vindicate the transferor's subjective intent. *See* HANOCH DAGAN, THE LAW AND ETHICS OF RESTITUTION 40–45 (2004).

53 *See* RIPSTEIN, *supra* note 6, at 107; *see also* Peter Benson, *Contract, in* A COMPANION TO PHILOSOPHY OF LAW AND LEGAL THEORY 24, 37 (Dennis Patterson ed., 2d ed. 2010). ("Autonomy theories view contract law as a legal institution that recognizes and respects the power of private individuals to effect changes in their legal relations *inter se*, within limits.").

54 *See* Stewart Macaulay, *Non-Contractual Relations and Business: A Preliminary Study*, 28 AM. SOC. REV. 55 (1963); *see also* HUGH COLLINS, REGULATING CONTRACTS 104, 108 (1999); Anthony T. Kronman, *Contract Law and the State of Nature*, 1 J. L. ECON. & ORG. 5 (1985).

55 DORI KIMEL, FROM PROMISE TO CONTRACT: TOWARDS A LIBERAL THEORY OF CONTRACT 55, 58, 60, 65 (2003). *See also, e.g.,* Michael G. Pratt, *Promises, Contracts and Voluntary Obligations*, 56 L. & PHIL. 531, 572 (2007).

56 *Cf.* Hanoch Dagan & Michael A. Heller, *The Liberal Commons*, 110 YALE L.J. 549, 578–79 (2001).

57 *Cf.* JAMES GORDLEY, THE PHILOSOPHICAL ORIGINS OF MODERN CONTRACT DOCTRINE 234 (1991).

58 *See generally* ROBERT NOZICK, ANARCHY, STATE, AND UTOPIA (1974).

59 *See* Hanoch Dagan, *The Utopian Promise of Private Law*, 61 U. TORONTO L.J. 392 (2016).

60 *See* ROBERT NOZICK, THE EXAMINED LIFE: PHILOSOPHICAL MEDITATIONS 286 (1989) ("*The Zigzags of Politics*").

61 *See supra* Chapter 2, text accompanying note 2.

CHAPTER 4

1 *See* Joseph Raz, *Promises and Obligations, in* LAW, MORALITY, AND SOCIETY: ESSAYS IN HONOUR OF H.L.A. HART 210, 228 (P.M.S. Hacker & J. Raz eds., 1977).

2 *See infra* Chapter 8, text accompanying notes 29, 31–33.

3 JOHN RAWLS, JUSTICE AS FAIRNESS: A RESTATEMENT 19 (2001).

4 H.L.A. Hart, *Between Utility and Rights*, 79 COLUM. L. REV. 828, 836 (1979).

5 This section draws on Hanoch Dagan, *Liberalism and the Private Law of Property*, 1 CRIT. ANALYSIS L. 268 (2014). For a similar conceptualization of the relationship between autonomy and efficiency, albeit one which is differently reasoned, see Jody S. Kraus, *Legal Theory and Contract Law: Groundwork for the Reconciliation of Autonomy and Efficiency, in* LEGAL AND POLITICAL PHILOSOPHY 385, 422–44 (Enrique Villanueva ed., 2002).

6 *See* JOSEPH RAZ, THE MORALITY OF FREEDOM 177 (1986).

7 *Cf.* WILL KYMLICKA, CONTEMPORARY POLITICAL PHILOSOPHY 123–24 (1990).

8 Isaiah Berlin, *Two Concepts of Liberty, in* Four Essays on Liberty 118, 126, 132–33 (1969).

9 Raz, *supra* note 6, at 177–78. As the text implies, we interpret Raz's category of intrinsic value in line with what Christine Korsgaard would call extrinsic non-instrumental value, that is, a value that derives its value from some other source, but is nonetheless valued for its own sake. *See* Christine M. Korsgaard, *Two Distinctions of Goodness*, 92 Phil. Rev. 169, 170 (1983).

10 Hart, *supra* note 4, at 834.

11 *Id.* at 835.

12 *Id.* at 834–35.

13 Peter Benson, *Contract, in* A Companion to Philosophy of Law and Legal Theory 24, 41 (Dennis Patterson ed., 2d ed. 2010).

14 Peter Benson, *Misfeasance as an Organizing Normative Idea in Private Law*, 60 U. Toronto L.J. 731, 731 (2010).

15 Arthur Ripstein, Private Wrongs ch.3 (2016).

16 *See* Hanoch Dagan & Avihay Dorfman, *Just Relationships*, 116 Colum. L. Rev. 1395 (2016).

17 *See, e.g.*, Robert L. Hale, *Prima Facie Torts, Combination, and Non-Feasance*, 46 Colum. L. Rev. 196, 214 (1946).

18 *See respectively, e.g.*, Douglas J. Den Uyl, *The Right to Welfare and the Virtue of Charity, in* Altruism 192, 192–93, 197, 205, 222–23 (Ellen Frankel Paul et al., eds., 1993) *and* Saul Levmore, *Waiting for Rescue: An Essay on the Evolution and Incentive Structure of the Law of Affirmative Obligations*, 72 Va. L. Rev. 879 (1986).

19 *See* Dagan & Dorfman, *supra* note 16, at 1451–59.

20 Alan Brudner with Jennifer M. Nadler, The Unity of the Common Law 247, 253 (2d rev. ed. 2013).

21 *See* Hanoch Dagan, The Law and Ethics of Restitution 43 (2004).

22 *See supra* Chapter 3, text accompanying notes 49–51.

23 *Cf.* Daniel Markovits, *Making and Keeping Promises*, 92 Va. L. Rev. 1325, 1328, 1348 (2006) (Markovits claims that this means the essence of all contracts is relational, a claim we criticize in Chapter 6, *infra*).

24 *See* Hanoch Dagan, Reconstructing American Legal Realism & Rethinking Private Law Theory ch. 5 (2013) (developing this argument).

CHAPTER 5

1 For opposing views regarding the possible impact of distributive justice on contract law, compare Richard Craswell, *Passing on the Costs of Legal Rules: Efficiency and Distribution in Buyer-Seller Relationships*, 43 Stan. L. Rev. 361 (1991) with Aditi Bagchi, *Distributive Justice and Contracts, in* Philosophical Foundations of Contract 193 (Gregory Klass et al., eds., 2014).

2 *See respectively infra* Chapter 8, text accompanying notes 37–45, and Chapter 12, text accompanying note 7.

3 *See* Hanoch Dagan, Reconstructing American Legal Realism & Rethinking Private Law Theory ch. 5 (2013).

4 For a preliminary account, see Hanoch Dagan & Avihay Dorfman, *Just Relationships*, 116 Colum. L. Rev. 1395, 1428–29 (2016).

5 *See* Robert Cooter & Thomas Ulen, Law & Economics 307 (6th ed. 2011). *See also, e.g.,* Richard Posner, Economic Analysis of Law 123 (8th ed. 2011). Critics of this scholarship also characterize the work this way. *See, e.g.,* Stephen A. Smith, Contract Theory 108 (2004); Peter Benson, *Contract, in* A Companion to Philosophy of Law and Legal Theory 24, 54–60 (Dennis Patterson ed., 2d ed. 2010).

6 *See, e.g.,* Ernest J. Weinrib, Corrective Justice 297–333 (2012).

7 *See* Avery W. Katz, *Economic Foundations of Contract Law, in* Philosophical Foundations of Contract, *supra* note 1, at 171, 186–87 (arguing "consent-based theories of contract" have "considerable affinity with the economic approach, which is also grounded in both normative and methodological individualism"); *see generally* Michael J. Trebilcock, The Limits of Freedom of Contract 241–70 (1994) (chapter on autonomy and welfare).

8 Alan Schwartz & Robert E. Scott, *Contract Theory and the Limits of Contract Law,* 113 Yale L.J. 541 (2003). A firm, for Schwartz and Scott, is "(1) an entity that is organized in the corporate form and that has five or more employees, (2) a limited partnership, or (3) a professional partnership such as a law or accounting firm." *Id.* at 545.

9 *See* Hugh Collins, Regulating Contracts 9–10 (1999) (arguing that "legal systems are in a process of transition from the dominance of traditional private law regulation to one where welfarist regulation increasingly provides the basic discourse of legal regulation of contracts," so that the "new regulation is a type of hybrid" of "private law and public regulation.").

10 Schwartz & Scott, *supra* note 8, at 549.

11 *Id.* at 545.

12 *Id.* at 545–46.

13 *See id.* at 544.

14 *Id.* at 619.

15 *See id.* at 568–94; *see also* Alan Schwartz & Robert E. Scott, *Contract Interpretation Redux,* 119 Yale L.J. 926 (2010).

16 *See* Schwartz & Scott, *supra* note 8, at 594–609. They note, however, two business contract settings where legal facilitation is crucial. *Id.* at 544; *see also infra* Chapter 7, text accompanying note 25 (discussing these settings).

17 We admit that there may be other possible readings of their framing of the role of efficiency in business settings. Thus, in their response to critics, they also emphasize other reasons to adopt efficiency above all. *See* Schwartz & Scott, *supra* note 15, at 934–35.

18 Schwartz & Scott, *supra* note 8, at 556.

19 *See id.* at 544.

20 *Schwartz & Scott, supra note* 15, at 939.

21 "Party sovereignty" is mentioned twice, for example, in the short conclusion of their piece. *See* Schwartz & Scott, *supra* note 8, at 618-19.

22 *See, e.g.,* VICTOR GOLDBERG, FRAMING CONTRACT LAW: AN ECONOMIC PERSPECTIVE 2 (2006). Interestingly, this may also be the (or a) way to read STEVEN M. SHAVELL, FOUNDATIONS OF ECONOMIC ANALYSIS OF LAW 296–99 (2004).

23 *See* Schwartz & Scott, *supra* note 8, at 556.

24 Liam Murphy, *The Practice of Promise and Contract, in* PHILOSOPHICAL FOUNDATIONS OF CONTRACT, *supra* note 1, at 168.

25 *See, e.g.,* T.M. SCANLON, WHAT WE OWE TO EACH OTHER 118–23 (1998).

26 Schwartz & Scott, *supra* note 8, at 550.

27 *Id.*

28 *See generally* Alon Harel & Ariel Porat, *Commensurability and Agency: Two Yet-to-Be-Met Challenges for Law and Economics,* 96 CORNELL L. REV. 749, 751–67 (2011).

29 *See supra* text accompanying note 5.

30 *See infra* Chapter 6, text accompanying notes 20–22.

31 Schwartz & Scott, *supra* note 8, at 544.

32 *Id.*

33 *See* Eyal Zamir, *Contract Law and Theory: Three Views of the Cathedral,* 81 U. CHI. L. REV. 2077, 2119–21 (2014).

CHAPTER 6

1 *See* Samuel Scheffler, *Relationships and Responsibilities,* 26 PHIL. & PUB. AFF. 189, 200 (1997).

2 *See* Joseph Raz, *Promises and Obligations, in* LAW, MORALITY, AND SOCIETY: ESSAYS IN HONOUR OF H.L.A. HART 210, 228 (P.M.S. Hacker & J. Raz eds., 1977).

3 Joseph Raz, *Promises in Morality and Law,* 95 HARV. L. REV. 916, 928, 936 (1982) (reviewing P.S. ATIYAH, THE RISE AND FALL OF FREEDOM OF CONTRACT (1979)); *see also* Joseph Raz, *Voluntary Obligations and Normative Powers* (pt. 2), 46 PROC. ARISTOTELIAN SOC'Y 79, 101 (Supp. 1972). *Cf.* HUGH COLLINS, REGULATING CONTRACTS 28 (1999) ("When two individuals enter a contract ... they create a discrete communication system, which serves to specify some particular undertaking that the parties commit themselves to observe. At the same time, it focuses the relationship by implicitly excluding any other expectations not included in the reciprocal undertakings. The contractual frame of reference prises the relation out of its context of personal relations, and insists upon narrow criteria of relevance and significance of events.").

4 *See* Daniel Markovits, *Contract and Collaboration,* 113 YALE L.J. 1417, 1419–21 (2004). *See also* David Campbell, *Ian Macneil and the Relational Theory of Contract, in* THE RELATIONAL THEORY OF CONTRACT: SELECTED WORKS OF IAN MACNEIL 3, 5, 9–10, 14 (David Campbell ed., 2001).

5 *See* STEPHEN A. SMITH, CONTRACT THEORY 77 (2004).

6 *See generally* Robert E. Scott, *The Promise and the Peril of Relational Contract Theory*, *in* REVISITING THE CONTRACT SCHOLARSHIP OF STEWART MACAULAY: ON THE EMPIRICAL AND THE LYRICAL 105, 108 (Jean Braucher et al., eds., 2013).

7 *See, e.g.*, Robert E. Scott, *The Case for Formalism in Relational Contract*, 94 NW. U. L. REV. 847, 852 (2000) ("We are all relationists now").

8 *See, e.g.*, Ian Macneil, *Relational Contracts: What We Do and Do Not Know*, *in* RELATIONAL THEORY, *supra* note 4, at 257, 261.

9 *See, e.g.*, Julia Tomassetti, *The Contracting/Producing Ambiguity and the Collapse of the Means/Ends Distinction in Employment*, 66 S.C. L. REV. 315, 349–53 (2014) (highlighting the differences between commercial and employment contracts, including bargaining power disparities and indefiniteness).

10 Campbell, *supra* note 4, at 16, 22. *See also, e.g.*, Ian Macneil, *Exchange Revisited: Individual Utility and Social Solidarity*, 96 ETHICS 567, 578–79 (1986).

11 Campbell, *supra* note 4, at 22.

12 For a particularly sophisticated example of contract governance in the context of commercial collaboration, see Ronald J. Gilson, Charles F. Sabel & Robert E. Scott, *Braiding: The Interaction of Formal and Informal Contracting in Theory, Practice, and Doctrine*, 110 COLUM. L. REV. 1137 (2010).

13 Ian Macneil, *The New Social Contract: An Inquiry into Modern Contractual Relations*, *in* RELATIONAL THEORY, *supra* note 4, at 144.

14 *Id.*

15 *See id.* at 143, 151.

16 *Id.* at 136, 146; *see also* Ian Macneil, *Restatement (Second) of Contracts and Presentation*, 60 VA. L. REV. 589, 595 (1974) (claiming that "[t]he entangling strings of friendship, reputation, interdependence, morality and altruistic desires are integral parts of the relation").

17 Macneil, *supra* note 13, at 148.

18 *See, e.g.*, MARGARET GILBERT, LIVING TOGETHER: RATIONALITY, SOCIALITY, AND OBLIGATION 2, 8 (1996).

19 *See* Brian H. Bix, *Contract Rights and Remedies, and the Divergence between Law and Morality*, 21 RATIO JURIS 194, 203 (2008); Brian H. Bix, *Private Ordering and Family Law*, 23 J. AM. ACAD. MATRIMONIAL LAW. 249, 264–65 (2010).

20 *See* Elizabeth S. Scott & Robert E. Scott, *Marriage as Relational Contract*, 84 VA. L. REV. 1225, 1271–73 (1998).

21 *Id.*, at 1273–74.

22 *See* HANOCH DAGAN, PROPERTY: VALUES AND INSTITUTIONS 200–01, 212–13 (2011).

23 Markovits, *supra* note 4.

24 *Id.* at 1420 ("[C]ontract participates in this ideal of respectful community even though contracts typically arise among self-interested parties who aim to appropriate as much of the value that contracts create as they can.").

25 *Id. See also* Daniel Markovits, Promise Made Pure 26 (unpublished manuscript).

26 Markovits, *supra* note 4, at 1450–51.

27 *Id*. at 1462.

28 *See* Daniel Markovits, *Promise as an Arm's-length Relation, in* PROMISES AND AGREEMENTS, 255, 295 (Hanoch Sheinman ed., 2011).

29 Markovits, *supra* note 4, at 1450. *See also id*. at 1462 (re, marriage contracts).

30 *Id*. at 1465.

31 *Id*. at 1464–66.

32 *Id*. at 1451.

33 *Id*. at 1451. "By sharing ends in this fashion the parties to contracts come, as Kant would say, to treat each other as ends, which is to say that they cease to be strangers and enter into a moral community together." *Id*. at 1463.

34 *Id*.

35 *Id*. at 1471–72.

36 *Id*. at 1421.

37 *Id*. at 1450; *see also id*. at 1465 ("contracts involving individuals properly occupy the center of our intuitive conception of contract.").

38 *Id*. at 1467.

39 *Id*. at 1472.

40 *See* Ethan J. Lieb, *On Collaboration, Organizations, and Conciliation in the General Theory of Contract*, 24 Q.L. R. 1 (2005).

41 *See* RESTATEMENT (THIRD) OF AGENCY (2006) §§ 2.01–2.02 (scope of agent's authority), and §§ 2.04, 7.08 (scope of respondeat superior liability).

42 Markovits, *supra* note 4, at 1472.

43 *Id*. at 1434–35, 1440–41.

44 *See infra* Chapter 7, text accompanying notes 22–24, and Chapter 8, text accompanying notes 4–6.

CHAPTER 7

1 *See respectively* ALAN BRUDNER, CONSTITUTIONAL GOODS 25 (2004) *and* Martha C. Nussbaum, *Perfectionist Liberalism and Political Liberalism*, 39 PHIL. & PUB. AFF. 3 (2011).

2 *See* JONATHAN QUONG, LIBERALISM WITHOUT PERFECTION 85–96 (2011).

3 *See* JOSEPH RAZ, THE MORALITY OF FREEDOM 372 (1986).

4 *Id*. at 398.

5 *Id*. at 381, 399.

6 *Id*. at 395.

7 *See* Joseph Raz, *Promises in Morality and Law*, 95 HARV. L. REV. 916, 934 (1982) (arguing that by and large "the law of contracts operates predominantly in a supportive ... role").

8 *See* RESTATEMENT (THIRD) OF EMPLOYMENT LAW § 1.01 cmt. g (2015).

9 *See* RESTATEMENT (SECOND) OF AGENCY § 220(2) (1958); *see also* Richard R. Carlson, *Why the Law Still Can't Tell an Employee When It Sees One and How It*

Ought to Stop Trying, 22 BERKELEY J. EMP. & LAB. L. 295 (2001); Julia Tomassetti, *The Contracting/Producing Ambiguity and the Collapse of the Means/Ends Distinction in Employment*, 66 S.C. L. REV. 315, 336–40 (2014) (economic realities test is "hopelessly imprecise and unwieldy").

10 *See* Teresa J. Webb et al., *An Empirical Assist in Resolving the Classification Dilemma of Workers as Either Employees or Independent Contractors*, 24 J. APPL. BUS. RES. 45 (2008) (deducing three dominant criteria: employer control, integration of services, and payment of assistants); *see also, e.g.*, Robert W. Wood, *Do's and Don'ts When Using Independent Contractors*, BUSINESS LAW TODAY (June 16, 2011) *available at* http://apps.americanbar.org/buslaw/blt/content/2011/06/article/wood .shtml; U.S. Chamber of Commerce, *Tips for Using Independent Contractors*, *available at* www.uschambersmallbusinessnation.com/toolkits/guide/P05_0092.

11 Greg Bensinger, *Startups Scramble to Define "Employee*," WALL ST. J., July 30, 2015.

12 That is, it applies where a seller who "regularly solicits, engages in, or enforces consumer transactions" deals with a buyer purchasing for "personal, family, or household" purposes. UNIFORM CONSUMER SALES PRACTICES ACT § 2(1), (5), 7A U.L.A. 69 (2002). Consumers, typically, cannot opt out of these protections. *See* CAROLYN L. CARTER & JONATHAN SHELDON, UNFAIR AND DECEPTIVE ACTS AND PRACTICES § 4.2.19.4, at 257–61 (8th ed. 2012); DEE PRIDGEN & RICHARD M. ALDERMAN, CONSUMER PROTECTION AND THE LAW § 5:21 (2014 ed.).

13 *See* Gisela Rühl, *Consumer Protection in Choice of Law*, 44 CORNELL INT'L L.J. 569, 571–75 (2011).

14 *Canal Elec. Co. v. Westinghouse Elec. Corp.*, 548 N.E.2d 182, 187 (Mass. 1990).

15 TEX. BUS. & COM. CODE ANN. § 17.42(a) (West 2011).

16 *See* Hanoch Dagan, *Autonomy, Pluralism, and Contract Law Theory*, 76(2) LAW. & CONTEMP. PROBS. 19 (2013).

17 *See* Raz, *supra* note 3, at 265.

18 *Id.* at 162.

19 *Id.* at 133, 265.

20 STEPHEN A. SMITH, CONTRACT THEORY 139 (2004).

21 *Id.*, at 140.

22 DORI KIMEL, FROM PROMISE TO CONTRACT: TOWARDS A LIBERAL THEORY OF CONTRACT 78 (2003).

23 *Id.* at 79.

24 *See infra* notes 42–49.

25 Alan Schwartz & Robert E. Scott, *Contract Theory and the Limits of Contract Law*, 113 YALE L.J. 541, 544 (2003).

26 *See, e.g.*, Ian Ayres & Robert Gertner, *Filling Gaps in Incomplete Contracts: An Economic Theory of Default Rules*, 99 YALE L.J. 87 (1989); Russell B. Korobkin & Thomas S. Ulen, *Law and Behavioral Science: Removing the Rationality Assumption from Law and Economics*, 88 CAL. L. REV. 1051 (2000).

27 *See* Ronald J. Gilson, Charles F. Sabel & Robert E. Scott, *Braiding: The Interaction of Formal and Informal Contracting in Theory, Practice, and Doctrine*, 110 COLUM. L. REV. 1137 (2010).

28 *Cf.* Charles J. Goetz & Robert E. Scott, *The Limits of Expanded Choice: An Analysis of the Interactions between Expressed and Implied Contract*, 73 CAL. L. REV. 261, 286–88 (1985); Michael Klausner, *Corporations, Corporate Law, and Networks of Contracts*, 81 VA. L. REV. 757, 766, 788 (1995).

29 *Cf.* Eyal Zamir, *The Inverted Hierarchy of Contract Interpretation and Supplementation*, 97 COLUM. L. REV. 1710, 1758–59 (1997).

30 Manfred Rehbinder, *Status, Contract, and the Welfare State*, 23 STAN. L. REV. 941, 955 (1971).

31 *Id.*, at 953.

32 RESTATEMENT (THIRD) OF SURETYSHIP & GUARANTY (1996).

33 *See, e.g.*, Frank S. H. Bae & Marian E. McGrath, *The Rights of a Surety (Or Secondary Obligor) Under the Restatement of the Law, Third, Suretyship and Guaranty*, 122 BANKING L.J. 783, 787–89 (2005).

34 *See* RESTATEMENT (THIRD) OF SURETYSHIP AND GUARANTY § 22(1)(A) (1996).

35 *See* SAMUEL WILLISTON, THE LAW OF CONTRACTS iii (1st ed. 1920) ("However vague may be the boundaries of contract, it fills so large a space in the law that the most formidable obstacle presented to one who chooses the subject is its magnitude ... The simplest applications of fundamental principles of contracts when found in an insurance policy or a contract of suretyship are often considered by writers on those topics as peculiarities of the law of insurance or of suretyship, controlled by no general rules. It therefore seems desirable to treat the subject of contracts as a whole, and to show the wide range of application of its principles").

36 *See* 72 C.J.S. PRINCIPAL AND SURETY § 3 (Mar. 2013); THE LAW OF SURETYSHIP AND GUARANTY § 3:4.

37 *See, e.g.*, Robert W. Gordon, *Unfreezing Legal Reality: Critical Approaches to Law*, 15 FLA. ST. U.L. REV. 195, 212–14 (1987).

38 *See respectively, e.g.*, ROBERT E. KEETON & ALAN I. WIDISS, INSURANCE LAW 628 (1988); Eugene R. Anderson & James J. Fournier, *Why Courts Enforce Insurance Policyholders' Objectively Reasonable Expectations of Insurance Coverage*, 5 CONN. INSUR. L.J. 455 (1998).

39 *See* Ronald J. Gilson, Charles F. Sabel & Robert E. Scott, *Text* and *Context: Contract Interpretation as Contract Design*, 100 CORNELL L. REV. 23, 82–83 (2014).

40 *Id.*

41 *Id.* at 84.

42 *See infra* Chapter 8, notes 5–6, and accompanying text.

43 *See* PRIDGEN & ALDERMAN, *supra* note 12, at §§ 3:1, 3:15 (discussing general ambit of state-law prohibitions on unfair and deceptive trade practices).

44 *See id.*, at §§ 7:1 (role of state attorneys general), 7:28 (municipal enforcement).

45 *See id.*, at §§ 11:1 (misleading advertising), 9:10 (coercive sales techniques), 10:1 (deceptive trade practices), 9:11 (commercial exploitation of children, elderly, and

infirm). For an overview of the FTC's efforts to regulate advertising to children, see generally J. Howard Beales, III, *Advertising to Kids and the FTC: A Regulatory Retrospective That Advises the Present*, 12 GEO. MASON L. REV. 873 (2004).

46 *See What Does FDA Do?*, FOOD AND DRUG ADMINISTRATION (April 20, 2015), www.fda.gov/AboutFDA/Transparency/Basics/ucm194877.htm; *About Us*, CONSUMER FINANCE PROTECTION BUREAU (March 25, 2015), www.consumerfinance.gov/the-bureau/.

47 *See* 15 U.S.C. §§ 1–38 (2013) (antitrust regulation); 15 U.S.C. §§ 77a–78lll (2013) (securities regulation); 15 U.S.C. §§ 1601–1693(r) (2013) (consumer credit protection).

48 *See, e.g.*, STEPHEN G. BREYER, REGULATION AND ITS REFORM 7–8 (1982).

49 *See* JOSEPH WILLIAM SINGER, NO FREEDOM WITHOUT REGULATION 64 (2015).

50 *See* Ian Ayres, *Menus Matter*, 73 U. CHI. L. REV. 3, 8 (2006) (arguing that even "statutory menus that merely reiterate what the private parties could have done contractually by other means can have a big effect").

51 *See infra* Chapter 11, text accompanying notes 11–14.

CHAPTER 8

1 *See* Philip Pettit, *The Cunning of Trust*, 24 PHIL. & PUB. AFF. 202, 209–10 (1995).

2 *Cf.* Eyal Zamir, *Contract Law and Theory: Three Views of the Cathedral*, 81 U. CHI. L. REV. 2077, 2086–87 (2014).

3 The cautionary language of the text is deliberate. It is intended to clarify that our conception of consumer contract law does not rely on a thick perfectionist conception of autonomy.

4 This reconceptualization of consumer transactions, which emerges from our discussion of Kimel's account of contracts, *supra* Chapter 7, text accompanying notes 22–24, was to some extent anticipated by Karl Llewellyn. *See* Robert A. Hillman & Jeffrey J. Rachlinski, *Standard-Form Contracting in the Electronic Age*, 77 N.Y.U. L. REV. 429, 455 (2002).

5 Rules imposing on businesses' heightened duties of disclosure seem also relevant here but are trickier, because in order to be effective, disclosure does require some consumer attention. *See* OREN BAR-GILL, SEDUCTION BY CONTRACT: LAW, ECONOMICS, AND PSYCHOLOGY IN CONSUMER MARKETS (2012).

6 *See respectively* Omri Ben-Shahar & Eric A. Posner, *The Right to Withdraw in Contract Law*, 40 J. LEGAL STUD. 115 (2011); Alan Schwartz & Louis L. Wilde, *Imperfect Information in Markets for Contract Terms: The Examples of Warranties and Security Interests*, 69 VA. L. REV. 1387 (1983).

7 *See* Tess Wilkinson-Ryan, *Intuitive Formalism in Contract*, 163 U. PA. L. REV. 2109, 2121, 2126–27 (2015).

8 *See supra* Chapter 5, text accompanying note 25.

9 *See* Fred H. Miller, *Consumers and the Code: The Search for the Proper Formula*, 75 WASH. U. L.Q. 187, 187–99 (1997); *see generally* Anthony T. Kronman, *Paternalism and the Law of Contracts*, 92 YALE L.J. 763 (1983).

10 *See infra* text accompanying note 30.

11 *See supra* Chapter 7, text accompanying notes 12–15.

12 JOSEPH RAZ, ETHICS IN THE PUBLIC DOMAIN: ESSAYS IN THE MORALITY OF LAW AND POLITICS 105 (1994).

13 *Id.*

14 *See supra* Chapter 5, text accompanying note 25.

15 On some of the difficult questions this commitment raises, see Omri Ben-Shahar, *Forward: Freedom from Contract*, 2004 WISC. L. REV. 261.

16 *See* Lon L. Fuller, *Consideration and Form*, 41 COLUM. L. REV. 799 (1941).

17 *See* PRINCIPLES OF EUROPEAN CONTRACT LAW § 2:101 cmt. B (Communication on European Contract Law, Ole Lando & Hugh Beale eds., 2000); PRINCIPLES, DEFINITIONS AND MODEL RULES OF EUROPEAN PRIVATE LAW: DRAFT COMMON FRAME OF REFERENCE (DCFR), OUTLINE EDITION § II: 401 (Christian von Bar et al., eds., 2009); EU COMMISSION, PROPOSAL FOR A COMMON EUROPEAN SALES LAW § 39(2) (2011).

18 *See, e.g.*, Steven M. Haas, *Contracting Around Fraud Under Delaware Law*, 10 DEL. L. REV. 49, 50–51 (2008); Melissa T. Lonegrass, *Finding Room for Fairness in Formalism – the Sliding Scale Approach to Unconscionability*, 44 LOY. U. CHI. L.J. 1, 1–6 (2012).

19 *See, e.g.*, Eric A. Posner, *The Parol Evidence Rule, the Plain Meaning Rule, and the Principles of Contractual Interpretation*, 146 U. PA. L. REV. 533, 534 (1998).

20 *See, e.g.* Gregory Klass, *Intent to Contract*, 95 VA. L. REV. 1437, 1480–87, 1488–97 (2009).

21 *See supra* Chapter 3, text accompanying notes 10–12.

22 *See supra* Chapter 3, text accompanying notes 41–51.

23 *See* Martijn W. Hesselink, *Private Law Principles, Pluralism and Perfectionism, in* GENERAL PRINCIPLES OF EU LAW AND EUROPEAN PRIVATE LAW 21 (Ulf Bernitz & Xavier Groussot eds., 2013).

24 *See* BASIL MARKESINIS ET AL., GERMAN CONTRACT LAW: A COMPARATIVE TREATISE 162–63 (2006). Italian contract law (according to some interpretations) provides an example for a – troublesome – exception to this rule by requiring parties to such transactions affirmatively to show that they are designed to realize worthy interests. *See* Arthur Von Mehren, *A General View of Contract, in* 7 INTER-NATIONAL ENCYCLOPEDIA OF COMPARATIVE LAW 28–29 (Arthur Von Mehren ed., 1982).

25 It is, however, debatable whether this distinction is justified. *See* Hanoch Dagan, *The Challenges of Private Law, in* PRIVATE LAW IN THE 21ST CENTURY 67, 78–79 (Kit Barker et al., eds., 2016).

26 *Cf.* HUGH COLLINS, REGULATING CONTRACTS 176–77 (1999) (arguing that in order to permit "novel types of transaction to be supported by law," what is needed

is not "a uniform set of rules for all types of contracts," but rather sufficiently abstract rules that "escape[s] the confines of particular types of agreement.").

27 *See* Yuval Feldman & Doron Teichman, *Are All Contractual Obligations Created Equal?*, 100 GEO. L.J. 5, 31, 38–39 (2011).

28 *See* Stephen A. Smith, *Future Freedom and Freedom of Contract*, 59 MOD. L. REV. 167 (1995).

29 *See generally* Leslie Green, *Rights of Exit*, 4 LEG. THEORY 165 (1998); Dori Kimel, *Promise, Contract, Personal Autonomy, and the Freedom to Change One's Mind, in* PHILOSOPHICAL FOUNDATIONS OF CONTRACT 96, 101–03 (Gregory Klass et al., eds., 2014); Aditi Bagchi, *Contract Law as Procedural Justice*, 2015 JURISPRU-DENCE 1, 16–17.

30 *See* MEIR DAN-COHEN, RIGHTS, PERSONS, AND ORGANIZATIONS: A LEGAL THEORY FOR BUREAUCRATIC SOCIETY 77–78 (1986).

31 *See* Ronald J. Gilson, *The Legal Infrastructure of High Technology Industrial Districts: Silicon Valley, Route 128, and Covenants Not to Compete*, 74 N.Y.U. L. REV. 575, 594–619 (1999) (attributing Silicon Valley's dynamism in part to limited enforcement of noncompete agreements); *see also* Ruth Simon & Angus Loten, *When a New Job Leads to a Lawsuit*, WALL ST. J., Aug. 15, 2013, at B1 (discussing national variation in enforceability).

32 *See, e.g.*, Douglas Belkin, *More College Students Selling Stock – in Themselves*, WALL ST. J, Aug. 5, 2015 (discussing income share loan contracts).

33 *See, e.g.*, Deborah A. DeMott, *The Fiduciary Character of Agency and the Inter-pretation of Instructions, in* PHILOSOPHICAL FOUNDATIONS OF FIDUCIARY LAW 321, 333–36 (Andrew Gold & Paul Miller eds., 2014).

34 *Cf.* Richard H. Pildes, *Conceptions of Value in Legal Thought*, 90 MICH. L. REV. 1520, 1557 (1992).

35 *Cf.* EYAL ZAMIR & BARAK MEDINA, LAW, ECONOMICS, AND MORALITY 1–8, 79–104 (2010) (defending "threshold deontology").

36 *See generally* Cass Sunstein, *Incommensurability and Valuation in Law*, 92 MICH. L. REV. 779 (1994).

37 *See* Hanoch Dagan & Avihay Dorfman, *Just Relationships*, 116 COLUM. L. REV. 1395 (2016), on which this subsection relies.

38 *See, e.g.*, Peter Benson, *The Unity of Contract Law, in* THE THEORY OF CON-TRACT LAW: NEW ESSAYS 118, 130–31 (Peter Benson ed., 2001); Daniel Markovits, *Contract and Collaboration*, 113 YALE L.J. 1417 (2004).

39 *See* RESTATEMENT (SECOND) OF CONTRACTS § 12 (1981).

40 *See id.* § 177.

41 *See id.* § 208.

42 Seana Valentine Shiffrin, *Paternalism, Unconscionability Doctrine, and Accommo-dation*, 29 PHIL. & PUB. AFF. 205, 206 (2000).

43 Stephen M. Waddams, *Unconscionability in Contracts*, 39 MOD. L. REV. 369, 369 (1976).

44 *Patterson v. Walker-Thomas Furniture Co.*, 277 A.2d 111, 113 (D.C. 1971).

45 *See* Dagan & Dorfman, *supra* note 37, at 1438–45; *see also* Hugh Collins, *The Vanishing Freedom to Choose a Contractual Partner*, 76(2) LAW & CONTEMP. PROBS. 71, 74, 77 (2013).

46 National Labor Relations Act, 29 U.S.C. § 151 (1935).

47 *See* Mark Barenberg, *The Political Economy of the Wagner Act: Power, Symbol, and Workplace Cooperation*, 106 HARV. L. REV. 1379, 1423 (1993).

48 *Cf.* Roberto Mangabeira Unger, *The Critical Legal Studies Movement*, 96 HARV. L. REV. 561, 629–30 (1983).

49 *See* Paul Weiler & Guy Mundlak, *New Direction for the Law of the Workplace*, 102 YALE L.J. 1907, 1911 (1993) ("Under the auspices of the New Deal labor law policy, union representation of the private nonagricultural work force ... soared to nearly 40% by the mid-1950's. From that base, collective bargaining strongly influenced employment conditions for nonunion staff at unionized firms or at non-union firms in largely unionized industries.").

50 *See id.* at 1912–13 (discussing the decline in unionization due to corporate union avoidance policies).

51 *See* Rebecca J. Livengood, *Organizing for Structural Change: The Potential and Promise of Worker Centers*, 48 HARV. C.R.–C.L. L. REV. 325, 340 (2013) (explaining that the Section 14(b) of the Taft-Hartley Act allows states to pass right-to-work laws, proscribing agency shop provisions, and that twenty-three states have done so).

52 Lonnie K. Stevans, *The Effect of Endogenous Right-to-Work Laws on Business and Economic Conditions in the United States: A Multivariate Approach*, 5 REV. L. & ECON. 595 (2009); *see also Communications Workers of America v. Beck*, 487 U.S. 735, 745 (1988) (reaffirming that employees may not be required to support union activities outside collective bargaining, contract administration, and grievance adjustment). *See also* PAUL C. WEILER, GOVERNING THE WORKPLACE: THE FUTURE OF LABOR AND EMPLOYMENT LAW, 72–78 (1990) (suggesting that many non-union workers would prefer "for-cause" guarantees, but that "a number of features of the nonunion labor market obstruct ... this preference").

53 *See, e.g.*, Robert W. Gordon, *Unfreezing Legal Reality: Critical Approaches to Law*, 15 FLA. ST. U.L. REV. 195, 209–10 (1987).

54 *Cf.* JEDEDIAH PURDY, THE MEANING OF PROPERTY: FREEDOM, COMMUNITY, AND THE LEGAL IMAGINATION 88, 112 (2010).

55 This paragraph draws substantially from Avihay Dorfman, Private Law Exceptionalism? Part II: A Basic Difficulty with the Argument from Formal Equality (2015) (unpublished manuscript).

56 On this distinction, see Peter De Marneffe, *Liberalism, Liberty, and Neutrality*, 19 PHIL. & PUB. AFF. 253 (1990). Our discussion brackets broader (familiar) qualms about neutrality and attempts to establish that whatever the concerns are about neutrality writ large, choice theory provides the most neutral path one can take as to contracts in particular.

57 *See* Hesselink, *supra* note 23.

58 *See supra* text accompanying notes 16–21.

59 *See generally* Tom Ginsburg et al., *Libertarian Paternalism, Path Dependence, and Temporary Law*, 81 U. CHI. L. REV. 291, 302–25 (2014); Cass R. Sunstein & Richard H. Thaler, *Libertarian Paternalism Is Not an Oxymoron*, 70 U. CHI. L. REV. 1159, 1161, 1171–83 (2003).

60 *See* Manfred Rehbinder, *Status, Contract, and the Welfare State*, 23 STAN. L. REV. 941, 951 (1971).

61 *Cf.* Martijn W. Hesselink, *Democratic Contract Law*, 11 EUR. REV. CONTRACT L. 81 (2015).

62 *Cf.* Hanoch Dagan, *Judges and Property, in* INTELLECTUAL PROPERTY AND THE COMMON LAW 17 (Shyam Balganesh ed., 2014).

63 *See supra* Chapter 3, text accompanying note 50. Furthermore, even if we are proven to be wrong and – in the name of neutrality – it is more legitimate for a liberal contract law to rely on *freestanding*, as opposed to autonomy-based, structural pluralism, it should be noted that the practical implications of these two approaches largely converge. *See* Hanoch Dagan, *Pluralism and Perfectionism in Private Law*, 112 COLUM. L. REV. 1409, 1424 (2012).

64 *See supra* text accompanying notes 31–33.

65 *See* SAMUEL SCHEFFLER, EQUALITY AND TRADITION: QUESTIONS OF VALUE IN MORAL AND POLITICAL THEORY 50 (2010).

66 *See supra* Chapter 5, text accompanying note 3. *Cf.* STEPHEN A. SMITH, CONTRACT THEORY 76–77 (2004).

CHAPTER 9

1 *See* Roy Kreitner, *Multiplicity in Contract Remedies, in* COMPARATIVE REMEDIES FOR BREACH OF CONTRACT 19, 19–20, 38, 49 (Nili Cohen & Ewan McKendrick eds., 2005); Alan Schwartz, *The Default Rule Paradigm and the Limits of Contract Law*, 3 S. CAL. INTERDISCIPLINARY L.J. 389 (1994); Ronald J. Gilson, Charles F. Sabel & Robert E. Scott, *Text* and *Context: Contract Interpretation as Contract Design*, 100 CORNELL L. REV. 23 (2014). *See generally* Roy Kreitner, *On the New Pluralism in Contract Theory*, 45 SUFFOLK U. L. REV. 915 (2012).

2 *See* R.M. Helmholz, *Bailment Theories and the Liabilities of Bailees: The Elusive Standard of Reasonable Care*, 41 U. KAN. L. REV. 97, 99 (1992).

3 *See* Daniel Markovits, Promise Made Pure (unpublished manuscript), at 5; *cf.* Seana Valentine Shiffrin, *Enhancing Moral Relationships through Strict Liability*, 62 U. TORONTO L.J. 353 (2016).

4 *See* Tony Weir, *Contracts in Rome and England*, 66 TULANE L. REV. 1615, 1642–43 (1992).

5 *See* Helmholz, *supra* note 2, at 109–29 (describing expansion of strict liability exceptions).

6 *Id.* at 99.

7 *See, e.g.,* Melvin Aron Eisenberg, *The Limits of Cognition and the Limits of Contract*, 47 STAN. L. REV. 211, 225–36 (1995).

8 *See, e.g.,* Alan Schwartz, *The Myth That Promisees Prefer Supracompensatory Remedies: An Analysis of Contracting for Damage Measures,* 100 YALE L.J. 369 (1990).

9 *See supra* Chapter 8, text accompanying notes 40–54.

10 *See* Meredith R. Miller, *Contract Law, Party Sophistication and the New Formalism,* 75 MO. L. REV. 493, 512 (2010).

11 *See* Avery Katz, *Virtue Ethics and Efficient Breach,* 45 SUFFOLK U. L. REV. 777, 794–97 (2012) (discusses the doctrinal basis of efficient breach, particularly noting the moral objections arising from the introduction of efficient breach in the non-market contexts); Margaret F Brinig, *"Money Can't Buy Me Love": A Contrast between Damages in Family Law and Contract,* 27 J. CORP. L. 567, 572–79, 589 (2002) (details how a number of contracts theories, particularly efficient breach, are not and should not be applicable in the family law context).

12 *See also, e.g.,* Brett E. Lewis, *Secondary Obligors and the Restatement Third of Suretyship and Guaranty: For Love or Money,* 63 BROOK. L. REV. 861 (1997) (criticizing suretyship law for not distinguishing between compensated and uncompensated sureties).

13 *See* HUGH COLLINS, REGULATING CONTRACTS 181 (1999) (arguing that contract law "has to resist the universalizing tendency of formal logical rationality to apply the same rules to every type of transaction because a single rule may fail to make the kinds of differentiation between types of transaction and business relation which the parties expect.").

14 *See* COLLINS, *id.,* at 78.

15 *See generally* HANOCH DAGAN, RECONSTRUCTING AMERICAN LEGAL REALISM & RETHINKING PRIVATE LAW THEORY ch. 6 (2013) (discussing this methodological commitment).

16 *See* P.S. ATIYAH, THE RISE AND FALL OF FREEDOM OF CONTRACT 102–03 (1979); Duncan Kennedy, *The Structure of Blackstone's Commentaries,* 28 BUFF. L. REV. 205, 327–50 (1979).

17 *See supra* Chapter 8, text accompanying note 50.

18 We deliberately use the adjective "normatively attractive" to describe the contract types the state must supply because – although we do not commit ourselves to full-blown Razian autonomy (*see supra* Chapter 7, note 1) – we believe that it is "a mistake to lose sight of the value of the activity that is being chosen through one's exercise of autonomy." Youngjae Lee, *Valuing Autonomy,* 75 FORDHAM L. REV. 2973, 2987 (2007).

19 *See generally* J. William Callison, *Benefit Corporations, Innovation and Statutory Design,* 26 REGENT L. REV. 143 (2014).

20 *See* Henry Hansmann & Reinier Kraakman, *Property, Contract, and Verification: The* Numerus Clausus *Problem and the Divisibility of Rights,* 31 J. LEGAL STUD. 373, 374–75, 380–84, 416–17, 419 (2002). *See also, e.g.,* Glenn O. Robinson, *Personal Property Servitudes,* 71 U. CHI. L. REV. 1449, 1484–88 (2004).

21 HANOCH DAGAN, PROPERTY: VALUES AND INSTITUTIONS 18–20, 31–35 (2011).

22 *See* Jody Freeman, *The Contracting State,* 28 FLA. ST. U. L. REV. 155, 164–165 (2000) (discussing the difficulty of bargaining for favorable terms with the government).

23 *Id.* at 201–202 ("Despite posing considerable cause for concern, contractual instruments also represent potentially useful accountability instruments. Conceivably, public-private contracts could function not only as mechanisms for delivering social services or effecting regulatory purposes, but as vehicles for achieving public law values, such as fairness, openness, and accountability."); *see also* Gillian Hadfield, *Of Sovereignty and Contract: Damages for Breach of Contract by Government*, 8 S. Cal. Interdisc. L.J. 467, 488–492 (1999) (discussing the benefits of termination for convenience clauses for the democratic process).

24 *See* Curtis A. Bradley, *The Treaty Power and American Federalism*, 97 Mich. L. Rev. 390 (1998) (detailing constitutional concerns with expansive federal control over international affairs).

25 *See* Pierrick Le Goff, *Global Law: A Legal Phenomenon Emerging from the Process of Globalization*, 14 Ind. J. Global Legal Stud. 119, 130–136 (2007) (recognizing the importance of public and private international organizations in developing global contract law).

26 *See* Tai-Heng Cheng, *Power, Authority, and International Investment Law*, 20 Am. U. Int'l L. Rev. 465, 515–517 (2005) (discussing the difficulty of creating a coherent body of international investment law due to forum shopping and weak *res judicata* in the current international arbitration regime).

CHAPTER 10

1 *See supra* Chapter 5, notes 14–16 and accompanying text.

2 *See supra* Chapter 6, notes 14–16 and accompanying text. *See also, e.g.*, Hugh Collins, Is a Relational Contract a Legal Concept? (2015) (unpublished manuscript).

3 *See, e.g.*, Ian Ayres & Richard E. Speidel, Studies in Contract Law 719 (7th ed. 2008).

4 *See supra* Chapter 7, text accompanying note 39.

5 On the agent's authority to bind the principal, see Restatement (Third) of Agency §§ 6.01–6.02, 2.01–2.02 (2006); on the principal's liability, see *id.* § 7.03–7.08.

6 *See id.* § 8.09 cmt. b.

7 *Cf.* Deborah A. DeMott, *The Fiduciary Character of Agency and the Interpretation of Instructions, in* Philosophical Foundations of Fiduciary Law 321, 337 (Andrew Gold & Paul Miller eds., 2014) ("direction, supervision [and] authority [are] all highly significant to the functioning of agency relationships.").

8 Restatement (Third) of Agency § 8.11 (2006); *see also* Restatement (Third) of the Law Governing Lawyers § 20(1) (2000).

9 *See* Restatement (Third) of the Law Governing Lawyers § 20(1) (2000).

10 *See* Restatement (Third) of Agency §§ 4.01–4.08 (2006); (discussing how adjustments of relations between the principal and agent are governed in part by the doctrine of ratification); *see also* Peter Tiersma, *The Language of Silence*, 48 Rutgers L. Rev. 1, 31–43 (1995) (analyzing the ways in which an agent's acts and

a principal's silence may change the agency relationship by imposing duties on a principal).

11 *See supra* Chapter 8, note 65 and accompanying text.

12 For the claim that lawyers should turn their attention to the way law functions in people's daily lives, instead of focusing on its pathologies, see H.L.A. HART, THE CONCEPT OF LAW 79–88 (1961). *See also* Lisa Bernstein, *Merchant Law in a Merchant Court: Rethinking the Code's Search for Immanent Business Norms*, 144 U. PA. L. REV. 1765, 1796–98 (1996) (distinguishing, in a commercial law context, between "relationship-preserving norms" and "end-game norms").

13 *See* Hanoch Dagan & Michael A. Heller, *The Liberal Commons*, 110 YALE L.J. 549, 597–98 (2001); Carolyn J. Frantz & Hanoch Dagan, *Properties of Marriage* 104 COLUM. L. REV. 75, 95–98 (2004).

14 *See* HANOCH DAGAN, THE LAW AND ETHICS OF RESTITUTION 278–82 (2004).

15 Ori Aronson, *The How Many Question: An Institutionalist Guide to Pluralism*, *in* INSTITUTIONALIZING RIGHTS AND RELIGION: COMPETING SUPREMACIES 147, 147 (Leora F. Batnitzky & Hanoch Dagan eds., 2017).

16 *Id.*

17 *See infra* Chapter 12, text accompanying notes 1–8.

18 *See* Aronson, *supra* note 15, at 162.

19 *Id.* at 158, 161 (noting that a particularly complex challenge of such a process is to assess the meaning of long-term convergence notwithstanding the availability of multiple options: Does it derive from the designers' failure to create the appropriate contract types or to communicate properly their potential virtues to contracting parties? Or maybe it means that choice is less important than they thought it to be in this sphere?).

20 *See generally, e.g.*, WILLIAM T. ALLEN ET AL., COMMENTARIES AND CASES ON THE LAW OF BUSINESS ORGANIZATION (3d ed. 2009); LARRY E. RIBSTEIN, THE RISE OF UNINCORPORATION (2010).

21 *See, e.g.*, FRANK H. EASTERBROOK & DANIEL R. FISCHEL, THE ECONOMIC STRUCTURE OF CORPORATE LAW 34–35 (1991).

22 *See* Edward P. Welch & Robert S. Saunders, *Freedom and Its Limits in the Delaware General Corporation Law*, 33 DEL. J. CORP. L. 845, 846–47 (2008).

23 *See* Terry A. O'Neill, *Toward a New Theory of the Closely-Held Firm*, 24 SETON HALL L. REV. 603, 605 (1993).

24 Victor Li, *The End of Partnership?*, ABA J., Aug. 2015, at 48.

25 *Id.*, at 71 (quoting Robin Gibbs).

26 *Compare* 1 FRIEDMAN ON LEASES § 1:2.1 (Patrick A. Randolph, Jr. ed., 5th ed., rel. 20, 2012) (describing modern approach to residential leases), *with id.* § 1:2.2 (describing commercial leasing).

27 *See* Hanoch Dagan & Sharon Hannes, *Managing Our Money: The Law of Financial Fiduciaries as a Private Law Institution*, *in* PHILOSOPHICAL FOUNDATIONS OF FIDUCIARY LAW, *supra* note 7, at 91, 103–05, 118, 121.

28 This rule is relatively new, to be sure, and by now controversial. Addressing this complex controversy is beyond the scope of this book. For our purposes, it is

enough to say that insofar as it is problematic, its difficulties derive from the detrimental impact of the traditional way trustees (and trust advisers) are compensated. *See* Dagan & Hannes, *supra* note 27, at 113–14.

29 *See id.* at 111–12.

30 *See supra* Chapter 8, text accompanying notes 12–22.

31 *See, e.g.,* STEVEN M. SHAVELL, FOUNDATIONS OF ECONOMIC ANALYSIS OF LAW 207–14 (2004); Stephanie M. Stern, Psyched-Out: The Implications of Comparative Institutional Expertise for Psychologically-Informed Law (unpublished manuscript).

32 Note that in this section we use the terms "regulate" and "regulation" in a broad sense, rather than in the more technical, administrative sense we employed in Chapter 7.

33 *See* Hanoch Dagan, *Pluralism and Perfectionism in Private Law*, 112 COLUM. L. REV. 1409, 1436 (2012).

34 *See* Melanie B. Leslie, *Trusting Trustees: Fiduciary Duties and the Limits of Default Rules*, 94 GEO. L.J. 67, 69–70, 91, 116 (2005). *Cf.* Dagan, *supra* note 33, at 1436 (referring to a prenuptial agreement providing that a given marriage would last for a week or a month).

35 Gerald Dworkin, *Paternalism, in* PATERNALISM 19, 20, 23, 27–29 (Rolf Sartorius ed., 1983). For the distinction between weak and strong versions of legal paternalism, see Joel Feinberg, *Legal Paternalism, id.* at 3, 8–11, 17.

36 *See supra* Chapter 8, text accompanying note 6.

37 *See* Thomas J. Stipanowich, *The Third Arbitration Trilogy:* Stolt-Nielsen, Rent-A-Center, Concepcion *and the Future of American Arbitration*, 22 AM. REV. INT'L ARB. 323, 408 (2011) ("the U.S. Supreme Court's arbitration jurisprudence makes the U.S. less protective of the procedural rights of consumers and employees than almost any other jurisdiction in the world.").

38 *See* Judith Resnik, *Diffusing Disputes: The Public in the Private of Arbitration, the Private in Courts, and the Erasure of Rights*, 124 YALE L.J. 2804, 2810–11 (2015).

39 *See supra* Chapter 7, text accompanying notes 12–14, and Chapter 8, text accompanying notes 4–11.

40 *See* Ian Ayres, *Regulating Opt Outs: An Economic Analysis of Altering Rules*, 121 YALE L.J. 2032, 2097 (2012) (sticky defaults can minimize the costs of party error (or judicial error) as well as channel contractors' efforts towards means that better control externalities).

41 *See supra* text accompanying note 34.

42 Ayres, *supra* note 40, at 2086.

43 *See* Dagan & Hannes, *supra* note 27, at 107–11, 115–18.

CHAPTER 11

1 *See infra* Chapter 12, notes 1–8, and accompanying text.

2 *See* Ronald J. Gilson, Charles F. Sabel & Robert E. Scott, *Contract and Innovation: The Limited Role of Generalist Courts in the Evolution of Novel Contractual Forms,*

88 N.Y.U. L. Rev. 170 (2013). *But cf.* Hugh Collins, Regulating Contracts 77–78 (1999) (conceding that "over time legal doctrine has developed specialized regulation for certain types of recurrent and familiar contracts," but insisting that "the list of nominate contracts remains short compared to the potential variety of business transactions").

3 For example, long-standing market failures in design of mortgage derivative contracts catalyzed recent legislative interventions in new types of real estate contracting. *See generally* Michael Heller, The Gridlock Economy: How Too Much Ownership Wrecks Markets, Stops Innovation, and Costs Lives xvi (2008).

4 William N. Eskridge Jr., *Family Law Pluralism: The Guided Choice Regime of Menus, Default Rules, and Override Rules,* 100 Geo. L.J. 1881, 1891 (2012).

5 In this, we diverge from Nathan B. Oman, *A Pragmatic Defense of Contract Law,* 98 Geo. L. J. 77, 94–105 (2009) where he argues that pluralist contract law inhibits experimentalism.

6 *See supra* Chapter 8, text accompanying notes 24–27.

7 *See supra* Chapter 7, text accompanying notes 8–10.

8 *See* Jesse Rudy, *What They Don't Know Won't Hurt Them: Defending Employment-at-Will in Light of Findings That Employees Believe They Possess Just Cause Protection,* 23 Berkeley J. Emp. & Lab. L. 307, 309–10 (2002).

9 *See* Restatement (Third) of Employment Law § 2.01 cmt. b (2015); Barry D. Roseman, *Just Cause in Montana: Did the Big Sky Fall?,* American Constitution Soc'y, Sept. 2008 *available at* https://secure.acslaw.org/files/roseman%20issue%20brief_0.pdf.

10 Charles J. Muhl, *The Employment-at-Will Doctrine: Three Major Exceptions,* Monthly Labor Rev. 3 (2001) (discussing the exceptions and listing them by state).

11 *See* Seth D. Harris & Alan B. Krueger, *A Proposal for Modernizing Labor Laws for Twenty-First-Century Work: The "Independent Worker,"* Brookings Institution Working Paper, Dec. 2015; *see also* Justin Fox, *Your Uber Driver Should Be an "Independent Worker,"* BloombergView (Dec. 8, 2015), www.bloombergview .com/articles/2015-12-08/labor-laws-need-modernizing-for-the-gig-economy-worker; Justin Fox, *Uber and the Not-Quite-Independent Contractor,* BloombergView (June 23, 2015), www.bloombergview.com/articles/2015-06-23/uber-drivers-are-nei ther-employees-nor-contractors [http://perma.cc/LU8Q-99N6]; Lauren Weber, *What If There Were a New Type of Worker? Dependent Contractor,* Wall St. J., Jan. 28, 2015; Lauren Weber & Rachel E. Silverman, *On-Demand Workers: "We Are Not Robots,"* Wall St. J., Jan. 27, 2015.

12 *See, e.g., McKee v. Reid's Heritage Homes, Ltd.,* 2009 ONCA 916 (Can. Ont.) (defining dependent contractors as "an intermediate category … which consists, at least, of those non-employment work relationships that exhibit minimum economic dependency" and are "owed reasonable notice upon termination").

13 *Cotter v. Lyft Inc.,* Civil Action No. 13-cv-04065-VC (N.D. Cal., Mar. 11, 2015) (order denying cross-motions for summary judgment).

14 *Cf.* Benjamin Sachs, *A New Category of Worker for the On-Demand Economy*, OnLabor Blog, June 22, 2015, http://onlabor.org/2015/06/22/a-new-category-of-worker-for-the-on-demand-economy (discussing difficulties in designing new employment contract type).

15 As opposed to job-sharing programs, which are voluntary agreements designed to accommodate reduced working hours, work-sharing programs provide an alternative to unemployment during economic downturns. Work-sharing programs allow an employer to forego layoffs by reducing working hours and wages of all employees. Instead of paying unemployment benefits to newly laid-off workers, the government subsidizes the wages paid to these reduced-hour workers. These programs have been employed with great success to combat job loss in Germany, but still only make up 2 percent of unemployment paid by the United States government. For more information, see Megan Felter, *Short-Time Compensation: Is Germany's Success with Kurzarbeit an Answer to U.S. Unemployment?*, 35 B.C. INT'L & COMP. L. REV. 481, 487 (2012); William B. Gould IV, *A Century and Half Century of Advance and Retreat: The Ebbs and Flows of Workplace Democracy*, 86 ST. JOHN'S L. REV. 431, 441 (2012).

16 For a general overview of flexible work arrangements, discussion of pros and cons, and a rich selection of secondary sources, see CHRISTINE AVERY & DIANE ZABEL, THE FLEXIBLE WORKPLACE: A SOURCEBOOK OF INFORMATION AND RESEARCH 37–80 (2001).

17 Joan C. Williams et al., *Better on Balance? The Corporate Work/Life Report*, 10 WM. & MARY J. WOMEN & L. 367, 410–11 (2004) (noting "island" type, whereby two attorneys share one position but maintain separate caseloads and "twins" type in which two attorneys act as one and share a single caseload).

18 Marion Crain, *"Where Have All the Cowboys Gone?" Marriage and Breadwinning in Postindustrial Society*, 60 OHIO ST. L.J. 1877, 1952 (1999).

19 For an outline of the government's job-sharing policies, see U.S. OFFICE OF PERSONNEL MANAGEMENT, www.opm.gov/employment_and_benefits/worklife/officialdocuments/handbooksguides/pt_employ_jobsharing/pt08.asp.

20 *See* Robert C. Bird, *Why Don't More Employers Adopt Flexible Working Time?*, 118 W. VA. L. REV. 327, 341–342 (2015).

21 *See* Erika C. Collins, *Labor and Employment Developments from around the World*, 38 INT'L LAW. 149, 169 (2004).

22 *See, e.g.*, ARCHIBALD COX ET AL., LABOR LAW: CASES AND MATERIALS (15th ed. 2011); ROBERT A. GORMAN & MATTHEW W. FINKIN, LABOR LAW: ANALYSIS AND ADVOCACY (2013) (leading labor law textbooks which discuss unions to the exclusion of alternative labor law structures).

23 *See* Priya Baskaran, *Introduction to Worker Cooperatives and Their Role in the Changing Economy*, 24 J. AFFORDABLE HOUSING & COMMUNITY DEV. L. 355, 370 (2015); *What is a Worker Cooperative?*, US Federation of Worker Cooperatives (Mar. 24, 2016), https://usworker.coop/about/what-is-a-worker-coop.

24 *See generally* David Ellerman & Peter Pitegoff, *The Democratic Corporation: The New Worker Cooperative Statute in Massachusetts*, 11 N.Y.U. Rev. L. & Soc. Change 441 (1982–1983).

25 Kathleen, O'Malley, AB 816 Bill Analysis, at 11 (Cal. 2015), www.leginfo.ca.gov/pub/15–16/bill/asm/ab_0801-0850/ab_816_cfa_20150715_173239_asm_floor.html.

26 *See* Cal. Worker Coop. Pol'y Coal., Fact Sheet (June 24, 2015), https://d3n8a8pro7vhmx.cloudfront.net/theselc/pages/226/attachments/original/1439488297/AB816_Fact_Sheet_vs_3.pdf?1439488297.

27 Christina Oatfield, Governor Brown Signs California Worker Cooperative Act, AB 816, Sustainable Econs. Law Ctr. (Aug. 12, 2015), www.theselc.org/governor_brown_signs_california_worker_cooperative_act [http://perma.cc/K393-3KLN].

28 *See* Stephen Machin & Stephen Wood, *Human Resource Management as a Substitute for Trade Unions in British Workplaces*, 58 Indus. & Lab. Rel. Rev. 201, 205 (2005) (noting that "[t]he practices that most directly constitute alternatives to unions are those that can replace bargaining and voice roles. More specifically... forms of individualized pay determination such as individual bargaining or imposed merit- and performance-related pay awards").

29 *How an Employee Stock Ownership Plan (ESOP) Works*, National Center for Employee Ownership (Mar. 24, 2016), www.nceo.org/articles/esop-employee-stock-ownership-plan.

30 *See* Henry Hansmann, *When Does Worker Ownership Work? ESOPs, Law Firms, Codetermination, and Economic Democracy*, 99 Yale L.J. 1749, 1797 (1990).

31 *See id.* at 1758–59.

32 *See* Mark Barenberg, *Democracy and Domination in the Law of Workplace Cooperation: From Bureaucratic to Flexible Production*, 94 Colum. L. Rev. 753, 758 (1994) (noting that union membership had fallen from 37 percent in 1953 to less than 12 percent in 1994).

33 *See id.* at 759.

34 *See* National Labor Relations Act, 29 U.S.C. § 158(a)(2).

35 *See* Barenberg, *supra* note 32, at 928–46 (discussing the various proposals and rationales posited for eliminating the ban on company unions).

36 *Id.* at 948–960 (discussing how a majority vote among workers should be implemented to decide between unionism, autonomous teams, strategic councils, and non-unionism as a means to maximize democratic labor empowerment). For a failed attempt to repeal the ban, see the Teamwork for Employees and Management Act, H.R. 1529, 103d Cong., 1st Sess. (1993); *see also* Barenberg, *supra* note 32, at 761 (discussing problems with this version of a repeal).

37 Interestingly, the French legislature has been particularly active in providing new employment contract types to solve problems caused by insufficient choice and to face emerging challenges and opportunities. *See* Types of Job Contracts in France, Angloinfo.com, http://france.angloinfo.com/working/employment/contract-types/.

38 *See generally* Martha Field, *Compensated Surrogacy*, 89 WASH. L. REV. 1155 (2014) (noting rise of same-sex couples seeking surrogacy).

39 *See* Elizabeth S. Scott, *Surrogacy and the Politics of Commodification*, 72 LAW & CONTEMP. PROBS. 109 (2009).

40 Anemona Hartocollis, *And Surrogacy Makes 3*, NYT, Feb. 20, 2014, at E1.

41 *See id.* (surrogacy "has long been the path taken by the affluent and celebrities, partly because it takes good legal advice and money to accomplish").

42 *See, e.g.*, the website of the American Academy of Assisted Reproductive Technology Attorneys, www.aaarta.org/aaarta/surrogacy/surrogacy.

43 *See* Amy M. Larkey, *Redefining Motherhood: Determining Legal Maternity in Gestational Surrogacy Contracts*, 51 DRAKE L. REV. 605, 608 (2003) (noting differences between commercial and altruistic surrogacies).

44 For a conceptualization of cohabitation along these lines, see Shahar Lifshitz, *Married against Their Will? Toward a Pluralist Regulation of Spousal Relationships*, 66 WASH. & LEE L. REV. 1565, 1569 (2009).

45 *See supra* Chapter 6, text accompanying note 19.

46 *See, e.g.*, ELIZABETH BRAKE, MINIMIZING MARRIAGE: MARRIAGE, MORALITY, AND THE LAW (2012).

47 Ralph Wedgwood, Is Civil Marriage Illiberal? (2015) (unpublished manuscript).

48 *Id.*

49 *Cf.* Elizabeth S. Scott & Robert E. Scott, *From Contract to Status: Collaboration and the Evolution of Novel Family Relationships*, 115 COLUM. L. REV. 293, 369 (2015).

50 *Id.* at 369–73.

51 *See* Robert J. Shiller & Allan N. Weiss, *Home Equity Insurance*, J. REAL EST. FIN. & ECON. 21 (1999) (introducing the idea); *See also* Lee Anne Fennell, *Homeownership 2.0*, 102 NW. U. L. REV. 1047, 1049 (2008) (summarizing and elaborating equity insurance in a legal context).

52 For an elaborate discussion, see Ora Bloom, Shared Equity Homeownership Models: The Individual, Corporation and Community Perspectives (unpublished manuscript).

53 *See* Fennell, *supra* note 51, at 1069.

54 *See id.* at 1064, 1067.

55 *See id.* at 1065, 1069.

56 *See id.* at 1070, 1087.

57 *See id.* at 1103, 1107 (discussing further issues for this contract type such as the respective roles of the homeowner and offsite risk investor in resolving questions of local politics and policy and in the treatment of property taxes).

58 *See respectively* David H. Kirkpatrick, *Cooperatives and Mutual Housing Associations*, J. AFFORDABLE HOUSING & COMMUNITY DEV. L., Spring 1992, at 7, 8; Andrew Caplin et al., *Shared-Equity Mortgages, Housing Affordability, and Homeownership*, 18 HOUSING POL'Y DEBATE 209, 209 (2007). For variations abroad, see Mike Berry et al., *Financing Affordable Housing: A Critical Comparative Review of*

the United Kingdom and Australia, in Australian Housing and Urban Research Institute (Nov. 2004), www.ahuri.edu.au/publications/download/ahuri_30206_fr; Robert Mowbray & Nicholas Warren, *Shared-Equity Home-ownership: Welfare and Consumer Protection Issues, in* Shelter NSW (July 2007), https://web.archive.org/web/20120320114107; http://www.shelternsw.org.au/docs/rpt07sharedequity-sb33.pdf.

59 John E. Davis, *More than Money: What Is Shared in Shared Equity Homeowner-ship?,* J. Affordable Housing & Community Dev. L., Spring/Summer 2010, at 259, 260.

60 *See* David M. Abromowitz, *An Essay on Community Land Trusts: Toward Perman-ently Affordable Housing, in* Property and Values: Alternatives to Public and Private Ownership 213, 218–219 (Charles Geisler & Gail Daneker eds., 2000) (describing ways to evade "self-enforcing" affordable housing deed restric-tions and need for monitoring); Julia B. Milne, *Will Alternative Forms of Common-Interest Communities Succeed with Municipal Involvement?: A Study of Community Land Trusts and Limited Equity Cooperatives,* 38 Real Est. L.J. 273, 278–279, 283 (2009) (discussing difficulties of oversight and good stewardship for certain models of shared-equity homeownership); John E. Davis, *Shared Equity Homeownership, in* National Housing Institute 75 (2006), www.nhi.org/pdf/SharedEquity Home.pdf (noting shift from nonprofit to public sector in this sphere).

61 *See supra* Chapter 7, text accompanying notes 42–49.

62 Jan M. Smits, *A Radical View of Legal Pluralism, in* Pluralism and European Private Law 161, 171 (Leone Niglia ed., 2013).

63 *See* Martijn W. Hesselink, *How Many Systems of Private Law Are There in Europe? On Plural Legal Sources, Multiple Identities and the Unity of Law, in* Pluralism and European Private Law, *supra* note 62, at 199.

64 *See* Ralf Michaels, *Why We Have No Theory of European Private Law Pluralism, in* Pluralism and European Private Law, *supra* note 62, at 139, 149–53.

65 *Cf.* Stefan Grundmann, *The Future of Contract Law,* 7 Eur. Rev. Contract L. 490, 513, 517 (2011).

CHAPTER 12

1 *See generally* Barry Schwartz, The Paradox of Choice: Why More Is Less (2004). A complicated – and complicating – effect along similar lines can emerge when adding choices serves as a manipulative strategy that hinders, rather than enhances, meaningful choice. *See* Ohad Somech, Contractual Regret: A Psychological Perspective (2016) (unpublished manuscript).

2 On these disutilities, see Maytal Gilboa & Omer Y. Peled, Reassessing Autonomy (2016) (unpublished manuscript).

3 *See* Martijn W. Hesselink, *Non-Mandatory Rules in European Contract Law,* 1 Eur. Rev. Contract L. 43, 48–49 (2005).

4 Thus, in German law the decisive question for such cases of "mixed" or "hybrid" contracts is whether to apply the "absorption" or "combination" method. The absorption method applies to (a) "typical contracts with atypical complementary obligations," in which one main obligation clearly dominates the contract despite atypical elements and (b) for the most part, to "fused" or "merged" contracts, in which the main obligations belong at the same time to different types (according to the dominant type). The combination method is used for (c) "combined contracts," in which one party owes multiple main obligations of different types, but the obligations are not independent; (d) "coupled contracts," where the main obligation of one contract type for one party is coupled with the main obligation of another contract type for the other party; and (e) "comprised" or "connected" contracts, where the different contract parts could each form a freestanding separate legal agreement. *See* Volker Emmerich, Münchener Kommentar zum Bürgerlichen Gesetzbuch § 311 para 28 (7th ed. 2016); Barbara vor Grüneberg, Palandts Kommentar zum Bürgerlichen Gesetzbuch, prologue to § 311 (75th ed. 2016); Manfred Löwisch & Cornelia Feldmann, Staudingers Kommentar zum Bürgerlichen Gesetzbuch § 311 para 33 (2012).

5 *Cf.* Barry Nicholas, The French Law of Contract 57 (2d ed. 1992) (noting that because French lawyers are conscious of the traits of different *contrats nommés*, contracting parties can intentionally attempt to choose their preferred contract type).

6 For an important example, dealing with law's facilitation of same-sex intimate relationships, see Allison Anna Tait, *Divorce Equality*, 90 Wash. L. Rev. 1245 (2015).

7 *See generally* Alan Manning, Monopsony in Motion 3–10 & tbl.1.1 (2003) (compiling economic literature on monopsony).

8 *See* Nathan B. Oman, *A Pragmatic Defense of Contract Law*, 98 Geo. L.J. 77, 86–90 (2009).

9 *See* Alan Schwartz & Robert E. Scott, *Contract Theory and the Limits of Contract Law*, 113 Yale L.J. 541, 598–609 (2003); Alan Schwartz & Robert E. Scott, *The Political Economy of Private Legislatures*, 143 U. Pa. L. Rev. 559 (1995); *see also* Alan Schwartz & Robert E. Scott, *The Common Law of Contract and the Default Rule Project*, 102 Va. L. Rev. 1523 (2016).

10 *See generally* Neil K. Komesar, Imperfect Alternatives: Choosing Institutions in Law, Economics, and Public Policy (1994).

11 *See supra* Chapter 11, text accompanying note 44.

12 Ann Laquer Estin, *Ordinary Cohabitation*, 76 Notre Dame L. Rev. 1381, 1399–1402 (2001).

13 *See* Hanoch Dagan, *Restitution and Relationships*, 92 B.U.L. Rev. 1035, 1040 (2012).

14 *See* Elizabeth S. Scott & Robert E. Scott, *From Contract to Status: Collaboration and the Evolution of Novel Family Relationships*, 115 Colum. L. Rev. 293, 359–64 (2015).

15 *See supra* Chapter 11, text accompanying note 11.

CONCLUSION

1 *See supra* Chapter 5, notes 26–33 and accompanying text.
2 *See supra* Chapter 7, text accompanying notes 22–24; Chapter 8, text accompanying notes 4–6; and Chapter 10, text accompanying notes 37–38. Consider also, along these lines, the way we analyzed the choice between contracts of franchise and commercial agency. *See supra* Chapter 6, text accompanying note 41.
3 *See supra* Chapter 7, text accompanying notes 12–14.
4 *See supra* Chapter 7, text accompanying notes 32–35, and Chapter 10, text accompanying note 34.
5 *See supra* Chapter 8, text accompanying note 33.
6 *See supra* Chapter 9, text accompanying notes 2–6.
7 *See supra* Chapter 9, text accompanying notes 7–8 and 11–12.
8 *See supra* Chapter 10, text accompanying note 14.
9 *See supra* Chapter 10, text accompanying notes 30–44.
10 *See supra* Chapter 11.
11 Recall also, along these lines, our analysis of marriage contract and agency contracts. *See supra* Chapter 6, text accompanying notes 19–22, and Chapter 10, text accompanying notes 5–11.

Index

absorption method, 172
agency contract types, 104–105
  under Delaware corporate law, 107
altering rules, 113
American Law Institute (ALI), 15
Anarchy, State, and Utopia (Nozick), 40
arbitration clauses, 112
Aronson, Ori, 106
at will employment, 117
Atiyah, Patrick, 20
autonomy
  choice theory and, 4, 46–47, 68–69, 113
  in consumer transactions, 81–82
  in contract law, 7, 39, 72
  contract types and, 111–113
  contract values and, 84–85
    instrumental values, 43–45
    intrinsic values, 43–45
    ultimate value, 43–45
  instrumental values for, 43–45
  intrinsic values for, 43–45
  low-demand contracts and, 99–100
  mandatory rules for enhancement of, 111–112
  personal independence and, 41–43
  in promise theory, 26
  self-determination and, 41–43
  as side constraint, 84–85
  utility and, 52–53, 55
  welfarist interests compared to, 55
Ayres, Ian, 113

bailee contracts, 74–75
bailment doctrine, 93–94
  transfer theory and, 94
bargaining, in freedom of contracts, 2–3
Barnett, Randy, 35–36

Benson, Peter, 22
Berlin, Isaiah, 1, 43–44
binary transfer of authority
  promise types and, 30
  transfer theory and, 27
business contracts, 53–57
  as challenge to choice theory, 131–132
  contract values and, 80
  limits of, 55–57
  party sovereignty and, 54, 56
  relations contracts compared to, 104
  as sub-sphere of commerce, 98–99

Campbell, David, 60
categories
  for deciding, 13–14
  for thinking, 13–14, 130
Chhabria, Vincent, 117–118
choice theory
  autonomy and, 4, 46–47, 68–69, 113
  consumer goods purchases and, 71
  deciding in, 13–14
  development of, 67–68
  employment types and, 70–71
  family contracts and, 119–122
  freedom of contracts and, 1–2
  freestanding contracting and, 84
  as general theory, 4–6
  horizontal coexistence in, 79–80
  incremental expansions of, 132–133
  interpretive approach, 12–13
  intra-sphere multiplicity and, 5, 69–71
  mandatory rules in, 4
  methodological approaches to, 12–15
  minimal obligations of, 133
  neutrality and, 88–90

Kimel, Dori, 73
Klass, Gregory, 38
Korsgaard, Christine, 151
Kraus, Jody, 23–24

labor contracts, 60
    employment types and, 70–71
labor law, 87–88, 96–97. *See also* employment
        contracts
    innovative contract types in, 118–119
Langdell, Christopher Columbus, 8
The Law of Contracts (Williston), 8
lending contracts, 98–99
liberal contract law, 3–4
liquidated damages, 94
Llewellyn, Karl, 158
low-demand contract types, 99–100

Macneil, Ian, 60
market demand
    for contract types, 114–115
    intra-sphere multiplicity and, state's
        obligation to, 115–116
Markovits, Daniel, 25, 27–28, 61–63, 145–146.
        See also thin community
marriage contracts, 60
    alternatives to, 121
    equal division rule in, 61
mistaken payments law, 46
mixed contracts, 172
morality
    of contract theory, 22
    of promise theory, 26
Murphy, Liam, 54

NCCUSL. *See* Uniform Law Commission
negative liberty view, 11
neutrality, 88–90, 161–162
    voluntariness and, 89
no class-action clauses, 112
no community contracts
    commercial contracts as, 73
    consumer transactions and, 73
    relation-based contracts, 73–74
no community model, 64
nominate contracts, 84, 141–142
nonunion collaborative structures, 119
Nozick, Robert, 10, 40

Owens, David, 25, 27–28
ownership, property and, 36

partnership law, 107–108
paternalism, 111
Perdue, William, 20
power, in contract law, 37–38
principled multiplicity, 136
principled uniformity, 136
private law, 10, 152
    affirmative duty in, 45–46
    regulatory measures and, 77
promise principle, 21, 23–24
promise theory, 10
    autonomy in, 26
    contract law and, 28–29
    liberal theories of, 30–31
    morality of, 26
    normative implications of, 28–29
    reforms for, 29, 32
    roots of, 29
    stakes of, 25–26
    transfer theory and, 25–28
promises
    binary transfer of authority and, 30
    contracts compared to, 31
    liberal theories of, 30–31
    types of, 30–31
property
    contracts and, 36–37
    Kantian theory, 149
    ownership and, 36
    theory, 149

Rawls, John, 1, 42
Raz, Joseph, 68
regulation
    of contracts, 76–78
    private law and, 77
relational contracting, 59–60
relational equality, 52. *See also* vulnerable
        parties
    as contract value, 86–88
    formal, 86–87
    labor law and, 87–88, 96–97
    sphere of employment and, 87–88
    substantive, 86–87
relation-based contracts, 73–74
relations contracts, business contracts
        compared to, 104
Ripstein, Arthur, 33–35, 147–148. *See also*
        transfer theory
risk contracts, 98–99
Roman contract law, 8, 141–142